ST. DENIS

A FRENCH-CANADIAN PARISH

ST. DENIS

A FRENCH-CANADIAN PARISH

HORACE MINER

U D' OF O   HORS - CAMPUS
            OFF - CAMPUS

PHOENIX BOOKS
THE UNIVERSITY OF CHICAGO PRESS

CHICAGO & LONDON

This book is also available in a clothbound edition from

THE UNIVERSITY OF CHICAGO PRESS

THE UNIVERSITY OF CHICAGO PRESS, CHICAGO & LONDON
The University of Toronto Press, Toronto 5, Canada

FOREWORD

A QUARTER-CENTURY has elapsed since this study of St. Denis was made. The passage of time has added historical interest to whatever value existed in the description and analysis of traditional French-Canadian culture. As the study was also concerned with the social forces which were changing that culture, events in the subsequent years have provided a test of these original formulations. Only the unpredicted impact of World War II on the whole Dominion of Canada produced an acceleration of change in St. Denis along unforeseen lines.

The author and his family have maintained intermittent but warm contacts with their friends in St. Denis. During a two-week visit to the parish in 1949, an attempt was made to document the major changes which had occurred since the original study and to explain their cause. The results of this brief inquiry were published as an article, "A New Epoch in Rural Quebec," in the *American Journal of Sociology*, LVI (1950), 1–10. With the permission of the *Journal*, portions of that article have been used as the basis of the Postscript which has been added in this new edition of the study. Gratitude for the assistance received from Professor Charles Gagné and Curé Joseph Laforet, in 1949, is reiterated here.

So far as the adequacy of the original description of St. Denis is concerned, it is remarkable that the volume has become involved in an academic controversy. Professor Philippe Garigue has attacked our analysis of French-Canadian rural culture, along with the comparable findings of Léon Gérin, Everett Hughes, Jean-Charles Falardeau,

Marcel Rioux, and Hubert Guindon. A summary of the disagreement appears in Guindon, "The Social Evolution of Quebec Reconsidered," *Canadian Journal of Economics and Political Science*, XXVI (1960), 533–51. Essentially, Garigue appears to object to the conceptualization of the old rural life-ways as being akin to those of "peasants" and resembling those of "folk" societies, as Professor Robert Redfield came to conceive them. In contrast to our observation that St. Denis was a relatively isolated, family-oriented, and self-sufficient community, Garigue sees the traditional culture of Quebec as having been "that of a mainly commercial and urban society" (Bernard Blishen *et al.* [eds.], *Canadian Society: Sociological Perspectives*, p. 523).

We have no intention to pursue the interpretation of the facts in these prefatory remarks, but the reader of *St. Denis* would be rightly concerned had the description of the community been distorted to fit a preconceived concept, as has also been implied. The legitimate social scientist does, of course, select data which are relevant to his conceptual scheme of analysis, but he does not exclude relevant data because they do not conform to the scheme. Still, as selective observation is always involved, the conceptual tools with which the investigator approaches his research do influence what he sees. In this connection, one point seems to have escaped attention with regard to the objectivity of the study in hand. Although the author was a student of Redfield, the analysis of St. Denis was made along ethnological and structural-functional lines, strongly influenced by the teaching of A. R. Radcliffe-Brown. Culture change was conceptualized as resulting from social structural forces and from diffusion, not as a shift away from a folk type of culture. It is in the widely quoted Introduction to the study, written by Robert Redfield, that the data from St. Denis were put into the context of peasant culture. Although his discussion appears sound to us, the more relevant consideration with regard to the accuracy of the study is that the research was not undertaken to illustrate or to "test" any social typology. While the data are clearly relevant to the consideration of such types, the facts are independent of them and remain as stated.

HORACE MINER

UNIVERSITY OF MICHIGAN

PREFACE

THE objectives of the study reported in this volume were threefold: the ethnographic description of the old rural French-Canadian folk culture in its least-altered existent form, the analysis of the social structure of the society, and the consideration of the factors responsible for culture change in the direction of urbanization and anglicization. The first two aspects are basic to the adequate diagnosis of the third. The facts concerning the period, kind, and causes of social change in French Canada were determined through the examination of the history of the whole ethnic group and through the intensive analysis of the culture of a single parish, St. Denis de Kamouraska.

To satisfy the requirements of the study a long-established agricultural community was sought which had maintained the old culture to a great degree. St. Denis admirably suited these requirements. Other parishes in Quebec which are more physically isolated are more recently settled or are dependent upon a varied economy. Many of the older parishes have permanent or summer English residents and were, therefore, avoided. Still others have specialized in certain crops because of proximity to large cities. Many more have become towns and cities. St. Denis was selected as possessing none of these drawbacks.

The actual field work consisted of a preliminary month at McGill University, Montreal, and continuous residence in the parish from July 1, 1936, to June 1, 1937. The writer's own language and creed were no bar to social contact and full participation in the life of the community. The field methods included writing up observed behavior, direct interviewing, and analyzing family and parish records. Personal names in the following text are largely fictitious.

In this volume the materials on each phase of life are related to the basic problem concerned with an understanding of the causes and modes of the culture change which is going on. Relevant material is indicated in the various chapters dealing with history, family, religion, medicine and magic, routine of life, and orientation of children. The processes working toward urbanization are drawn together from these various considerations and summarily analyzed in the concluding chapter.

In the selection of the parish the author is indebted to M. Georges Bouchard, M.P., and Colonel Wilfrid Bovey, whose wide knowledge of the province was of great assistance. The field work was made possible by a grant from the Social Science Research Council, for which the author is very grateful. During the field period, contacts with Dr. Everett C. Hughes were extremely profitable. Dr. Robert Redfield was of continual help, and his painstaking criticism of the manuscript for this volume has led to the clarification and improvement of many sections. Acknowledgment must be made of the field assistance and the aid in the preparations of materials rendered by Dr. Agnes Murphy Miner. Others whose co-operation was enjoyed were Dr. C. A. Dawson, Dr. Marius Barbeau, and Sir Thomas Chapais. The friendship and assistance of the vicar and parishioners of St. Denis made the study both a pleasant and a profitable one.

Chapters iv and xi have already appeared in altered form in the *American Sociological Review* and the *American Journal of Sociology*, respectively.

HORACE MINER

TABLE OF CONTENTS

LIST OF ILLUSTRATIONS

INTRODUCTION

FOR the comparative study of societies the peasant peoples occupy a strategic position. They form a sort of middle term in the equation of culture and civilization. On the one hand, they resemble the primitive peoples with whom the ethnologist is characteristically acquainted; and on the other, they belong to that modern urbanized world which lies in the foregound of attention of most American sociologists. To study the peasant peoples is to help to draw into a single field of investigation all the societies of the earth from the simplest to the most complex. This unity of subject matter must be realized if we are to develop the science of society and culture, whatever that science may be called. For their importance the peasant societies have been relatively neglected; careful field studies of such groups are to be welcomed.

The reader of Dr. Miner's excellent book will note the respects in which this French-Canadian peasant society resembles the primitive peoples. The *habitants* live in terms of common understandings which are rooted in tradition and which have come to form an organization. The fundamental views of life are shared by almost everyone; and these views find consistent expression in the beliefs, the institutions, the rituals, and the manners of the people. In a word, they have a culture. Furthermore, the sanctions which support conduct are strongly sacred: the faith which all share provides indorsement of certain behavior and condemnation for other behavior. The priest tells them this is right and that is wrong; but the point here is that the people feel the right and the wrong and act from such a feeling, not from mere expediency. And, also, this society, like many others more primitive and outside of the European world, is strongly familial. The fabric of society is woven of threads of consanguineous and connubial connection; the family system is strong, pervasive, and certain in its effects. The activities which the individual will perform—in work, in getting married, in finding a career, in politics—are largely determined by his position in a family. The familial organization, as analyzed by Dr. Miner, though made up of no exotic elements but of terms and customs perfectly familiar to most readers, has the definition of outline, the importance of role in the total society, and the intimacy of connection with other parts of the total social structure which we are accustomed to find in the study of aboriginal simple societies. There is little disorganization and little crime. "The only death by violence in the parish happened so long ago that even the ballad about it is forgotten." Viewed in one light, the isolated peasant group is comparable with American Indian or native African societies. Even the political behavior of the people of St. Denis may be so regarded; the division into two political parties the members of each of which exhibit strongly expressive and competitive behavior toward each other suggests the dual divisions of some simpler folk.

But to look at these *habitants* as another Melanesian or American Indian society would be, of course, to ignore the fact that they form a part of the modern urbanized world. The peasant participates in a money economy, produces a surplus for sale in city markets, pays taxes, sometimes goes to school, votes, and otherwise participates in a wider economic and political structure which includes not only the peasant but the townsman. The peasant makes some use of literacy, while the aborigine does not. Moreover, peasant and city man constitute one single society that is organized in terms of status. Each is aware of the other; each allows a place for the other in his world of recognized social relations; each accepts the other as a member of a larger society in which both are members. It is the nature of the peasant that he accords prestige to the city man and to the sophisticated members of his own group. The peasant may, through education, enter the world of the city, while the city man has kinsmen among the peasants. In the case of St. Denis the immediate connection between the *habitant* and the city of Quebec is made by certain residents of the local community: the *curé* and his relatives, and the senator and his kinsmen. Dr. Miner provides a diagram of this relationship on page 250. These persons, having risen from the people, are nevertheless "socially so far removed from the society of the parish that they can not carry on normal social life with the other parishioners. . . . . These persons do not owe their position to anything within the immediate society. Their position is due to contacts which they have had with the world outside the parish, from which sphere they have received recognition far higher than anything the parish can give." The *habitants*, in turn, accord them the prestige which these educated persons have won in the city.

In Durkheim's terms the peasant society forms a special type of relatively stable compromise between the social segment and the social organ. It is the adjustment of local culture to the civilization of the cities. The solidarity of the tribe is preserved in conjunction with the market and within the nation.

The condition of the peasant is often regarded as something to be escaped, an ignominy to be shunned. A consideration of the French Canadians herein described, who are almost the only North American peasants, may give pause to such a judgment. Certainly their form of life in-

vites comparison with other rural agriculturalists with low
standards of living. If the sharecropper be brought to
mind, the difference between the mode of life of the latter
and that of the *habitant* is evident, and who will say that
the comparison is to the disadvantage of the latter? If the
habitant has order and security and faith and confidence,
it is chiefly because he has a culture. It cannot be validly
said that his advantages arise from a relatively greater
wealth of natural resources in the region he occupies; it is
doubtful if such an advantage could be demonstrated. It
is not simply that the one owns land and the other does
not. The *habitant*'s life is orderly and relatively secure
largely because it is lived in terms of an organized body
of common understandings that authorize his conduct and
explain and justify his impulses. Culture is not to be identified with the artifacts of a tribe or the tools of a farmer.
The *habitant* has culture not because he has something to
live with but because he has something to live for.

The double character of peasant societies brings it
about that they offer to students of social change a combination of advantages of which, in this case, Dr. Miner has
not failed to avail himself. Like other primitive or folk
societies they have a definiteness of outline and a relative
simplicity which facilitates the work of the reporter and
student. One can say what their institutions are, one can
fix upon the essential characters of their culture, and one
can often recognize the elements that are today promoting
change. On the other hand, being a part of a literate na-
tionality, these societies have each a recorded past. One
can consult documents about them and learn something
about how they have come to be what they are. The his-
tories of nonliterate peoples are far less accessible. But
when one has trustworthy information on the past, the

present is clarified and one may venture to consider probable future trends.

In the case of the French-Canadian rural communities Dr. Miner's account makes plain some of the special circumstances that have there tended to preserve the local and traditional organization and some other factors that are tending to disrupt it. Like the members of other societies on the peripheries of expanding civilization, the *habitant* has been exposed to the existing and disorganizing example of the outsider and more citified person. There has been the usual tendency to modify old local ways and take over customs and points of view of the outsider. But here the Catholic church has acted as a regulator upon this tendency. She has stood between the changing world and the *habitant*, preventing the admission of elements which she condemns and interpreting admitted elements in accordance with the faith and with the local culture. The reader of this book cannot fail to be impressed with the completeness with which this local folk culture is articulated with the doctrines and the practices of the church. The church provides sacred justifications and explanations for the necessary toil of the native, offers rituals to carry the individual from birth to death, and supports and sanctifies the large-family system. In its local institutions and in the local priest it provides the framework for community government and the moral leader of the community. And when the local ways are threatened by such a danger as the example of the summer colony, the church is there, in the sermons of the priest, to minimize the danger of contagion. The church has gradually eliminated from the magic of the people those forms which are not consistent with Catholic Christianity, while allowing the society to accept certain approved novelties, such as scientific agriculture. One might think that under this tutelage the traditional culture of the French Canadian, preserving its essentials, might continue substantially intact for many centuries.

Dr. Miner's analysis indicates some of the important reasons why, nevertheless, the traditional organization is threatened. The system, as a body of beliefs and practices, is static; but as an adjustment between sources of wealth and means of exploitation, it is expansive. It required the settlement of excess children upon marginal lands. The large-family system produced more children than could be established in the local community. The culture could persist without important change so long as there were marginal lands. In Dr. Miner's language, "French-Canadian culture was one which had a high degree of internal social integration based on a short-term adjustment to the environment." As accessible lands gave out, a readjustment had to be made. In old France the large-family system gave way to one of small families. So far, in Quebec, this adjustment has not taken place. Other adjustments have. Some of the children have been placed in the professions; some have emigrated to the factories of the outside world. But to educate children requires money, and the need for money has brought changes of technology and dependence upon a wider economy. And the children that go out to factories return to bring city ways into the rural community. The old organization was one of land and church; the new ways of dealing with excess children, turning them into factory hands abroad or into local day-laborers, puts them outside of the land-church system. And this tends to disrupt the system. It is the same thing that happens when an oceanic native is given a job and a daily wage on a plantation: it disrupts the tribal life. Only, in this case no invader with a plantation was necessary. The system, based on expansion into new lands, contained its own future problems. The *habitant* had a folk culture, but he came as a pioneer into a new world. It is this combination of a self-consistent and well-organized culture with a new habitat and open resources that makes the situation of the French Canadian particularly interesting. A study such as we have here preserves our confidence that social change may be subjected to orderly study and reduced to a more systematic understanding.

ROBERT REDFIELD

UNIVERSITY OF CHICAGO

CHAPTER I

HISTORY

FRENCH CANADIANS are proud of their history, bring their children up on it, and admonish each new generation to follow in their ancestors' footsteps. The "glorious age" of French Canada precedes the cession of Canada to England, for since then its history has been a story of struggle for ethnic rights. For a proper understanding of French-Canadian life as it exists today, a knowledge of origins is necessary. The fundamental structure of the rural parish goes back to the earliest days, and the structural upheaval with the growth of cities after the English conquest can be understood best in the light of the development of the province of Quebec.

As a reminder to every French child that priority rights in Canada are his, rustic crosses bearing the *fleurs-de-lis* escutcheon of France stand before schools in all the parishes of the province. They represent the cross planted by Jacques Cartier in Gaspé four hundred years ago, when he first laid eyes on the St. Lawrence. Not until eighty years later did a small group of French settlers attempt to establish themselves in what is now Nova Scotia. A few years later Champlain and his small party of twenty-seven wintered at the site of Quebec. This settlement had a continual struggle against the wilderness, its aborigines, and the English. Twenty years later the population was only eighty-five.[1] Settlements were pushed farther up the St. Lawrence; Trois Rivières was founded; and Maisonneuve moved to establish himself at Montreal with that courage

[1] Dominion Bureau of Statistics, *Chronological List of Canadian Censuses* (Ottawa, 1933), p. 2 (mimeographed).

which prompted his statement: "I will settle Montreal, even if every tree from here to there were an Iroquois."[2] The first act upon his arrival was the celebration of a Mass on a rustic altar. The religious aspect of the settlement cannot be too greatly emphasized. Of the numerous religious orders which were actively interested in expansion and conversion, the Jesuits were by far the most powerful and active. The whole colonial enterprise was charged with the crusading spirit. Martyrs died in their attempts to Christianize the Iroquois. Miraculous intervention from heaven was not unusual: Indian attacks were thwarted, healings performed, apparitions seen. When Father Dablon wanted an escort home, the desire of the Onandagas to pursue a beaver hunt was overcome by nine Masses to St. Jean Baptiste and the intercession of the Canadian martyr, Brébeuf.[3] This general acceptance of the miraculous as a natural result of prayer and religious activity continues only slightly diminished to the present day. Frontier conditions were ideal for its maintenance.

The early days of the colony were marked by the struggle for dominance between Laval, later bishop of Quebec, and the intendant and other civil authorities. Laval usually prevailed in his fervent attacks. It was he who founded a seminary so that Canada could provide its own priests. There was also considerable strife among the orders, particularly between the Jesuits and the Sulpicians. They openly attacked one another, carrying their fights even to the pulpit. Huguenot difficulties in France only served to make the Canadian clergy more militantly Catholic than ever. Care was taken that Huguenots should not get to

[2] Jean C. Bracq, *The Evolution of French Canada* (New York: Macmillan Co., 1924), p. 19.

[3] Francis Parkman, *The Old Régime in Canada* (8th ed.; Boston: Little, Brown & Co., 1880), p. 19.

the country; and when they did succeed, they were there-
with converted. In one instance, to bring about conversion it was necessary for a nun to mix a ground fragment
of Brébeuf's bones in the gruel of a sick Huguenot who
refused to be converted.[4]

When Louis XIV ascended the throne of France in 1661,
there were less than twenty-five hundred persons settled in
Canada, a third of these being in Quebec city.[5] This king
and his minister, Colbert, were largely responsible for the
immigration to Canada.[6] Up until the outbreak of the
Dutch war in 1672 Colbert conducted a systematic settlement of New France. The population a year later is given
as 6,705, an increase of over four thousand in ten years.[7] A
few proprietors of *seigneuries* granted in the name of the king
brought over colonists to settle their estates; the Sulpicians
of Montreal so peopled their grants. Still, the government
was responsible for the greatest part of colonization. According to a letter from Laval to Rome, the king had promised to send three hundred men a year for ten years. The
men came in groups on merchant ships. Some of these im-
migrants were bound to serve previous settlers for three
years, although they received wages. After this period they
were free to establish themselves. French agents located
and collected the men and sent them out from Dieppe and
Rochelle. At first the agents took men from around
Rochelle, but Laval objected that he wanted none from
that ancient stronghold of heresy. In an effort to "sow
good seed" in the new colony most of the emigrants were

---

[4] Parkman, *op. cit.*, p. 180.

[5] Dominion Bureau of Statistics, *op. cit.*, p. 3.

[6] Source for settlement of Canada and seignorial system is Parkman, *op. cit.*,
chaps. xiii and xv.

[7] Dominion Bureau of Statistics, *op. cit.*, p. 3.

drawn from northwestern France: Normandy, Poitou, Pay-d'Aunis, Brittany, Picardy, and Paris.

In addition to this emigration almost a complete regiment was discharged to become settlers. The officers and men were offered tracts of land and grants of money and provisions to encourage them to remain in Canada. This exclusive attention to the introduction of men into the country soon created a sexual disparity which required remedy. The king had rather recently established the Hôpital général in Paris as a sort of tremendous paupers' home. The *archers de l'hôpital*, a body of special police who herded this collection together, had been so successful that in 1662 there were 6,262 paupers in the institution. When the request for girls came from Canada, it was not surprising that the king sent out a hundred from the Paris and Lyons institutions. They were soon married, and twice the number was promised for the next year. It shortly became apparent that it was necessary to stop sending girls from the cities, as they were incapable of becoming colonial farmers' wives. Peasant girls, accustomed to the land, were sent in their stead. These came largely from families overburdened with children and glad to establish some of them. A letter is on record from Colbert to the Bishop of Rouen asking him to find fifty or sixty girls. The girls were rather carefully selected, and those who became notorious upon arrival in Canada were deported. The Canadian intendant, Talon, requested strong, healthy, and reasonably comely girls of Colbert. According to Mother Mary, who chaperoned their transportation to Canada, they were "mixed goods"; but the worst were only rude and unmanageable. Through the process of selection in France and the weeding-out in Canada, the female element of the settlement was even more God-fearing and hard working than the male. Upon arrival these "king's girls" were put together in large halls to which the men repaired and made their selections without ceremony or delay. The girls had the right of refusal, and their first question to any applicant was to inquire if he had a house and farm. In addition to the peasant girls, over a hundred girls from Dieppe and Rochelle were sent over as wives for the officers of the disbanded regiment. These included several actual *demoiselles*. During the seven-year period of immigration, about a thousand girls were sent over to the new country.

Likewise there was stimulus for the early marriage of settlers. Bounties were offered to boys who married before twenty and girls who wed before sixteen. This was in addition to the dowry, or "king's gift," which was given to each of the "king's girls." Fathers of families who did not "marry" their children by the time they reached the foregoing ages were fined and forced to report twice a year, like culprits. Bachelors were barred from hunting, fishing, and trading. Special bounties were offered to families having ten, twelve, or fifteen living children not in religious orders. From the statement of Talon that there were six to seven hundred births in the year 1671 the birth-rate appears to have been the prodigious figure of 100 per 1,000 population, over double the greatest in the world in 1931.[8] This pattern of early marriage, made possible by available land and large families, is the basis of French-Canadian social structure. The unified background of the colonists gave to the pattern of life in the whole province the homogeneity which existed down to the beginning of the movements of the *habitants* to the towns and cities. This fundamental pattern still prevails in rural Quebec. All the settlement was accomplished before the French Revolution and the

[8] Quebec Department of Municipal Affairs, Trade and Commerce, *1935 Statistical Year Book* (Quebec: Printer to the King's Most Excellent Majesty, 1936). Also Dominion Bureau of Statistics, *op. cit.*

subsequent growth of freethinking which separated French Canada in tradition and ideology from France.

The basis of the system of land settlement was a type of feudal tenure differing greatly in character from that of Europe. Canadian feudalism, started by Richelieu with the charter of the Hundred Associates, was practically a method of land distribution. It also faintly reflected the class divisions of France. The age-old abuses had been removed from the system. The greatest part of the land was given outright to *seigneurs* by the king. The *seigneur* receiving the fief was denied any voice in the direction of the government and was forced to render faith and homage to the crown at given intervals or whenever the *seigneurie* changed hands. The *seigneur*, in turn, granted portions of land to his vassals, or *habitants*. He never had the right to call upon them for military service—the right which was the heart of European feudal history. The *seigneur* was obliged to clear his land within a certain length of time or forfeit it to the crown. This was usually an impossible task for the *seigneur* alone, as he was rarely wealthy; so he was obliged to grant the land to farmers for a small perpetual rent and the duty of clearing it. The grants to the *habitants* were usually four *arpents* wide and forty long.[9] They ran back from the river and, as they were almost one and a half miles long, they included a combination of meadow and wooded upland. These grants, which the lord made to the *habitants*, passed freely to their heirs; but if the rights were sold, the *seigneur* received mutation fines, known as *lods et ventes*. From such a transaction the *seigneur* received one-twelfth of the purchase money. This operated to keep the land in the same families. If the *seigneur* sold his fief, he was likewise obliged to pay his superior a fifth of the price received for the *seigneurie*. This, of course, constituted a

---

[9] One *arpent* is 192 feet.

A Quebec Farmhouse

The *Route* from the Village to the Rang des Bras

tax on all improvements and therefore was abolished with the remainder of the system, except for the rents, in 1854.

The rents due the *seigneur* annually by the *habitants* were exceedingly low, rarely more than two *sous* per *arpent* in the early days. Payment was commonly on St. Martin's Day, and it was usual to pay the rents in kind. As long as the rents were paid, the *habitants'* titles were clear. In addition to these obligations there were others, which were customarily included in the agreement when the grant of land was made. The *habitant* usually had to have his grain ground at the *seigneurie* mill, work for the *seigneur* one or more days a year, give him one-eleventh of the fish taken from the river, and bake his bread in the *seigneur*'s oven. The last-named duty was rarely enforced, and the construction of the mill often became a weight around the neck of the *seigneur*. The *seigneur* had a little judicial power but rarely a prison.

Varying again from the old European feudal pattern, the receipt of a fief from the king carried with it no title of nobility. According to Parkman, only half of the *seigneurs* were of the *noblesse*, and many of these sold their fiefs to persons of very humble social rank. Thus, an investigation of ninety-one *seigneuries* in 1712 showed ten belonging to merchants, twelve to husbandmen, and two to masters of river craft. The rest belonged to religious corporations, judges, discharged officers and their sons, widows, councilmen, and crown officials. In addition to the French nobility there were the untitled *gentilhommes* in France. These persons constituted a group apart. The *noblesse* of Canada came largely from the disbanded regiment of Carignan. Intendants asked the king for patents of nobility for the more prominent colonists. Any *seigneur* could take on the country-gentlemen airs of the *gentilhomme*, and many did. Titles were actually bought in some cases. But unless a

man were rich enough to support such a life, he had to farm
like his *habitants*. The true nobility was worse off financially than the spurious, and fraternizing between lord and
vassals was the usual thing. The Canadian *gentilhomme*
wore his sword, tried to mimic court fashions, and had
some Jesuit education. Although never forgetful of his position, he was perfectly at home with his *habitants* or on an
Indian war-party.

The history of St. Denis and the most important of its
parent-parishes, Rivière Ouelle, is well recorded.[10]   The
first *seigneur* of Rivière Ouelle was one Jean-Baptiste
Deschamps, who was only twenty-eight years old when he
received the grant. He had been an officer in the regiment
of Carignan-Salières; and he was a *gentilhomme*, his father
being the Seigneur de Landes in Normandy. Desiring to
settle in New France, the young man had married a
sixteen-year-old *canadienne*, the daughter of a settler. A
few days after his marriage, in October, 1672, the intendant Talon granted him a seignorial fief in the name of Louis
XIV. His grant was two leagues[11] in frontage on the St.
Lawrence on either side of the Rivière Ouelle and a league
and a half in depth. Two leagues farther in depth were
granted to his widowed daughter-in-law in 1750. The *seigneurie* was officially named after three of his father's pos-
sessions in Normandy: La Bouteillerie, Flamandville, and
Boishébert; but the *seigneur* was known simply as Seigneur
de la Bouteillerie. The name Rivière Ouelle persisted as
the appellation of the *seigneurie*. This river's name has
been attributed to the Indian name of the eel, which the
tortuous stream resembles; but the better supposition is
that it honors M. Ouel, who accompanied Champlain and

    [10] Information on the history of Rivière Ouelle is taken from *Une Paroisse
canadienne au XVIIe siècle* by l'Abbé H. R. Casgrain (Montreal, 1912).

    [11] Five English miles.

who was a member of the *Cent-Associés* and a benefactor of the Recollets. The earliest censuses report a few persons from the region of this river, so that the name was fixed before the fief was established. At first, written indifferently "Ouel" or "Houel," the orthography finally became "Ouelle." This river name outlived not only the *seigneurie* designation but also the parish name which the settlement later received, so that today there are natives of the general region who do not know to whom the parish is dedicated.

There seems to have been little doubt in anyone's mind that the fief would be granted, for a manuscript in the Dieppe library stated that Jean Deschamps embarked for Canada in 1671 with two carpenters, two masons, and four laborers. A letter of the same year, written by the intendant Talon says of him: "Si les gens de cette qualité prennent aisément cette route, bientôt le Canada se remplira de personnes capable de le bien soutenir."[12]

The *seigneur* came to his fief with his little party and, after examining the area, selected and started clearing land for himself. A log house with steep roof was built the same year. In the years that followed, the clearing of the land was continued and a mill was built. It was ill-fated and was but the first of six constructed before the abolition of seignorial tenure. Settlers came and established themselves on grants of land. Within nine years after the founding of the fief there was a population of sixty-two persons. There were eleven families—thirty-six men and twenty-six women. The average age of the heads of households was only thirty-eight, varying from forty-six to twenty-nine, a normal situation in frontier communities. They had an average of only four children. The men married rather late, but to young wives. As further evidence of the early marriage of girls and the utility of boys, there were fifteen

[12] Casgrain, *op. cit.*, p. 32.

girls in the community to twenty-five boys. The average household had a twelve-*arpent* frontage of land,[13] nine head of cattle, and three guns. This little community, gathered around the *seigneur*, counted among its number a carpenter, three masons, a wheelwright, and a baker. These men were all pioneer farmers, and fishers in addition. In understanding the lack of social division between the *seigneur* and his *habitants* it is interesting to note that the *seigneur* had one servant boy of fifteen, twelve head of cattle, fifteen *arpents* of land, and three guns, whereas one of his *habitants*, a man of thirty-four, who had just married a nineteen-year-old girl, had two men servants of forty and nineteen, a girl servant of twelve, sixteen head of cattle, fifty *arpents* of land, and fourteen guns. Hired hands were necessary with a large farm when there were no children.

Of these settlers, three heads of families came directly from the region of Rouen with the *seigneur*. At least two others were second-generation Canadians from near Quebec. As the best lands around Beaupré and Ile d'Orléans were taken, there was a considerable movement of settlers away from that area. Of the families named in the 1681 census of Rivière Ouelle, half are still represented in the same settlement.

A few years after the granting of the fief of La Bouteillerie, the *seigneurie* of Kamouraska was granted farther down the river, and the fief of St. Denis, a strip of land a league wide between Kamouraska and Rivière Ouelle was granted to Nicolas Juchereau de Saint Denis in 1679. The settlement of the entire south shore in the Bas du Fleuve was so sparse that Father Morel was charged with the spiritual administration of the whole string of incipient parishes from Rivière du Loup to Rivière du Sud, a distance of seventy miles. This included the fiefs mentioned

---

[13] About 500 acres.

above. The settlement of these fiefs was slower than that of Rivière Ouelle. From a report on the missions made in 1683 we find that among Father Morel's charges there were eight families in Rivière Ouelle, eleven persons in two families in St. Denis, and one resident of Kamouraska.[14] This is the earliest record of settlement on the land of St. Denis.

Father Morel at forty-eight was the oldest of the country *curés*. He paddled up and down his area in a birch canoe with a pioneer companion. Each year he made his retreat to the seminary of Quebec for meditation and prayer, but the rest of the time was spent in making his rounds. The settlements were so scattered that the people often heard Mass only two or three times a year; the sick died without absolution; and infants without ritual baptism. Between these infrequent visits the *habitants* assembled at the house of the *seigneur* to say prayers or celebrate a *messe blanche*, which consisted of the prayers of the Mass, followed by rosaries. When the priest did arrive, he was received with joy and installed in the house of the *seigneur*, if the latter resided in the settlement, or in the home of one of the *habitants*. Here, on a rustic altar, Masses were said for the benefit of the community. The principal parts of the service were sung by some of the *habitants*. Infants were baptized, services read over old graves, confession heard and penance imposed, catechisms recited, and possibly a couple married.

Soon there was to be more regular religious administration. In 1685 Rivière Ouelle constructed, on land given by the *seigneur*, a small wooden chapel, dedicated to Notre Dame de Liesse. A year later a Recollet missionary from France settled in the community. He remained only two years, to be followed by another native French mission-

---

[14] The two families mentioned are possibly included in the Bouteillerie census of 1681, explaining the discrepancy in the population given for that *seigneurie*.

ary. This latter one weakened and soon left to die in peace, as had the first one. Abbé Pierre Francheville, a native Canadian, was then sent to the parish. It was he who, on an October morning of 1690, learned that an English fleet was coming up the St. Lawrence. In the absence of the *seigneur*, Abbé Francheville led his armed parishioners to the Point of Rivière Ouelle when the fleet anchored off this landmark. Schooled by the savages, they lay in ambush until the first boats of the landing-party were grounded. "Feu!" cried the priest, and a fusillade of shots rang out. A number of the Bostonian enemies of God and France fell dead, and the others hastily rejoined their ships. This was just the beginning of the difficulties of Phipps, who sailed on to Quebec, only to be repulsed again.

As the settlements in Rivière Ouelle and Kamouraska increased, new families pushed into the land between them. This was the fief of St. Denis. The Gagnon family is the first which is recorded as having settled on the land of what is now the parish of St. Denis. Two Gagnon brothers came to the parish of Rivière Ouelle from Ile d'Orléans in 1695. One of them settled in the fief of St. Denis. Their father had emigrated from Perche, and after nine generations the blond racial stock is still marked. Equally noticeable is the brunette strain in the Raymond family after nine generations. In 1709 one Phaucas dit Raymond came from Gascony and established himself in Kamouraska on what is now the Cap of St. Denis. Slightly later a second-generation Canadian, Jean Dionne, took up land in that part of the *seigneurie* of Kamouraska which now lies in St. Denis. These families grew, and sons took up concessions adjoining the parental *terre*. The *seigneurs* of St. Denis never settled on their *seigneurie*, and so it was left much to its own devices. The *habitants* of the eastern section of the fief went to the church of Kamou-raska, and those of the west to Rivière Ouelle.

Another English fleet sailed up the river in 1759 and anchored off the Point of Rivière Ouelle. With the memory of the first ambuscade still in the minds of the old men, another one was organized. But this time the *habitants* were overcome by the landing-party, and the commander of the fleet was so enraged by the unexpected resistance that he ordered the burning of settlements along the river for twenty miles. This was but the beginning of the French reverses. Quebec fell the same year, and Montreal the next. The Treaty of Paris in 1763 turned the whole country over to the English. The first years after the cession brought bitterness to the hearts of the most remote *canadiens*, for so the French considered themselves in contrast to *les anglais*. It was the history of any conquered people; and not until the Quebec Act, eleven years later, were the rights of the 150,000 French guaranteed against the 1,200–2,000 English residents of Quebec. During this time the English policy changed, and it was decided that "Canada would remain British by becoming French."[15]

The rights of the Catholic clergy were guaranteed—a wise move on England's part. Two years later, when public sentiment ran in favor of the American uprising and the invading forces were helped with supplies and even enlistments, Bishop Briand ordered the Canadians to defend their country. Such was the power of the church that, after that, all the coercion of the Americans went to naught. In 1812 the French again remained faithful to the English and served well against the States.

In both Lower and Upper Canada, roughly corresponding to the provinces of Quebec and Ontario today, unrest was growing against the form of government in operation

[15] Bracq, *op. cit.*, p. 70.

in both provinces. The system placed all the power in the hands of a few British families. Dislike of the form of government was very outspoken in the papers of the day and finally culminated in the abortive revolt of 1837, led largely by non-French. Separation was not even a consideration of the general movement. In spite of the handful actually concerned in the uprising, the suppression and reprisal were so horrible that they called forth even English protests. In rural Quebec there was no actual contact with the English, even as there is none today. For this reason bitterness was less personal; but public opinion and indignation followed the pattern of the cities, and *curés* made the most of it to combat all that was Protestant. The conversation of the long *veillées* kept feelings high, and politics became the absorbing interest it has always remained.

During these times there came to St. Denis one Jean Charles Chapais, a son of Rivière Ouelle, who had taken the classical course at the seminary of Nicolet. He established the first store for those settlers who had taken up lands along the *coteau* between Rivière Ouelle and Kamouraska. This settlement, including contiguous parts of the two parishes which lay in the *seigneurie* of St. Denis and parts of Kamouraska and La Bouteillerie, were designated canonically as a separate parish in 1833.[16] The parish was put under the protection of St. Denis d'Alexandrie in honor of the first *seigneur*. Popular opinion had it, however, that the parish was named after Denis Blanchet, son of the Seigneur de la Bouteillerie. The name St. Denis de la Bouteillerie stuck, only to be replaced in the last generation by the county name, St. Denis de Kamouraska. Arriving in the new parish, M. Chapais prospered and

---

[16] For the history of the parish of St. Denis see Joseph A. Lavoie, *La Famille Lavoie au Canada* (Quebec, 1922).

married the daughter of the *seigneur* of the parish adjoining Rivière Ouelle. He took an active interest in the community and had a small wooden chapel built in 1839 with material furnished by the *habitants*. It was not until three years later that the parish received civil recognition and

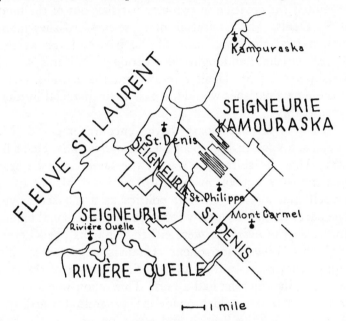

Kamouraska

SEIGNEURIE KAMOURASKA

FLEUVE ST. LAURENT

St. Denis

SEIGNEURIE

St. Philippe

SEIGNEURIE Rivière Ouelle

ST. DENIS

Mont Carmel

RIVIÈRE-OUELLE

⊢——⊣ 1 mile

MAP OF THE LOCAL *Seigneuries* AND PARISHES

the first *curé* came to reside there. He immediately started the erection of the stone church which was to take fifteen years to complete. Rural French Canada had a well-earned reputation for heavy drinking; and Curé Quertier, a reformed drunkard, became an enthusiastic apostle of temperance. Two years after his arrival he founded the Société de la Croix de Tempérance and had all his parishioners sworn to its rules. The black cross which symbolized his movement soon spread to the houses of surrounding parishes. The whole parish assisted at the erection of a great cross overlooking the river, and the *croix noire* became permanently associated with the daily prayers and customs of inhumation.

The second *curé* despite the protests of his parishioners, promoted the creation of two new parishes out of the land of St. Denis. The separation of these new parishes more than halved the population of the parish. Even as the parent-parishes had fought the creation of St. Denis, so the parishioners of St. Denis foresaw that the establishment of these new parishes would increase their financial burden considerably.

Owing in no small part to the encouragement of M. Chapais, his son-in-law opened a *fromagerie* in St. Denis in 1881. This cheese factory was at the same time the first milk-industry school in North America.[17] M. Chapais himself had already entered politics as a Conservative. The party name was locally replaced by his personal name. For years the *habitants* were either "Chapais" or "Letellier," his Liberal opponent. Chapais represented his county continuously from 1851 until the union of the two Canadas, in which he had a part. This union was an artificial, formal one which made no progress toward the assimilation of the French and was soon broken, so that Quebec took up its independent government under the Dominion. M. Chapais remained active in Quebec politics until his death. To his son Thomas he gave a legal education at the University of Laval, where Thomas later occupied the chair of history. Being defeated in his first election in his own county, Thomas Chapais was appointed senator in the province, later senator in the Dominion government. He is the only man holding the two offices. Honored with ministerial positions and knighthood, he has

[17] *Ibid.*, p. 321.

continued the tradition of his father and represents to the St. Denisians their highest attainments.

Less than thirty years after the foundation of the parish, difficulties arose over the position of a new school. The old school was a house to which went children from the whole parish. The dispute arose over where the new schoolhouse should be built. Parishioners at each end of the parish wanted the school closer to them. The quarrel grew bitter, and classes were continued in the large old house in the village. Family animosities arose, and one group shifted its political affiliation so as further to oppose its rivals. The fourth *curé* of the parish tried to settle the matter, but by then the quarrel was too intense. The *curé* himself was removed from the parish as a result of opposition to his desire to have the gallery in the church torn down.

The term of the next *curé* was marked with disaster. One year there was an earthquake, and another year the church was completely gutted by fire. The *bedeau* had been burning spruce branches behind the altar in order to make ashes for use on Ash Wednesday. Apparently, when he departed for the night, the fire was not completely out. When a passing parishioner noticed the smoke, the fire was already so advanced that there was barely time to take out the *bon Dieu*. Fearing that the steeple might fall to the east onto the presbytery and set it afire, the *habitants* started to move out the furniture. The *curé* told them to stop, saying that the steeple would not fall that way.[18] It actually did fall in the opposite direction; and as it fell, the bell miraculously rang out. The stone walls of the church remained standing. While the rest was being rebuilt, Masses were heard in the *salle publique*. Another

[18] The actual *curé* was on a trip to Rome. The details of the fire are according to a traditional account of a nonwitness. For other miracles associated with fire see chap. vii.

bell was borrowed from the neighboring parish of Kamouraska and set up outside, so that the life of the parish could go on as usual.

After the church was rebuilt, the school dispute assumed new proportions. The most discontented faction had the old school house condemned as unsafe. They wanted to force the building of a new school closer to their end of the parish. Their means of pressing action so outraged other parishioners that the majority voted that the new structure be erected a hundred yards farther away from the condemning faction than the old house had been. The result of this move was the complete severance of the offended group from the school system and the erection of another school *municipalité* within the parish, a condition which persists along with the family animosities to this day.

At the outbreak of the World War, two young men from the parish volunteered. Later the draft took five more. The draft brought Anglo-French sentiments in conflict again. The English claimed that the French were cowards, while the French resisted the draft, being undesirous of fighting in a war in which they had no interest. They felt no patriotism for their English-dominated dominion. The principal effects of the war were not in terms of this ethnic dispute as much as the growth of industrial opportunities in Canadian and American cities. The good lands in Quebec had already been taken up; and even before the war, children of large families were finding a livelihood in industry. Post-war prosperity made the demand for their services even greater. In the twelve months from June, 1923, to June, 1924, 42,250 persons left the province for the United States.[19] Parishes with poorer land, which were

---

[19] Raoul Blanchard, *L'Est du Canada française* (Montreal: Beauchemin, 1935), I, 194.

on the direct road of emigration, were devastated. Half
of the people of St. Charles, in the county of Bellechasse,
went to the States; and present parishioners count as many
relatives there as in the parish. In a parish adjacent to St.
Charles half the houses were closed and the farms abandoned. No farms were left thus in St. Denis. The tempta-
tion of easy money could not root out the old secure
economy. Some one hundred persons did emigrate from
the parish, however, going to New Hampshire, Maine, and
Massachusetts.[20] The textile mills of Nashua, New Hampshire, drew the largest group. Most of these individuals
were in their late teens and early twenties. Both sexes
were attracted by the opportunity for self-establishment,
which was very difficult to achieve at home. A few entire
families, who were in debt, sold their lands and departed.
The usual procedure was for a young man to go to the
States, where, once established, he sent for his brothers
and sisters. It is clear that many left to work in industry
with the expectation of making enough money to return to
Quebec and buy a farm. Half of those who left returned
to St. Denis or neighboring parishes after about five years
in the States. Another pattern of movement was seasonal.
Particularly, brickyard work attracted men in summer,
who returned home in winter.

The industrial collapse and depression resulted in the
closing of the border to immigration. There was some return movement to Canada as a result of decreased employment. The youth that had hitherto found an outlet in the
cities was forced to remain in the rural parishes and attempt to make a living with neither land nor regular employment.

[20] This represents an emigration of over 10 per cent of the parish population.

CHAPTER II

THE LAND AND THE PEOPLE OF ST. DENIS

THE oldest parishes in Quebec are to be found along the St. Lawrence River. The narrow fertile lowlands bordering it were inviting to the farmers who entered New France over the broad stream, the highway of the settlement. North of the river the Laurentians, the oldest mountains in America, dip down almost to the river bank. To the south the Appalachians crowd in upon the strip of river lowland which becomes ever narrower to the east until the mountains of the Gaspé drop sheer into the St. Lawrence. The life of the province still clings to the lowland and the adjacent plateaus, except where tributaries have led man farther inland. The mountain hinterland on both sides of the river is wooded, and here are located the *chantiers*, where woodsmen work through the winter cutting timber for the spring drives. The province stretches vast, cold, and uninhabited north of this vital strip which has the St. Lawrence as its axis. The plateau region south of the stretch of river between Montreal and Quebec is more completely settled than the other back regions and joins the northeastern section of the States as the Appalachians stretch southward.

Along the south shore of the St. Lawrence below the city of Quebec the mountains rise abruptly only a few miles back from the river. Sharply faulted and folded rock beds rise out of the river and its lowlands, forming striking features on the landscape. In this region, some eighty miles downstream from Quebec, Rivière Ouelle empties its tributary waters into the St. Lawrence, which here has attained a width of over ten miles. The fertile lands around Rivière

Ouelle attracted an early farming settlement, just as they more recently attracted a provincial agricultural college and experimental farm. Adjoining the parish of Rivière Ouelle to the east is its daughter-parish, St. Denis, also on the St. Lawrence. The two are topographically connected by a broad, low ridge, the Coteau, which starts in Rivière Ouelle, follows the bank of the St. Lawrence along most of the frontage of St. Denis, and ends in a high rocky prominence, Cap au Diable, which juts out into the river. Beyond the Cap is a shallow bay and lowland which extend to the next ridge and parish to the east. The parishes of Rivière Ouelle and St. Denis are naturally separated where the ridge is met by the Grande Plaine, an extensive peat bog, which stretches southward. A road runs along the ridge between the two communities and dips down under the protection of the steep southern slope as it enters St. Denis. This road is an alternate highway from Quebec and Levis to Gaspé and follows the river, while its more traveled branch runs parallel three miles inland.

The parish of St. Denis extends five miles along the river. At its eastern edge it is separated from the adjacent parish of Kamouraska[1] by the sweep of lowland running south from the bay dominated by the Cap. This lowland is uncultivatable close to the river, and it is fully exposed to the winter winds blowing off the river ice, as the protecting Coteau ends at the Cap. Thus, the eastern and western boundaries of the parish are natural ones, there being no continuum of habitation from one parish to the next along the main road.

Topographically St. Denis constitutes one side and the bottom of a vast flat trough open at either end. The "side" is the Coteau, the shale cliffs of which rise abruptly only a few hundred feet back from the river. This ridge is low,

[1] Once Cap Mouraska.

ranging around thirty feet above the plain to its south. It is a mile wide in places, tapering toward the Cap. Parallel ridges break its surface for much of its length. The southern edge of the Coteau dips down to a fertile plain three miles wide. At the other edge of the plain the moun-

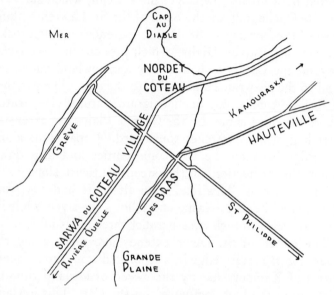

MAP OF ST. DENIS

tains rise abruptly, paralleling the Coteau and forming the other "side" of the trough. St. Denis extends two miles into this lowland, so that the irregular boundary of the parish is a mile from the mountain's edge, where lies the village of St. Philippe. Through the lowland and a half-mile south of the Coteau flows a stream called Des Bras because of its branches. This deeply cut rivulet finally empties into the bay to the north and east.

All St. Denis farmers recognize soil differences in the parish and know rather definitely the extent of each kind.

The land on the Coteau which is cultivatable is *terre sablée*, particularly good for potatoes and oats, and *terre d'avoine* or *terre grise*, which is good for oats, as the name implies, and other grains except wheat. The land of the plain is roughly *terre forte* in the western half and *terre d'avoine* to the east. The *terre forte* or *terre noire* is particularly good for hay and wheat. The relation of the soil type to the crop makes a knowledge of soil distribution important in this agricultural community.

Water facilities are likewise unevenly distributed. The families along the Coteau obtain an adequate supply from shallow wells. The spring thaw may make them muddy, but they quickly clear again. Water is obtained almost invariably by means of hand pumps in the houses. Running water is to be found only in a few of the richer homes of the village. The families in the plain have no adequate source of water. Some farmers take it from the stream Des Bras; one even filters it. There is an artesian well and a few deep cemented ones, but they are too expensive for most families. As a result, the farmers collect rain water and haul water for cooking from the Coteau.

The river on which the parish is located no longer plays as important a part in the life of the people as it used to. The road has supplanted water travel. There is still some commercial eel- and sardine-fishing, but this has declined with the stabilization of the economy on the cleared lands. Some men dig mussels along the shore when the ice breaks up in the spring, and the salvaging of billets of pulpwood still constitutes an irregular additional source of income for a few. The *habitant*'s major interests are in the land. The Coteau cuts the river off from his view, and months may pass when it is never visited. No parishioner has ever left the St. Denis shore and crossed over the expanse of water to the other side. For the fishermen the fact that the river turns salt some thirty miles upstream is important. He feels that the freshwater eels which he catches have a better flavor since they come from salt water. More vital are the tides which make his manner of fishing possible.[2] The tides recede more than a mile over the gently sloping river flats. The breadth, tides, and salt water cause the river to be designated as the *mer*. It is closed to navigation from the last of November to the last of April. The ice is not continuous across the river at St. Denis, as the tides keep it broken into huge blocks, leaving an open channel in the middle.

Snow entirely covers the ground for five months after the beginning of December. Snow flurries, or *bordées*, sufficient to cover the ground for short periods are common in October and May. St. Denis receives around nine feet of snow during the winter, so that when there are no melting periods the parish is deeply blanketed. The average length of the growing season is less than four months.[3] Precipitation is rather evenly distributed through the seasons, favoring the summer months to some degree.[4] The temperature is not extreme either in winter or summer. The winter mean temperature is 12.9° Fahrenheit, and that for the summer months is 64°.[5] Extremes of temperature during a fifty-year period range from −34° to 97°. Freezing weather

---

[2] Spring tide is 17.5 feet, and the neap tide 13 feet. For climate also see Raoul Blanchard, *L'Est du Canada française* (Montreal: Beauchemin, 1935), I, 111–33.

[3] Québec, Ministère de l'Agriculture, *Le Québec agricole 1932* (Quebec: Printer to the King's Most Excellent Majesty, 1933). The season is roughly June into September.

[4] Blanchard, *op. cit.*, pp. 111–33. A thirty-year average at Quebec is 42 inches of precipitation per year (snow reduced one-tenth), distributed: summer (June–August) 29.7 per cent, winter 24.4 per cent, spring 20.9 per cent. At St. Denis the average precipitation is lower, around 35 inches.

[5] *Ibid.* Fifty-year average from the city of Quebec. Somewhat colder as one progresses down the river.

during the three summer months is almost unheard of, but the farmer who has grain standing in the field in late September and early October may well awaken to find it frozen.

Houses are adapted to meet the rigors of winter. Those along the ridge crowd up close to its protecting southern edge. On the more exposed plain, houses have their doors on the south side to avoid the force of the strong north wind. This location of doors means that houses south of the *chemin* have doors which do not open on the road. If there are doors to the north, they remain sealed shut all winter. The large kitchen is the most continually occupied room in the house. It is usually located on the southern side of the building, while the small formal salon is often to the north. Storm doors or built-on entries are put on the houses in winter, and double windows are built into all the houses. Because the kitchen is the center of the social life in the house, airy summer kitchens, which do not retain the heat of the stove, are built onto the sides of the houses. Too exposed to be warm, these annex kitchens are evacuated in winter.

The typical house in St. Denis has a single full floor, often well raised off the ground, and a second floor under a ridge roof, the slope of which breaks into a curve as the roof extends out to form the eaves. The roof and front of the house are shingled; and the front is usually painted white, the windows and doors being outlined in color. An open gallery, supported from below, runs part way around the house under the protecting eaves. These galleries are now evolving into long covered porches. Thatch has entirely disappeared from housetops, although it is still to be found on a few barns. It is not being renewed, tin and iron roofs being used to replace it. Barns are both of the old single-floor variety, often a hundred feet long, and the newer double type with raised runways to the second floor. The straight pitched roof with no eaves, which was the original roof style in Canada, is retained in some of the barns. Newer barns are made with "French" roofs, a variety of mansard. This construction is to be seen in some of the houses also, but the trend in new houses is to two-story box-shaped structures with flat or low-peaked roofs. The *presbytère* and *salle publique* are good examples of this style. Conveniences in the houses are rare. Only a few villagers have plumbing or furnaces, and two-thirds of the houses still burn kerosene for light. There are twenty-eight radios in the parish, including two battery sets. One new feature has penetrated every house, that is, the most modern wood stove available. Made with the latest conveniences, including an oven thermometer, it is highly decorative with its enamel surface and built-in mirror. Such a stove is the one extravagance every farmer allows himself. A woman's housekeeping is judged first on the condition of her stove. It is the practice to clean the stove every day and to devote an hour to it on Saturdays.

The 9,000 acres of land in the parish include 650 acres of timber along the Coteau. Over 1,000 acres more are not tillable or fit for pasture, so that only 7,000 acres are used for farming purposes. They are divided among eighty farming families, who employ over a third of the land for pasturage and put the rest into equal parts of hay and grain, particularly oats.[6] The parish supports a population of 700 persons, or about 54 to the square mile.[7] Blanchard calculates that the "old parishes," or those of the lowland of this region, have an average population density of 53.3 per square mile.[8] Those actually on the river, excluding the three cities of Montmagny, Rivière du Loup,

---

[6] Dominion report on field crops for 1930.

[7] Church census for 1936.   [8] *Op. cit.*, I, 187–89. From 1931 census.

and Rimouski, have an average density of 52.6. St. Denis is, therefore, very typical of the section of the south shore between Quebec and the Gaspé. The population of St. Denis has actually declined over the past fifty years. Many families went to the States and did not return. Others left through failures due to poor management. Their lands have been incorporated into other farms or are being held for growing sons. There are three such farms being cultivated at present, but the houses are empty and the large families which they formerly contained are no longer there. The increasing loss of economic independence means that the farmer must use more land to produce cash crops in order to support his changed standard of living. The same amount of land, therefore, cannot support as many persons as it formerly did. Improvements in agricultural method have increased the yield per acre, but they have also taken many acres out of cultivation through the introduction of systematic rotation. The large pasturage evidences this fact.

The old, settled nature of the parish is seen in the age distribution of the population.[9] The excess of women and the number of individuals of extreme old age is typical of such a situation. The marked reduction in the number of persons in age groups over thirty bears out the basic principle of the rural French-Canadian family cycle—the elimination from the community of noninheriting children over this age. Of the total population of the parish, 68 per cent are single. This situation is typical in this region.[10] The predominance of unmarried women in the upper ages is of importance as indicating the recent failure of the social system to take care of this group.

The birth-rate in St. Denis over the past ten years was

[9] See Appen. I.

[10] For the county in the 1931 census, 67 per cent.

24 per 1,000.[11] It shows no decrease from the previous ten-year period. This is in marked contrast to the general situation in the county and province. The provincial rate has fallen 9.74 per 1,000 over a fifteen-year period, and the county rate 6.37 per 1,000.[12] It is a general tendency for the birth-rate to be higher in the rural regions, the cities being responsible for the marked decrease. Kamouraska County includes one town of 3,000. It will also be noted that the birth-rate in St. Denis approaches the 1934 figure for the entire province. The small number of procreative women relative to the population of the parish is responsible for this. The parish rate shows a decline over the past forty years owing to the increasingly large group of unmarried adults.

There is a noticeable tendency for fewer conceptions during the plowing and planting months of April and May and also during the month of February.[13] The explanation of the drop in this last month is difficult. It does, however, follow a month of general release popularly know as *les fêtes* and sometimes includes also the beginning of the Lenten period.[14] The months in which marriages occur

---

[11] From parish register of 1927–36. This is lower than that for the county in 1930: 32/1,000. Quebec Department of Municipal Affairs, Trade and Commerce, *1931 Statistical Year Book* (Quebec: Printer to the King's Most Excellent Majesty, 1932).

[12] Period from 1919–34:

	1919	1934
Quebec (province)........	35.04/1,000	25.3/1,000
Kamouraska County......	36.27/1,000	29.9/1,000

Note the close correspondence of rates in 1919.

[13] One-quarter fewer conceptions than the consistent number during the other months. Computed over thirty-nine-year period, as are marriages and deaths to be discussed.

[14] Robert Redfield, *Tepoztlán* (Chicago: University of Chicago Press, 1930). This is probably a feature of the cycle of "crises and lyses" of which the author makes a point.

show a more marked cyclical nature. Over a fifth of all marriages take place in July, following the spring farming activity. There is a subsequent drop during the rest of the busy cultivating and harvesting season, followed by another rise in October, after the harvest. Almost a sixth of the marriages are in this month. November, the Month of the Dead, begins a period during which the frequency of marriage declines. This period extends through the season of Advent, when there are no marriages. The *fêtes* of January mark the third most popular time for marriage, only

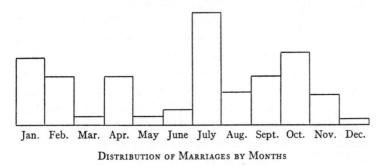

Jan.　Feb.　Mar.　Apr.　May　June　July　Aug.　Sept.　Oct.　Nov.　Dec.

DISTRIBUTION OF MARRIAGES BY MONTHS

slightly decreased in February. March and the Lenten period mark another period of decline during which there are almost no weddings. The ensuing month is one of release and marriage, followed by two months of spring work and practically no marriage. These cycles demonstrate how basic agriculture and religion are to the community.

The yearly distribution of deaths from all causes shows a surprising feature in the lack of correspondence with the climatically dangerous periods—autumn, winter, and spring. Deaths are more common during the summer months, the frequency in July and August each being twice that for November. Greater activity during the summer months, in comparison to the seclusion of the winter, is in part responsible for this situation. The probabilities of digestive trouble in infants are higher during this season also.[15] This is partially due to the fact that summer heat stimulates bacterial growth of all kinds. There are no doctors in St. Denis; but two reside in the immediate region, one fifteen miles away, the other three. The closer one is called more frequently than the other, who is requested largely by his relatives in the parish. In addition to this medical care, the provincial Bureau of Health has well-established contact with the parish. There are monthly baby clinics with a doctor and visiting nurse, and other special clinics and gratuitous services.[16]

According to these doctors, the high infant mortality is due largely to digestive ailments. Enteritis is the most common cause of such death. The use of unboiled water, the improper feeding of mother and child, and early weaning all contribute to the prevalence of this condition. Small children die of "convulsions," caused by eating too heavy food. Dietary deficiency causes numerous physical difficulties, the most obvious being rickets. At a public hospital in Quebec over 75 per cent of the cases were attributable to dietary insufficiencies. Among adults, pleurisy and pneumonia, resulting from lack of proper covering after physical exertion, are common causes of death. Two per cent of the people in the parish are tubercular in spite of free clinics.[17] Home treatment is advised for all but the most severe cases. Deaths from diphtheria, scarlet fever, measles, and smallpox are unusual now. Venereal diseases

[15] One-quarter of the children die before they are a year old. For infant mortality, see "Kinship and the Family Cycle," chap. iv.

[16] See "Control of Nature," chap. vii.

[17] Quebec Department of Municipal Affairs, Trade and Commerce, *1936 Statistical Year Book* (Quebec: Printer to the King's Most Excellent Majesty, 1937). Of the deaths in the province in 1935, 53.8 per cent were due to heart and arterial diseases, cancer, tuberculosis, nephritis, pneumonia, and diarrhea, in the order given.

are very rare. Syphilis is practically nonexistent, and the doctor treats only some five cases of gonorrhea a year in the whole county.[18] In spite of the rigorous climate and high death-rate in certain brackets, many people live to very old age. This is partially due to the vigorous selection at the infant level. The oldest local parishioners are a man of ninety and a woman of eighty-nine. Longevity is most marked in the women. Of the twenty-one parishioners over eighty years old, only one is a man.

Racially the people are mixed. Nordic strains, which originated in Normandy, are common in rather pure form. Blue-eyed blondes with long heads and thin hair are frequently encountered. Tall stature is rarer but does occur. In contrast to these types are shorter, extremely dark persons of marked Mediterranean appearance. Persons showing predominant Nordic characteristics are distinguished locally as "Normans," whereas the darker types may be called "Gascons." There is no racial antipathy and no consensus in preference for racial characters such as blondness. To the parishioner there are no sentiments organized around these physical characteristics. The word "race," however, is full of meaning, but in another context. "Race" has ethnic significance to the *habitant*. There are two principal "races" in this sense: the "Canadians," which is used synonomously with Catholic French-Canadians; and the "English," which means Protestant English residents of Canada.

All of the parishioners of St. Denis are Catholic and French-speaking. A few, who returned after living and working in the United States for a number of years, know a few English words and expressions, but they are gen-

[18] Not only is the aid of the doctor not sought but the effects of venereal disease are not recognizable in the population. In fifteen years the doctor has only seen two cases of syphilis, one a stranger in the region. This is but one evidence of the isolation of the people.

erally incapable of speaking or understanding English. The senator and his relatives who reside in St. Denis for varying periods have a real knowledge of English. They have a life in the Dominion which requires such bilingualism, but English has no part in their rural sojourns. The other parishioners have no contact with the English. English-speaking tourists pass through the parish, but few ever stop. Three houses have English signs making a bid for such travelers: "Lunch," "Room and Board," and "Rooms To Let." Only at the last of these is there anyone who can speak any English at all. Two or three American cars stop for the night each summer and constitute the entire contact. Advertising signs are largely in French, but the public notices at the post office and the labels on commercial goods are usually bilingual. Only French is seen in the local newspapers, but those homes with radios begin to feel themselves surrounded by a foreign tongue. The few French stations are preferred. Even music on English programs holds no appeal except to the senator, who enjoys the symphonies.

The schools attempt to teach a reading knowledge of English, although it is rarely employed after school is finished. In this respect the farmer is less likely to know English than the nonlanded villager. Being a farmer implies a sedentary life in a region where English is of no value. Nonfarmers have an eye constantly on the city, where there is employment. Bilingualism is a decided advantage in these centers; so this group expresses at least a desire to learn to speak English. Locally, there is no opportunity to learn, as even the schoolteachers do not know much English. The sentiment exists, however, that it is *commode* to know "the two languages."

In addition to the English words which individuals have acquired in travel, there are over three hundred English words in regular use.[19] Many of these words are actually believed to be French; others are used as an American might use "chauffeur," and still others with the self-consciousness which might accompany the use of an expression like *champ d'honneur*. The English words used in regular speech are associated with cultural borrowings from the English, largely technical and mechanical. This use of English words is decried by language purists in the province. The schools try to disseminate standard French by eliminating not only English words but also antiquated forms, local variations, and bad grammar.[20] However, the teachers are daughters of the local farmers and speak much the same dialect as their students. Such teachers can correct grammar and retard the use of some of the words and expressions on the lists of nonstandard French forms, but usually the substitute expressions are accepted as literary ones which have no particular bearing on common speech. This conscious revision of the local language has effected a few changes in pronunciation and choice of words. Such change is usually accomplished by attaching an aroma of humor to the nonstandard word and ridicule to its user. This method necessitates the development of a particular attitude on the part of the natives toward their speech. The priests, urban professional men, and governmental officers, and schools, newspapers, and radios have all, either by example or by crusading force, made the native feel that his traditional speech is a brogue, a patois. It symbolizes the uneducated *habitant;* a word which is gaining a derogatory significance. The *curé* preaches: "You are no longer *habitants;* you are *cultivateurs*."

Rural sons who go to the University of Laval in Quebec are forced to alter their speech, to omit much local idiom.

[19] See "Old and New," chap. xi.

[20] For French-Canadian vocabulary see Société du Parler français au Canada, *Glossaire du parler français au Canada* (Québec: L'Action sociale, 1930).

This sophisticated group speaks a dialect closer to the standard French. Whereas the farmer says that he realizes that he speaks a patois but it is the only thing he has ever known, the urban *canadien*, on the one hand, supports *bon parler français* movements and, on the other, defends the local speech as being only a mild dialect difference, as containing archaic expressions and pronunciation, and as being freer from English words than Parisian French. On the whole, the *bon parler français* aspect is what reaches the farmer. The defense of the speech is part of the urban English-French class picture with the French defending their heritage against criticism. A farmer, hearing his priest-son explain to an American that many of the local expressions were old French forms, commented: "We are not so bad then!" The rural Frenchman is usually apologetic about his speech. Corrective measures have succeeded in making him lose his pride in his language. He has no basis for judging which of the words he employs are standard French and which are not.[21] His acceptance of the fact that he speaks nonstandard French and will never learn anything else means that there is little resistance to the entrance of English words, the exactly opposite effect from that desired. Because of the value placed on learning English, there is no reticence in the use of words borrowed from that language. There is formal purist teaching in the school, but it goes no farther.

Language forms which are not in active association with their cultural context are not retained. Words learned in the study of English at school are not used outside the school. Words like "cat," "book," and "red" have their counterparts in French forms in constant use. "Cat" is the word to say for *chat* when in English class—such is

[21] Thus the county public-health nurse comments on the language and explains the local derivation of *tourtière* from *tourterelle*, a pure fiction based on two standard French words.

the association of the word. The word "boss," on the other hand, connotes an individual unknown in the region until the French came in contact with English "bosses" in industry. English words to be borrowed must then be associated with some new idea, object, or act which is of practical importance to the native. The words come in with the innovations. The schools attempt to supplant such English words with French ones. *Interrupteur* becomes the word to say to the teacher for "switch" during French lessons. As long as the French word has value only in the class, "switch" remains in common use. One teacher even complained that it was hard to teach the children from homes without electricity the French words they should use in place of English ones for electrical equipment. Being unfamiliar with the reference of the English word, they had to be taught both the wrong and right words. The chances are that, of the two strange words, the English one would be retained.

Girls are much more likely to receive supplementary education after finishing the local schools than are the boys. A girl may secure a *diplôme* after only two years of convent training, whereas a boy must attend college eight years to complete his *cours classique*. The tradition of sending girls to convent is far older. In addition, attendance at the parish schools is not altogether obligatory, and the services of even young boys are apt to be required on the farm. Because of all these factors the boys receive less schooling than the girls. A generation ago many of the men in the parish could not sign their names. The women have always been the scribes of the families.[22] They keep the

[22] During the ordinary week there is an average of fifty letters a day both entering and leaving the local post office. This number includes advertisements and business letters. The average of over two letters per week per household distorts the picture for the farm family. These households have little correspondence, the average being swelled by village tradesmen, *rentiers*, and village girls who correspond frequently with other girls.

farm accounts; and the local deputy to Ottawa says that it is invariably the women who write, requesting positions for their men. Since the turn of the century more importance has been attached to education, largely because it assists young men in securing positions in urban centers. The introduction of farm machinery in this same period made it possible for the farmers to let their sons finish the local school. Newspapers are taken in most of the homes; and although they may not be read by the father, the mother and children find them interesting.[23] Books are read almost exclusively by the women and girls.[24] Because of the six grades of school available for all, however, literacy is increasing. All the young men of the parish can read and write to some degree.

[23] The following were the newspaper subscriptions in the winter of 1936–37:

L'Action catholique	65	Le St. Laurent	5
Le Soleil	14	Le Journal	3
L'Evenement	8	La Presse	2
La Province	6	La Patrie	1
Le Devoir	5	L'Information	1

The great majority of these are printed in the city of Quebec. One hundred and ninety subscriptions were distributed among 8 religious monthlies sponsored by particular orders. Aside from these, there were 15 subscriptions to the provincial agricultural bulletin and a political monthly. The average daily makeup of L'Action catholique over a test week was as follows:

	Inches		Inches
Politics	216.5	Nationalistic (French-Canadian) editorials and stories	41.5
Religion	201.0		
Parish and town social notices	102.0	Accidents, sensationally reported	38.0
Quebec (city) social column	14.5		
Crime, largely court convictions	57.0	Advertising (75 per cent local, 12 per cent national, 13 per cent combined)	934.0

[24] There is a circulating library of 900 books in the church. During the last five years the reading has been distributed as follows: 79 per cent fiction, largely sentimental novels with religious content; 16 per cent specifically religion; 2.7 per cent history; 0.6 per cent travel; 0.1 per cent science. These percentages express preferences rather than library restrictions. This library is used by a small group of women and girls, 80 per cent of whom have had convent education and practically none of whom is married.

With the exception of the *école modèle*, all the schools are one-room frame buildings known as *écoles des rangs*. The *école modèle*, located in the village, has two classrooms and sleeping accommodations for the two teachers. The four other schools each have one teacher, who lives at home. Five of the parish teachers are local women, the sixth being the teacher for the upper grades of the *école modèle*, to which all the children of the municipality have access. Because the teachers have little training, usually only two years at convent, and because they live at home, they can be paid low salaries. They average $135 a year. The professional experience of the teachers ranges from one year to over twenty. Those teachers who have had long experience have taught outside the parish as well. There are in the parish several old-maid schoolteachers who have retired on pensions. School teaching used to be a prelude to marriage; now it is likely to create *rentières*.

A preparatory class and seven years of course work are available in the larger *municipalité* or school district, five years in the smaller. Children start preparatory work at five or six years. It is unusual for children to go farther than the fifth year; and, of course, in the local school of the smaller *municipalité* they cannot continue beyond that year. Enrolment is very evenly distributed among the ages up to this point. Girls are slightly more likely to go to school than boys, particularly after the age of thirteen.[25]

[25] Children of school age, by sexes and enrolment, in St.Denis, 1935-36:

AGES	BOYS		GIRLS	
	No. of School Age	No. Enrolled	No. of School Age	No. Enrolled
5 and 6 years.....................	12	9	11	10
7 through 13 years	47	44	54	54
14 and 15 years..................	18	6	15	11
Total......................	77	59 (75.1%)	80	75 (93.8%)

The average attendance of the girls is a little lower than that for boys.[26]

Certain nonfarming parishioners with urban backgrounds or who render special services are more literate than the farmers. The *curé* and senator and their relatives are cultured in an urban sense. Parish enterprises which necessitate the keeping of records may be conducted by literate men. The owner of the major store is a man who keeps his own accounts. His clerk, the son of a farmer, assists in keeping the books. The two other stores trade so little that they alone could not support their owners. One is run by a widow; the other, by a man who also owns a summer hotel at the beach. The local bank was started by a carpenter whose writing ability and character have gained for him the traditional post of secretary of the parish council. He soon turned the affairs of the bank over to an unmarried niece. The post office is handled by another widow, who writes with difficulty. In addition to her special function of sorting the three daily mails, she sells sweets, cards, tobacco, and various oddments. The owner and operator of the *beurrerie* keeps his own complicated accounts and renders a yearly report to the committee which represents the farmers whose milk he uses. The postilion who meets the mail trains and the two traveling salesmen from the parish make some use of their literacy.

Several young men, who have no employment and no land to inherit, live with their parents and gain a small income through special trades. One repairs radios; another makes tobacco pouches and fly-swatters from inner tubes; a third runs a small garage; and yet another does some photographic work and conducts a sort of taxi serv-

[26] Average attendance: boys, 85 per cent; girls, 80 per cent.

ice. None of these trades is sufficiently lucrative to allow the man to marry and set up his own household. All the trades are new to the parish, having been known less than ten years. The young men who ply them are no more or no less literate than their fellows. A number of the more traditional special services are rendered by older men with less need for literacy. The two blacksmiths, the cobbler, the spinning-wheel-maker are men of this type. Such trades are followed by nonlanded men. The farmer has neither time, inclination, nor need to do such work. The tradesmen, therefore, are drawn to the village, where small house lots are available. The village is composed of these tradespeople, *rentiers*, who are almost all single, and day-laborers, who have no land or trade and make a living by road work, peddling, and nonfarming day-labor.[27] A non-inheriting farmer's son may ply a special trade at home until he gets enough money to leave, and a nonlanded day-laborer's son is equally as likely to do so. The four cases in the parish of such marginal trades are divided equally between farm and village. In addition to these two farmer's sons and one of the smiths, who has his forge conveniently located on the main road, all the other tradesmen live in the village. Two fishermen and the *remmancheur*, or bone-setter, are farmers in addition. Their added specialties are the response to economic pressure. True, these services were performed by their fathers, but for the same reason. With increased economic stability on the farm the additional services are discontinued.

Besides these trades and services the parish supports a religious personnel consisting of a priest and *bedeau*. The

[27] The parish registration of property-owners and renters and their sons who are over twenty-one shows the following distribution of types of livelihood: 135 farmers, 30 special trades, 22 day-laborers, 22 *rentiers*, and 21 *rentières*.

parish priest, or *curé*, lives in the *presbytère*, a large frame building connected with the church by an inclosed passage for the cleric's use during inclement weather. The building was constructed from parish funds and is at the disposal of the *curé*. The *presbytère* is much too large for his own needs, the additional rooms being for the visiting priests. The mother and sister of the *curé* keep house for him. On the small strip of land adjoining the *presbytère* the priest raises a small garden for his own needs; he hires the labor for this garden and also to care for his few animals.

The attitudes toward the summer settlement of a dozen cottages on the river beach express a conflict between the parish and outsiders, between traditional mores and urban ways. These summer residents are largely from outside the parish, although a few parishioners go to the beach to serve them. There are two small stores and a hotel, which provide visitors with dancing and liquor. The *grève* has quite a regional reputation and is a favorite picnic and outing spot. One family from Montreal and two from Quebec have regular cottages. The local senator has a summer cottage somewhat aloof from the others. Aside from him, the parishioners who visit the beach are largely from the day-laboring families. They go to have a good time even if the means is openly disapproved by the *curé*. Only visitors from the city swim, and their immodest bathing suits cause public protest.[28] The parish is antagonistic to the beach and looks down on its own members who fraternize there. Gossip expands stories of drinking, of arrest, and

[28] A five- to twenty-dollar fine or imprisonment is posted on the beach by the *conseil* for the following: loitering; swearing; using injurious or immoral speech; conduct offensive to public morals; conduct causing scandal; disturbing the peace; bathing in suits which sin against decency and modesty; walking in a bathing-suit except between the house and beach, and then by the shortest route.

of visitors who are living with other men's wives. The *curé* preaches against the situation at the beach and threatens violence to the stores selling bootleg liquor. The beach represents the only contact the farmer has with other than his traditional ways, and its undesirable factors are under continual attack and public disapproval.

The *curé*'s parishioners are largely a quiet and honest people. Criminal cases are extremely rare. The only death by violence in the parish happened so long ago that even the ballad about it is forgotten. The beach house of a priest who resides in St. Denis during the summer was looted in the winter. The vandalism was attributed to returned discontented settlers whom he had sent to the cold new lands of Abitibi.[29] Minor thefts are infrequent and may be announced on the church steps after Mass, with a threat or a request for return. Transient beggars pass through the parish constantly but are credited with no particular dishonesty. During the day the doors of all houses remain open, and it is customary to enter even a strange house without knocking. While church vessels are frequently being stolen in the cities, the sacristy of the St. Denis church remains unlocked and unguarded. Fighting is rare except during elections. A provincial motor policeman is called in at such times. Arrests for drunkenness are occasionally made and are usually the result of particularly disorderly conduct on the part of an outsider.

The outside contacts of both children and adults are extremely limited. Around forty adult parishioners spent a few years working in New England, but even this gave them little that was novel enough to live in their memories. The French Canadians in the States set up their old life to a great extent. They never learned English, since they had

[29] Abitibi is a northern county in the province of Quebec.

French "bosses." They never went to moving-pictures or theaters, and they still attended the French Catholic church. They did a new kind of work, but after hours the women knitted and the men smoked and talked, just as they would have done in Canada. A few acquired a taste for conveniences, but those who returned to St. Denis were largely those whose modes of life had changed but little.

Aside from this movement to the States, the parishioners have not traveled. The senator is, of course, excluded, as he lives a life apart, only residing temporarily in the parish. Most of the parishioners have never been as far as Montreal or Gaspé. The times they have been to the city of Quebec they can count on the fingers of one hand. Such trips are taken almost exclusively by men. The younger men are traveling more than their fathers did. Travel is easier, and the need for finding employment forces the youth out of the rural parish. They go to lumbering and industrial centers in search of work. Special excursion rates on the railroad tempt an ever increasing group of young people to the city of Quebec, where they visit relatives. Travel still follows the family channels. A place where one has no relatives is particularly uninviting.

The newspaper and radio increase the rural consciousness of the wider sphere of life in the province. Two of the parish boys have motorcycles, which are used for commercial ventures and which also extend their personal contacts. Both boys are noninheriting sons of farmers. The buggy, carriage, and sleigh are still the general modes of travel; and their range maintains the traditional narrow scope of social intercourse. There are five automobiles in the parish; but they, like the motorcycles and train excursions, are part of nonfarming economies. The *curé*, the store-keeper, two traveling salesmen, and a private taxi-man own the cars. No farmer even wants a car, because of the upkeep. The work horse can be hitched to the buggy at no expense whatever and can draw the sleigh when autos cannot be used at all. An oxcart drawn up by the gasoline pump outside the local store is a common scene, which characterizes the disparity between the old economy, with its dependence on farm animals, and the new special economic adjustments.

CHAPTER III

THE SOCIETY UPON THE LAND

PARISHES always tend to be convenience areas and, therefore, to be limited topographically. The people who can conveniently go to a single church, which they support, constitute a parish. If the parish is too extensive, those people at an inconvenient distance from the church will try to separate themselves as a new parish. To do this they must be sufficiently numerous to support a new church; therefore population distribution is an obvious factor. This subdivision to form new parishes is the normal manner of parish creation in long-inhabited areas. The origin of St. Denis is typical. The families which first settled along the Coteau belonged to two different parishes whose churches were thirteen miles apart. As the division was about midway, this meant that many families were obliged to drive thirteen miles every Sunday. In case of birth or serious illness this distance had to be covered to reach the priest. Toward Rivière Ouelle, where the road passed up onto the Coteau, the winter snows often piled over ten feet deep. On the other hand, the parishioners of Kamouraska had to cross the unprotected lowland back of the bay to get to church. These natural barriers created an immediate need for a new parish. By the time the settlement had extended inland into the foothills, there were enough people to support a new parish. No sooner was it set up and the church built on the Coteau, where the majority of the parishioners lived, than people in the inland region, included in the parish territory, began to feel the inconvenience of coming down out of the hills and crossing the lowlands to get to church. As they grew in number,

44

two other parishes were split off—Mont Carmel in the mountains and St. Philippe at their foot. St. Denis now lies with the river to its north, parent-parishes separated by natural obstacles to east and west, and a daughter-parish to the south. Situated on the main highway and railroad, the daughter has far outstripped her parent in size and sophistication.

The parish land concessions were made following the customary system, that is, by *rangs*. Each *rang* parallels the river and is officially numbered, so that land in the strip next to the river is in the first *rang*, the next inland is the second *rang*, and so on. Locally the *rangs* develop special names. There are two *rangs* in St. Denis, separated roughly by the stream Des Bras. The first *rang* includes the Coteau and a portion of the lowland and is known as the Rang du Coteau. The second *rang* extends southward from the stream and is all plain. It is known as the Rang des Bras. A road runs the length of each *rang*. That through the Rang du Coteau is the main road coming from Rivière Ouelle and proceeding to Kamouraska. It lies a mile back from the river under the shelter of the south side of the Coteau for most of its length, except where it skirts the bay as it enters Kamouraska to the east. The road of the Rang des Bras has a blind end at the Grande Plaine to the west. To the east it continues into the next parish. Land holdings, unlike the *rangs* from which they are carved, run perpendicular to the river. The holdings are forty-two *arpents* long—in other words, the width of the *rang*.[1] The farms are extremely narrow, however, averaging two *arpents*, or about four hundred feet, in width. These farms are cut up into fields which divide them in width, not in length. The fields in a "two-*arpent* farm" (for such is the manner of reference, as the lengths of the

[1] About a mile and a half.

farms are constant) would be two hundred feet wide at most. This gives the countryside its characteristic appearance—long, narrow fields stretching away from the river. To the *habitant* there is nothing strange about fields a mile and a half long and a hundred feet wide. They are what he knows. The word "field" has that visual connotation to him. He thinks wide fields are strange and refers to them as "parks." His more sophisticated urban kinsmen joke about the *habitant* starting out in the morning with his lunch, plowing a furrow to the end of his land by noon and plowing back for supper at night.

There are both historic and ecological reasons for the long fields. Traces of an older historic pattern are to be seen around Charlebourg near Quebec. There the lands radiate from the central point which used to be the fort. But most of the settlement of Quebec was not on such a frontier pattern. The fiefs granted to the *seigneurs* were long and narrow. They started with a river frontage of several miles and ran inland many more miles, even into the mountains. The advantage of this system was that it provided fishing, a water outlet, level lands for farming, and hilly lands for timber and maple sugar. It provided a varied terrain with its combined advantages. The early farm concessions followed the same pattern, giving the *habitants* a river frontage and a variety of land. Had the lands been granted parallel to the river, one man would have received the whole beach, others the *coteau*, others the lowland, others the stream through the plain, and so on. Obviously, the farms that were granted did not run back as far as the mountains, but they did offer some variety. In the Rang du Coteau the fields are broken in length by the ridge, which is partially cultivated, and by the road. From Des Bras the lands stretch unbroken to the south. Now that most of the wood has long been cut off the land, farmers have bought wood lots in the mountains to the south, where they go to cut their winter's supply. Many of the long fields allow cattle to have access to the distant stream in addition to giving them large pastures, one end of which is close to the barns. The most vital reason for the long fences at such frequent intervals is that they hold the snow in great drifts over the soil. The protecting snow keeps the ground from freezing deeply. In the spring the snows melt quickly, the water rushing off in deep drainage ditches which parallel all the fences. The farmers fear a winter with little snow, for then the ground freezes deep and the spring plowing is greatly delayed. Where the growing season is so short, early plowing is necessary; therefore the fields are fenced to hold the snows.

The houses in which the farming families live string out along the road which goes through the *rang* and crosses every farm of that concession. As the farms are so narrow, the houses are only a few hundred feet apart. It was this appearance of a "continuous village" stretching unbroken along the river front which struck the invading English. There may be breaks for topographic reasons, such as we have described; but aside from places where there is marginal land, there is no reason for farms at the edge of the parish to be any larger than any others. As the length of the farms is constant and only width can vary, this means that farmhouses will be spaced regularly along the road except where nature or society interferes. Both interfere in St. Denis along the Rang du Coteau. As the road passes from Rivière Ouelle into St. Denis, houses are spaced very widely apart. There is actually a wide break where the Coteau and the Grande Plaine make farming impossible. At the other end of the parish there is not a house for several miles where the road traverses the lowland back of the open bay. Houses in the middle of the parish crowd to-gether along the road, forming the *village*. This is possible because the inhabitants of the houses are nonfarming and have only small pieces of land on which to live and raise a few vegetables. These small plots are cut off of the long strips of land which cross the road at this point. Farmers continue to cultivate the remainder, relinquishing the sec-tion adjacent to the road to the inhabitants of the village. The Rang des Bras, on the other hand, starts from nothing in the Grande Plaine, but it continues to the east with an unbroken line of farms. There is no natural break be-tween St. Denis and Kamouraska. The farmsteads run on in an unaltered row into the next parish.

Although the term *rang* technically refers to the land in a distribution plan, it has a somewhat different derived meaning. All the people with land holdings in one *rang* are identified with it. As the houses of that *rang* all lie along one road, the social aspect of the *rang* is identified with the road. "I went over to the Rang du Coteau," means that I went to the road through that *rang*, not just into the fields of that concession. This feeling of unity down the road along which are strung the houses of the *rang* is also shown in the special meanings given to the words *chemin* and *route*. A *chemin* is a road through a *rang*, crossing the farms and having houses along it. A *route* connects *chemins*, runs parallel to the fields, and therefore has no houses along it. This conceptualization is well illustrated in the mountain parish of Mont Carmel, where it became convenient to lay out two concessions with farms parallel to the river instead of the usual way. Thus, a road running to the south first passes parallel to the lands and has no houses along it, and then it is built up where it cuts across the farms. This single road is known as a *route* through the former region and becomes a *chemin* when it strikes the usual concessions.

The social cohesion is naturally much greater along a *chemin*, with its continuous stretch of neighboring houses. People know the parishioners of their own *rang* better than those of the other. They know them better because they have more contact up and down the *chemin* on which they live. A farmer of the Rang du Coteau may not visit the other *rang* a half a mile away once a year. He has been in all the houses of his own *rang* at some time or another, but there are several he has never entered in the other *rang*. From memory he can give the sequence of names of families along his own *rang* but not along the other, even though they are in the same parish. Farmers from the Rang des Bras have to go to the village store in the other *rang* or do their buying in the next parish. Farmers from the Coteau just cross the other *rang* on their way to St. Philippe; so these commercial contacts create no particular link between the *rangs*. Cohesion along the *rang* or *chemin* is also exemplified in the shape of parishes themselves. Where not distorted by topographic barriers or urban growth, parishes seem to have their longer dimension along the *chemins*.

The two *chemins* of St. Denis passing along its two *rangs* are connected by a *route* which starts at the river beach, crosses the Coteau and its *chemin*, and continues to the south over the lowland across the *chemin* of the Rang des Bras and on into the next parish. The intersection of this *route* with the Rang du Coteau marks the center of the village. On the crest of the hill above the intersection stands the church with its long silver spire. The village extends along the *chemin* in both directions. The village is not an organized social unit. It is simply a cluster of the houses of *rentiers*, craftsmen, and other specialists.

Its limits are generally accepted as being the end of the macadam-paved road which runs through the area of concentration. Highway signs naming the parish also stand at the junctures of the pavement with the gravel highway. The limits of the surfaced road were determined politically, having been extended slightly beyond the insurance company's village limits, based on the proximity of houses.

In addition to the village there is an even more ancient division within the parish, the geographical division into quarters. The primary division is between the two *rangs*— Du Coteau and Des Bras. These two halves are divided again by a line which crosses them both, cutting them roughly in half. Thus the Rang du Coteau is divided into Nordet du Coteau and the Sarwa du Coteau;[2] the second *rang* is divided into Hauteville in the east and Des Bras in the west.

Orientation, for the native of St. Denis, depends on the southwest-northeast base line paralleling the river. The early settlers used the terms *sarwa* and *nordet*, which designate the true orientation of the river valley.[3] The terms and their use have persisted. As the *rangs* and *chemins* parallel the river and the houses are oriented with these roads, it is obvious that the important directions for the St. Denisian are turned 45° from the cardinal points. Rarely are the terms "east" and "west" used. Altars in the church are designated as being on the northeast or southwest side; rooms in a house are similarly indicated; winds come from these directions. "North" and "south" are employed to mean "toward the river" and "toward the mountains." One might expect "northwest" and "southeast" to

[2] *Nordet* and *sarwa* are traditional pronunciations of *nordest* and *sud-ouest* attributed to Breton sailors. French orthography is not retained in one instance, to avoid the confusion that *saroua* would give English readers.

[3] This is not general in Quebec. The whole city of Montreal uses directional designations based on the supposition that the river flows east.

be the complementary pair, but this is not the case. The use of *nordet* and *sarwa* is the result of orienting in terms of the *rang*, which bears these traditional directional designations.

The road through the Hauteveille de St. Denis continues on into Hauteville de Kamouraska, part of the next parish. Actually, Hauteville is a flat part of the lowland through which the *rang* extends. The Coteau is the only eminence in the parish. Parishioners frankly do not know why Hauteville should be so named. What seems to have happened is that the name originated in Kamouraska, where the second *rang* is actually on high ground. Later the designation of the name spread down the road into St. Denis.

Each of the three most populous quarters of the parish has a cross erected beside the road and centrally located with respect to the limits of the quarter. These crosses are some fifteen feet high and are adorned by symbolic crowns of thorns at the intersections of the arms. Neighboring parishes sometimes have all of the instruments which were used in the crucifixion affixed to their crosses. These road crosses are symbols of the faith. Parishioners never stop to pray at them. Even the open-air altar for *fête-dieu* is never erected at the foot of one of them. No hat is raised, no head is bent, when they are passed. The parishioner actually does not know their purpose. He says: "They are to show passers-by that they are in a Catholic region." Such a statement shows a growing ethnocentrism but presents no really explicit purpose for the cross, as all travelers know the region is Catholic and the *habitant* cares little for the opinion of the tourist who whirls through in a car. In spite of apparent lack of purpose, these crosses serve a definite social function. They increase the internal unity of the quarters in which they stand.

A road cross is erected by the popular subscription of members of a quarter of the parish. In other parishes it may be a *rang* which thus acts as a unit. After the cross has been made and set up, the rest of the parish is invited to witness the ceremony of blessing and to hear the sermon by the *curé*. Every one comes, but parishioners of the host quarter feel a special pride and unity in this symbol which was erected through their common effort. It is their cross, their ceremony to which they have invited these other people. In later years the main sentiments attached to this cross are those which were brought out by the blessing ceremony—the distinction between the in-group and the out-group. As the crosses are wooden and uncovered, they must be replaced each generation with a new ceremony, re-expressing the unity of the quarter.

Two other crosses in the parish show the coincidence of purpose with this same sort of unifying function. The first *curé* of the parish started a temperance movement; and when the whole parish had taken the pledge, he had them erect a large black cross on the Coteau overlooking the river. The parish has renewed this cross four times since that first ceremony, reasserting its unity in the Société de Tempérance. Based on the same pattern of erecting crosses, parishes throughout Quebec recently set up, with fitting ceremony, large Jacques Cartier crosses in their school yards to mark the fourth centennial of French contact in America. This widespread movement had the effect of awakening ethnic pride and unity.

A few traditional attitudes have been developed by the quarters and *rangs* of the parish toward one another. Progressive farmers of the Coteau think that the farmers of Hauteville are not much interested in the education of their children. Many farmers of the Rang des Bras think that those of the Coteau are *petits habitants*, getting low

The Nordet du Coteau

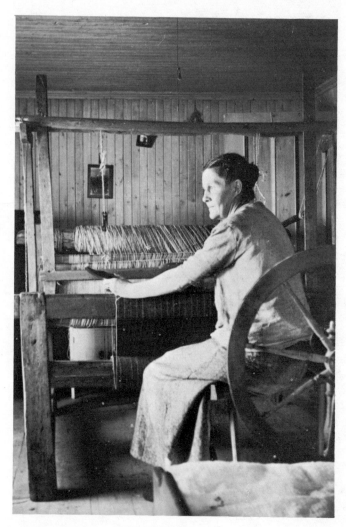

At the Loom

yield to their land. There is some truth in both statements. Fewer Hauteville farmers give their children convent and college education after local schooling. The farmers of the Coteau admit that the land in Des Bras is better, as there is no ridge to contend with. The difference in yield is questionable. The real function of these statements is to fortify local unities. *Rangs* in other parishes also have their typical features for the *habitant*. One new region of a poor mountain parish is typified by its numerous *veillées* and by its fighting and arguing. Another older, richer, and more settled *rang* of the same parish lives *comme il faut*. The distinction is based on fact, the newer *rang* having a louder, brusker frontier life. Again the difference is the basis for a mild contempt and the assertion of the superiority of one's own *rang*.

The religious, civil, and educational organization of the parish are separate and draw separate revenues. The upkeep of the priest is paid in part by the yearly *dîme*, or tithe. Every twenty-sixth *minot*[4] of grain belongs to the *curé*. The idea is definitely that this portion of grain is his, not that it is given to him. If a farmer is short of grain for his own use, he can pay the priest the value of the *dîme* in cash if such an arrangement is satisfactory. Such transaction is spoken of as "the *curé* selling the farmer the grain." The priest asks the price and sells the twenty-sixth portion of the grain, which is his own property. The payment of the *dîme* is a religious obligation, not a civil transaction. It is a sin to withhold the priest's share; and all the religious controls, such as refusing sacraments, can be used to collect the tithe. There is never any difficulty in collecting the share of grain. The farmers feel very consciously that their crops are direct blessings from God, and they would not think of denying him that which be-

---

[4] An old French measure equal to 39 liters.

longed to his church. There is no fixed date for turning
over the *dîme* to the *curé*. Most farmers give him his grain
in the spring, around March, as they thresh all winter.

The growth of a nonfarming group in the parish has
necessitated the establishment of another kind of tithe—
a head tax. Depending upon the size of the household, this
yearly head tax ranges from $3.00 to $5.00 per family.
This form of tithe is usually paid earlier in the year, as it
is in cash, not grain. The tithe supplements the money
the parishioners pay the *curé* to have special Masses sung.

The financial affairs of the church are handled by the
fabrique, a sort of church board composed of three *marguilliers*, who meet with the *curé*. The *marguilliers* are
elected for a three-year period, and the terms are staggered
so that one is elected each year. They normally come from
different quarters of the parish. The senior member is the
marguillier en charge, the highest prestige office in the parish organization. The retiring *marguillier* consults with
the *curé* and nominates his successor, who is rarely opposed.
The *marguilliers* are unpaid but sit in a special pew in the
front of the church. They also have religious ceremonial
roles at various times during the year. The *fabrique* is responsible for the upkeep and improvement of the church
property, including the church, *presbytère*, and cemetery.
It may take on special functions even of a nonreligious
nature. Thus, the *fabrique* of St. Denis owns a hearse; a
small cannon for celebrations; and a grain-sifter, used by
all the farmers for a small fee. To discuss particularly
momentous problems all of the retired *marguilliers* may
meet with the three active ones. The *fabrique* gets its
funds from the yearly "sale" of pews, from part of the
money paid for Masses, and from the sale of cemetery lots.
The money is used to pay off indebtedness on the church
structure itself, to heat and repair it, to insure it, to pay

the boys' and men's choirs, and to pay the *bedeau*. The auction of pews brings in about $400, $300 of which goes for insurance, so that there is not a large working balance.

The boys' choir consists of some thirty boys between the ages of seven and fifteen. These boys sit in the sanctuary in black and white vestments during all Masses of obligation, but they never sing. Chosen in rotation, they serve as acolytes throughout the week and receive a few cents for their services. Those not serving as acolytes follow the Masses of obligation from their sanctuary pews just like the parishioners. Boys are admitted to this choir as soon as they have learned the routine of the Mass from their schoolteacher, who decides when they are capable of participating. They may continue in the choir until they choose to leave, which is usually about the time they finish school. Not all the children in the parish are members of the boys' choir. Those families which have children in the choir consider it a mild honor; those that do not, simply lack interest in having their children serve the Mass. This ambivalent attitude is based on the necessity of seating all the children of large families in the church. Masses are sung only once a day, and pews must be "bought," so that seating a large family is a real problem.[5]

The men's choir has no relation to the boys'. It sits in the church loft without ceremony and sings the responses of the Mass. This choir is headed by the *maître chant*, designated by the *curé* to this almost permanent position. Traditionally this place is also one of parish prestige. The *maître chant* passes on the capabilities of applicants to choir membership. In addition to the *maître* there are ten

[5] The twenty families represented by the choir boys average 8.7 church-going persons, well above the parish average. Boys from larger families tend to stay in the choir longer. This reason for putting boys in the choir is never explicitly stated. It is too close to a religious matter to have commercial attitudes attached.

chants in St. Denis, all over twenty-five years of age. Members of the choir rotate for singing the Masses of the week. Two sing each day of the week and receive twenty-five cents the day they sing. None is paid for the Sunday Masses, which is also true for the boys' choir. For funerals all eleven sing; but only six, chosen in rotation, are paid the seventy-five cents received for first- and second-class *services*. For third-class funerals four *chants* are paid. The class is determined by the amount paid the church for the funeral and is evidenced in the elaboration of the service.

Exemplifying the close interrelation of religious and civil matters, the *bedeau* is paid a salary by the *fabrique* but is furnished a residence in the lower floor of the *salle publique*, the parish civil center located beside the church and cemetery on top of the Coteau. The *bedeau* is responsible for the heating and cleaning of the church, the ringing of the church bells, and the preparation of the paraphernalia and vestments for the Masses and sacraments. He sits with the choir boys during Masses and keeps them in order. There is no prestige attached to his role. The *bedeau* is selected by the *curé* and *fabrique* and usually holds the position for life. There is no tendency for the office to remain in one family. The present incumbent is the son of the long-established blacksmith.

The parish is not only a religious but also a civil unit. The village is in no way formally separated from the rest of the parish. All the parish constitutes a municipality directed by the mayor and *conseil*. This body consists of six councilors, presided over by the mayor, who votes only in case of a tie. The *conseil* elects a nonvoting secretary-treasurer from outside its own membership, who is paid around a hundred dollars a year for his services. The bachelor carpenter-banker has filled this post for thirty years. The mayor and councilors are chosen in January by popular vote of the property-owners and the adult sons of farm-owners. This special stipulation is supposed to balance the higher tax evaluation of the property of the farmers in comparison with that of the villagers. Here, again, is a special adaptation to the growth of a new type of economic household in the parish. Mayor and councilors are elected for two-year terms, three councilors being chosen each year.

The *conseil* decides evaluations and taxes parishioners accordingly. The money is largely used for road upkeep and improvement, primarily of the *route*. The *conseil* lets a contract for keeping snowdrifts on this road scraped down in winter. The *chemins* are maintained from provincial funds, and each farmer scrapes and levels the snow along his own frontage. Large projects are rarely undertaken by the *conseil*, as there is strong resistance to taxation. An important role of the *conseil* is to act as a contact with the provincial government. All government announcements reach the people through the secretary-treasurer. Although the province levies no direct taxes on the parishioners, it occasionally has money to spend in the parish. A $5,000 relief project was requested by the *conseil* in 1936. There was also an effort to secure a wood lot in the mountains to the south to furnish building material for public projects. The *conseil* meets monthly in the *salle* over the rooms of the *bedeau*. The meetings open with a prayer on the knees, led by the mayor. They are open to the public, and there is general banter and argument between spectators and councilors. Really important problems evoke long sessions, marked by lack of initiative in suggesting plans.

Provincial money is spent in the parish mainly through the *cantonnier*. This individual is appointed by the provincial government, so he fills a purely political post. He is in charge of the upkeep of the roads, particularly the main *chemin*. The post always falls to a farmer who has teams and wagons to use. The *cantonnier* makes around five hundred dollars a year.[6] Because of the road work he controls, he is the political boss of the parish. Only his own partisans are given work. The amount of the work is great around the time of provincial elections, and sandpits are invariably chosen on the land of party members.

Politics is a topic of continual interest and one which reaches fever heat during election time. The parish is traditionally Conservative, but long Liberal control in the province has converted many to that party. The whole parish is always divided between the "blues," or Conservatives, and the "reds." Party affiliations follow family lines and family cliques and antagonisms.[7] The long winter *veillées* are attended almost invariably by family groups of similar political belief. Constituents of each party have a genuine dislike for those of the other. Antagonism is frequently expressed by derision of the newspapers of the opposite political leaning. Election time is one of great tension, of taunts and shouting as parishioners get their evening mail. In the old days Conservatives even set fire to a load of hay on which a Liberal was riding. Insults are common, and many speaking acquaintances are dropped. During the last election the minority candidate had to have one meeting in the parish in secret, another open but under provincial police protection. The increase of interest during election time is shown in the increased subscription to newspapers and in the buying of radios.

Campaigns reach their climax with the *assemblée contradictoire*, at which both candidates speak. Characteris-

[6] Unverified.

[7] See "Kinship and the Family Cycle," chap. iv.

tically at these meetings there are organized strong-arm tactics, drinking, and attempts to make each opposing candidate's speech inaudible. Loud speakers, guarded by professional boxers, were the last innovation from the city. Subsequent to the election there is an organized *triomphe* by the victors. Houses are decked with flags, banners, and pictures; guns are fired; and there is a hilarious evening parade in which the young people dress themselves in all sorts of costumes. Bitter feeling and demonstration are particularly typical of the youth, even of many who are not yet old enough to vote. All the interests of the adults are also those of the children, from adolescence on. In this case political interests take on an aspect of decided youthful vigor. Another typical feature is the political interest displayed by unmarried women who do not have suffrage in provincial elections. Because of their lack of a man through whom to express their attitudes, they are more openly interested in politics than married women. Politics is generally conceived as being "too dirty" for women, who should be occupied in their homes. Women only vote in Dominion elections, "to equal the voting of the English women in Ontario." Elections are also felt to be secular matters in which the *curé* should not interfere. He does, nevertheless, wield a potent political hand through the indirect or direct support he can give from the pulpit. Although the newspaper *L'Action catholique* is not an official party paper, it gives a strong bias to its many subscribers.

Litigation is not an unusual outcome of bitter arguments. One spectator at a *conseil* meeting became angry with another over some current problem and called him a *fils de chienne*. For his slanderous use of the term he was sued for $50. This same man, a respected parishioner, was also sued for $20 for calling the Liberal *cantonnier* a "robber" within earshot of a "red" witness. It is little wonder that the intimate *veillées* include only members of one party. Land-infringement suits are rare in this long-settled region. In the wood lots of the mountains they are more common.

A deputy sued his defeated opponent for referring to him during the campaign as a "collector of *seigneurial* rents," in spite of the fact that the term was truly applicable to his father and brother. It is interesting that this reference should be considered slanderous. It is true that all parishioners still pay the *seigneur* a small rent. One dollar and a half per year for a two-*arpent* farm is not unusual, although high by the old standards. The *seigneurs* have long ceased to live on their concessions; and the fiefs have become a form of investment, often divided among a number of owners, who hire a "collector of rents." In such cases the names of the *seigneurs* are not even known by the *habitants*. A few *seigneurs* have a bad local reputation because of their attempts to collect rents in excess of those rightly owed. When one such man tried to make a widow two *seigneuries* away from his own pay him rent, even the *conseil* rose up in arms. A few *habitants* bought the rights to their farms from early *seigneurs*. Traditionally, they never paid rent after that; but some new *seigneurs* have taken advantage of lack of documentary evidence to force payment. Such incidents as these and the lack of any mutual interest between *seigneur* and *habitant* have led to the growth of a feeling of dislike for the institution which was once the backbone of the colony. The final remnants of the system are at present being eliminated by the Parliament.

The chicanery of politicians is a byword in the parish. Factional strife threatens the life of every organized association. Several years ago a branch of the popular provincial Association catholique de Jeunesse canadienne was organized in the parish. Politics and chicanery brought its brief life to a close. The Congrégation des Enfantes de Marie includes all the unmarried females over sixteen years old. Most of its activities are strictly religious. Within the organization there is constant quarreling between the old maids who control it and the young girls they try to direct. This same trouble immediately flared up when the *curé* tried to solve the conflict by appointing two presidents to a new *bon parler français* committee, one young and one old. The old one resigned. There are two agricultural clubs organized with provincial stimulus. One is for men, the other for women. They are the only associations with regular dues. The provincial Department of Agriculture is a constant stimulus to these groups. Les Enfants de St. Joseph is the male counterpart of the Enfantes de Marie, but its single meeting and Mass a year are not sources of trouble. Offices in the society are avoided because they entail making a collection among the members. Two other groups are societies in name only. One is the Société de Tempérance, which has neither meetings nor membership and represents a reformist movement. The other is the Forestiers catholiques, a life insurance organization with some twenty-five members and the regional court of claims in the parish.[8] On the whole the associational life of the community is weak. The people are not "joiners." The various societies are open to all, with the exception of sex and marriage restrictions and they have no other particular social role. They are not arranged in a series of increasing social importance, a common feature where associations are a vital part of social life. Even the formal school organization reflects family

[8] Central offices in Chicago. This was a boom-time organization. Young men are not joining.

animosities and political bickering. This small parish is divided into two separate school *municipalités*, each with its own board of commissioners, empowered to tax in its own area. Each board has five commissioners, elected for two-year terms. Elections are staggered, so that all do not change at once. From their own membership the commissioners yearly elect a president and secretary, the latter receiving a small salary. The school commissioners levy taxes to cover the expense of building, maintaining and heating their schools, and paying the salaries of the teachers. The entire system is under the jurisdiction of the provincial Comité catholique, which decides the curriculums and texts to be used and sends regular inspectors into the classes.

The two school districts are divided from one another by a north-south line through the parish, so that the Nordet du Coteau and Hauteville fall into one and the Sarwa du Coteau and Des Bras are in the other. The school division line is the only formal division between the halves of the two *rangs*. Each quarter of the parish constitutes a school *arrondissement*, with the exception of the populous Sarwa, which is divided into two. Each *arrondissement* has a small school building for the students of that area. "Were it not for this regulation all the children would go to the most popular teacher," comments one farmer.

Only in the separation of the parish into two school districts does formal organization fail to correspond with the parish territory. Even in this case it is a lack of correspondence by fission. The school organization is still independent of neighboring parishes. The parish is both a sacred and a secular unit. This is necessarily so because of the traditional interaction between the religious and civil elements.

CHAPTER IV

KINSHIP AND THE FAMILY CYCLE

THE unit of social life in French Canada is the parish. It is the natural division, the "society" for the purposes of this study. The parish is a partly autonomous local group, the whole ethnic group being made up of hundreds of parishes. A religious, civil, territorial, and economic unit, the parish is the first point of reference to everyone in it. "He is from Mont Carmel" immediately localizes a person under discussion. "He is the son of Jean Gagnon" further identifies the individual as to his most important role in Mont Carmel, that of a member of a certain family. So identified in the conversation, the person referred to is put in the focus of a whole set of attitudes of the listener. Since Mont Carmel is a mountain parish with poor lands and a more rustic life, its parishioners are generally conceived of as cruder in behavior than those of the older parishes. Jean Gagnon is known to be related to other Gagnons for whom the listener has a family enmity. Although the individual under discussion may be entirely unknown, he is put in a context of dislike. Thus, even in attitudes toward its constituent members, the family is a unit.

The real basis of rural life is the family. All its members of both sexes and all ages, share in the responsibilities. The grandmother, mother, and her daughters do the spinning, weaving, knitting, making of clothes, cooking, serving of the table, washing, vegetable-gardening, milking, and housekeeping. The men of the family raise the hay and grain, tend the animals, cut the wood, keep the house in repair, and attend to business contacts. The family economic unity was, until recently, shown in the tradition of always turning all money earned over to the head of the family. This custom has died out with the failure of the old system to function successfully under new conditions. Basic to this type of economy was the responsibility of the father to establish all his children economically. When children earned money on occasion, they did not hesitate to turn it over to their father, for they knew that he would use it most advantageously for the family and that he would take care of them when they grew up. As long as the land holdings were large enough to divide or there was land to be had for the clearing, children were assured the small material outlay to start them, as well as the co-operation of their brothers in the actual work. This co-operation is ingrained and is but another evidence of the tremendous strength of the family unity. A man whose farm was sixty miles from that of his brother wrote his kinsman that he was behind with his sowing and requested that the brother send a son to help. The uncle paid his nephew for this work. There were numerous other young men in his own parish who would have been glad to have the work, but he preferred to hire a relative. In securing the services of a stonemason, a man was willing to pay more to have a kinsman do the work. The family unity is stronger than selfish considerations. A man's remaining daughters married and quit the house, leaving the mother of the family to handle the female tasks for four men. The father wrote and told his eldest daughter, who was unmarried and had been teaching in the city for eighteen years, to come home to help her mother.

Not only is a unified family effort necessary, but a large family is essential. The short cultivating season of less than four months has made it impossible for a family to work large acreages with the traditional methods. The economic balance has been evolved on farms of about one hundred acres. Such an area can be farmed by two or three able males. Female labor is necessary to feed and clothe these men and boys and to help with the farm work. Both the male and the female labor is provided by large families. Not all the children can marry and raise their children on this same farm. It will support but one immediate family of parents and children. The particular social system affords a means of keeping the proper relation of individuals to the land. The system provides, through large families, the means of exploiting the given natural resources. It also provides a family cycle through which this number of individuals is not greatly augmented or decreased at any time. In each generation there are a few couples in each parish who bear no children. These couples sell their lands, as they are not able to cultivate them at a profit if they have to hire help to do the work. It is, therefore, a necessity that the social system furnish a method for keeping a continuum of able-bodied workers on the land. The sacred sanctions for the large family are explicit in the Roman Catholic doctrine. The *curé* frequently tells the parishioners that families with many children are blessed by God and experience no hunger. This is actually the fact under the local farm conditions, as has just been pointed out. Misery and hard work come from too few children. Sermons go on to point out that analysis of families on relief in the cities shows most of them to be childless or to have few children.

Family symbols play an important part in the whole sacred philosophy. The "earthly trinity"—Jesus, Mary and Joseph—is a family. Even the grandparent generation, Ste Anne. is tremendously important in Canada through her miracles and the fact that she is the mother of Mary. The attitudes toward these holy personages include the attitudes toward persons in similar family roles. God the Father is the director of life from whom one can expect justice, though it may be harsh. The Virgin is the Mother of all, full of compassion and the chief power to intreat God the Father for those who love her. The authority of the father of the family comes directly from God the Father, a fact which finds frequent expression from the pulpit. This gives the father additional power from the child's point of view and gives the father a sacred responsibility toward his children. With the mother it is the same, except that her special relationship is with the Virgin. Every morning and evening the family prays together on its knees, led by one or the other of the parents. The family comes to feel itself a sacred unit. Some of the prayers are always for the deceased members of the family. Part of the produce of their toil is used for Masses for these souls. The family economy goes beyond the grave. In essays written by twelve-year-old children on "What I would do if I had $1,000," all said they would use part of the money to have Masses sung for deceased relatives.

In reckoning the extent of the family, in the sense of including all relatives, direct descendents and collateral kin through third cousins are included.[1] In other words, if the relationship is not farther back than ego's great-great-grandfather, it is a family relationship. In normal usage the word "family" refers to the immediate family of direct descendents, usually in the same household. The other kin are thought of, and spoken of, as "relatives" rather

[1] This corresponds with degrees of consanguinity which the church used to recognize as impediments to marriage. The new code of law includes only second cousins, but the change of law is not generally known in St. Denis.

than as members of the family. Expressions of the restricted nature of the family group are not hard to find. Along one of the two roads in the parish there are eight consecutive farms, owned by families named Dionne. This was one of the earliest families in the parish, having settled here just after the beginning of the eighteenth century. Through the generations, land holdings adjacent to one another were acquired by kinsmen. Now the natives consider that there are several different families of Dionnes on these contiguous farms, although they are known to have common descent. The same conceptualization is shown by a native who complains that there is drunkenness at dances because "too distant" people are invited. "Distant" in this case does not refer to spatial distance but rather to kinship distance. Young men too distantly related are out of the family controls.

The common knowledge of extensive genealogical systems of one's family and also of others in the parish symbolizes the importance of the family relationships. Such knowledge requires no particular study for the native. Genealogies are bodies of knowledge in continual use. It is not uncommon for people to have personal recollections of great-grandparents. Questions of relationship are continually being referred to grandparents, who have ready answers because of their personal knowledge of the people under consideration. Thus is the knowledge passed from generation to generation. At the Mass the *curé* will ask the parishioners to pray for a certain woman who has died in the city of Quebec. Those who do not know the individual will ask grandmother who she was. Grandmother's answer may very well determine whether or not prayers are offered for the deceased. The walls of all the formal salons in the homes are hung with pictures of various ancestors. From frequent discussions of these relatives and their personal characteristics the smallest child comes to know them very well, not as mere names but as individuals in the family. Prayers may still be being said for some, and funeral mementos may hang on the salon wall as further reminders. Some of the family may still be wearing mourning for them, keeping them very much alive in the family memory.

Photograph collections help keep these personalities alive. Pictures are usually taken at life-crises: confirmation, marriage, ordination, death. Each marriage picture calls up a whole new set of collateral relatives or some further interrelation within the extended family itself. The cemetery is a constant expression of family unity through the generations. Here, again, each grave and stone represents a personality. Even children who died in youth are still part of the family. "I have fifteen children, ten living," is the normal way of speaking of one's offspring.

Families behave as units in all matters. Members all have the same political beliefs. The women feel no desire to vote because each is normally represented by a husband who expresses her opinion with his vote. The attitude is that it must be the unmarried women who are desirous of voting. Hatred between families usually follows political lines. People of a family toward which there is a standing dislike are characterized as drunkards, cheaters, and members of a certain political party. All the characteristics are on the same level and interrelated. There is a feeling that if a man changes to that party he will take on these personal characteristics and will throw his lot with the other set of families. Naturally, there is no consensus in the parish as to these beliefs, but the attitudes of opposing groups of families take the same pattern.

For this reason alone, one would not be tempted to marry into the other party or any of its constituent families.

Actually there would be little opportunity for such a union. Social contacts which might lead to marriage follow intimate family-friendship lines too closely. The long evening parties in winter are usually attended by the same group of relatives and approved neighbors. One's familiar contacts are only with friends who are part of this accepted inner circle. Sunday visits are from the same people or from relatives from other parishes. One might attend a succession of parties all winter without ever realizing that there were other people in the parish. There are, of course, many other equally exclusive parties in progress in other groups of families. Part of the entertainment and conversation of these very parties is of the gossiping type that builds up strong antagonistic sentiments between family factions. The effect of this talk as a control on the disliked families is nil but is a strong control within the gossiping families themselves.

Marriage is still by contract and with dowries, and no child would marry against the wishes of his parents. By marriage a new family is created. All the old alliances and interdependence remain, however; so the new spouse must fit into the whole without conflict. The family of the wife is joined by marriage with that of her husband. The two families must, in the first place, conclude the contract. The bride's parents may even eventually live with the new couple.

Not only do contacts within the parish follow family lines, but those without do also. A parish four miles away may never be visited if there are no relatives residing there. Travel is conceived of in terms of visiting relatives. Going to a strange place where one is unrelated is very undesirable. Travel abroad holds no excitement, although a certain amount of foreign news is constantly in the newspapers. "I would like to visit the grave of my brother in France," is the only reason a young, energetic girl could see for going abroad. When newly married couples go to the city of Quebec on their honeymoon, they visit around with relatives there or go to Ste Anne de Beaupré, where they feel at home with the saint and shrine with which they are so familiar. During the large immigration of French Canadians to New England at the beginning of the century, a great many of the men came back to their native parishes to marry or else found girls in the States whose families they already knew. The immigration itself followed the pattern of one man or family going out and others following, once the contact was made.

These family links which are made by marriage are important. The early death of either of the parties may well be followed by another marriage into the same family. When one widow with seven children married into another family, there was a hue and cry from the family of her deceased husband. His lands had passed out of the family name. Nephews of the dead man were confused as to whether or not they should continue to call her "aunt." Her children, down to a babe in arms, kept her first husband's name, which may eventually bring the land back into the old family. Marriage contracts often stipulate that the land is not to go out of the family of direct descent.

Because of the limited scope and familial nature of personal contact, such marriage patterns as these are very common: brother-sister exchange, brothers marrying sisters, brothers marrying girls who are cousins to one another, and so on. The ramifications such patterns can take are shown in the accompanying genealogical trees.[2]

There is general lip service to the belief that inbreeding is a bad thing. Frequent cases cited in proof are a robust family of a French Canadian "who married an Irish girl"

[2] All offspring are not shown on the charts.

and of an "inbred" family with a feeble-minded son and an infantile-paralysis case. The actual facts are that the "Irish" woman is French Canadian and the other family is not inbred. None of the three feeble-minded cases in a parish of seven hundred persons is in an inbred family.

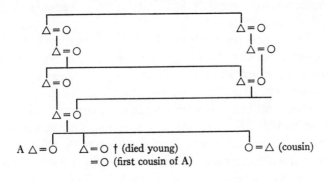

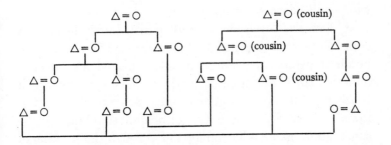

The stock which came to Canada was apparently good, and high infant mortality has only increased selection of good physical types. A member of one of the families shown on the kinship charts went into genealogical detail to demonstrate how terribly inbred was the family of the local drunk and good-for-nothing. Such expressions but demonstrate how subtle is the role of family in the selection of mates. A wife is chosen not because she is a first cousin; that would be bad because it would be inbreeding. The girl is selected because she went to the same parties as the boy and their families frequently called on one another. The boy also knows that he will be assured of parental approval in his choice. Her kin relationship makes her a logical choice, but for other reasons than the relationship.

The following analysis of family structure is based on the study of one of the oldest Quebec settlements, St. Denis, a parish which has maintained to a large degree the traditional ways of life. The parishioners still have no real money crop but cultivate a wide range of produce for their own consumption, selling any surplus. The family system here is that which was brought over from France in the seventeenth century and has remained unchanged. In the industrial centers and even the larger rural towns there has been marked alteration of this system, for reasons which will become apparent.

St. Denis is a relatively small parish but is lacking in none of the characters of the larger ones. There are seven hundred people distributed in one hundred and twenty households. The system of land establishment by which brothers took up contiguous lands was not always followed. However, the situation of neighboring lands in the same family name is a common one through the working of this system. Still, there has never been any feeling that opportunities such as better land or cleared farms for sale in other parishes should be passed by. The co-operative aspect of the family has acted as a check on this tendency to scatter. As the land was taken up more and more completely, the scattering tendency became stronger through sheer necessity; but farmers still like to buy near-by farms for their sons, if at all possible. In each generation a few families are obliged to sell their farms because of lack of healthy male outcome. Some families actually die out in certain regions through this cause, in spite of the large birth-rate.[3] The general family distribution picture is the result of the operation of all these forces, some of which are pure chance.

Every third person in the parish is named either Dionne or Garon. Three quarters of the people bear one or another of eleven family names. The remaining quarter has twice that number of names and represents new entrants to the parish and family lines which have played out through death, failure, or emigration. The larger, extended family groups include immediate families so distantly related that they do not consider themselves kin. Some of these may actually have moved into the parish later. In these cases families bearing the same name may belong not only to different cliques but to antagonistic ones. Similarities of name, where no known kinship exists, is such a common thing that persons having the same name feel no bond whatsoever when the kinship is not known. Genealogies are so well known and new personal contacts are so rare that there is seldom any attempt to relate one's self through kinship to someone of the same name.

The attitudes just considered show that family and name are far from synonymous. The former is a kin group which, through marriage, may include several surnames, although the male lines are always more important. The social function of names in this society is well demonstrated by the history of names in the parish. Until some fifty years ago literacy had but little utility in the parish. The literature of these people was in the form of songs and recounted stories. No commercial contacts necessi-

[3] About 10 per cent of the marriages are sterile.

tated reading or writing. The occasions when one was obliged to sign one's name were rare indeed—marriage contracts, records in the parish register, and that was about all. Even money was lent without notes. Many documents lack the signatures of some of the persons directly concerned. Even today, writing is left almost exclusively to the women, except for tradesmen. In this society a name did not serve as a means by which a man identified himself, but rather as a term by which he was identified by the society. In other words, a man had little opportunity to use his own name. He met new people infrequently and rarely under circumstances which would require him to give his own name. A surname did not necessarily pass down unchanged in a family. It was purely a term by which the society referred to a particular paternal unilinear family.

Some cases in point will clarify this function of names. The *curé* of the parish is called "Lallemand," the apostrophe having been dropped after the initial *L* and the article joined to the noun. The *curé* is, in fact, of German extraction; and his German surname of Fieber is still known by himself and a few of the more sophisticated parishioners, such as the local senator. Other parishioners remember having heard the name mentioned but cannot recall it. The phonemes being new and strange, the name was hard to use; and so he was called "The German" instead. Today he signs himself with this name that society gave him. Another name of the same type is "Langlais," which has very wide distribution. In another case a German named Franck settled in the parish with his family. Fully acculturated today, his descendants are still called by that name, as it had a phonetic counterpart in French.

There is another type of name change even more general

and pertinent to this discussion. To take three local cases: there are families called Roy and others Desjardins, whose ancestors were called Roy dit Desjardins; the man who opened the land for the Raymond family was named Phaucas dit Raymond; and the family of Beaulieu is related to Hudon through generations called Hudon dit Beaulieu. The origins of the secondary names are largely lost. The most logical supposition is that the secondary names are added by people trying to distinguish between persons of the same name. The majority of this type of name is descriptive, like Beaulieu; and even the linking word *dit* indicates that the secondary names arise popularly. Today in this and in surrounding parishes none of the double names is in use. However, everyone knows the history of the cases cited above.

There is another system for differentiating between persons with the same Christian and surnames; it is to state, in addition, the name of the father of each man. Two men named Paul Garon would thus be called Paul à Joseph and Paul à Baptiste, identifying them through their immediate families. This form is usually used only when the listener requests clarification.

In spite of the fact that all children are given the names of Joseph or Marie, only one in each family is ever called by this name. Three Christian names are given to most children, and even four may be given. The more names a child has, the more patron saints he has. Naming becomes difficult, particularly in families with common surnames, as the average number of children in a family is ten.[4]

---

[4] The figure for the average number of children per family, which happens to be 6.5. is useless, as it includes completed families, sterile families, and families of young couples. For this reason the 89 cases for which there was full information were divided into childless families, incomplete families (in which the mother was not yet 42 years old), and completed families (in which the mother was over 42). The average age of mothers at last childbirth was drawn from a group

Christian names are chosen by the parents for their children. Those selected may include traditional family names or the name of the saint on whose day the birth occurred. Names of recently deceased children and relatives are often employed. A name may be used simply because it strikes the parents as a nice one. Utter originality comes in at times with such names as Dieudonné and Angelique. The parents usually try to avoid duplicating the names of living persons with the same surname. Godparents for the infants are members of the family in most cases. Siblings of the parents serve most frequently in this capacity; but grandparents, cousins, or siblings of the child may also be chosen. This spiritual bond is a mild block to marriage, requiring a dispensation. Members of the family are in a position to watch after the spiritual needs of the child and have a greater natural interest in him. The solidarity of the family in the orientation of its young has resulted in the incorporation of the godparent role into the kin group.

With the relative immobility of the population and the pattern of marriage with kin or neighbors of kin who are in the approved family clique, we would expect marriages to

---

of mothers over 49, or over 40 and whose last children were over 4 years old. The average age at last childbirth was 40.8 years, with a maximum of 48 and a minimum of 34.

The 16 childless families were divided as follows:

Couples married after woman was 41 years old.......	2
Couples married for less than 2 years...............	5
Couples childless for biological reasons..............	9

For the incomplete families (25 cases):

Average number of married years...................	7.2
Average number of children per family..............	4.3
Interchild interval (years)........................	1.7

For the completed families (48 cases):

Average number of procreative married years (under 42 for the wife)................................	15.8
Average number of children per family..............	9.8
Interchild interval (years)........................	1.6

be local affairs. The parish marriage records bear out this assumption. Marriages are performed in the parish of the bride, so these records may be employed only for the women. Eighty-four per cent of the girls who marry take husbands from within twenty miles of St. Denis.[5] Of these, 29 per cent marry men in the parish of St. Denis itself. Another source of this type of material is the marriage notations entered after the birth records of the persons getting married. This is less reliable, because marriages in other parishes may not be completely entered. This is, however, the only source of comparison between the sexes. Among the women, 71 per cent marry men from within twenty miles, including 31 per cent who marry men from their own parish.[6] Only 53 per cent of the men marry girls from within twenty miles, and only 19 per cent take wives from their own parish.[7] The difference in the percentages of men and women who marry spouses from St. Denis is due to the fact that more men than women from the parish are getting married. Young men who are not going to inherit land must go elsewhere to establish themselves, with or without their father's aid. Because of these wider contacts, which the women do not have, men are more apt to take wives from distant parishes. The same lack of local opportunity which makes the men leave the parish keeps other men from coming in from a distance to establish and take wives in St. Denis.

[5] Drawn from 159 cases over the past 39 years.

[6] Material consists of 58 married girls born since 1898. The percentage which took marriage partners from St. Denis is substantially the same but that for the twenty-mile radius is lower than that derived from the other material. This may indicate a growing tendency for women to choose mates farther from home, as these figures represent marriages since 1917, whereas the others are marriages since 1898. The movement to the States during the latter period is not the reason, as only one husband came from the United States.

[7] Sixty-eight cases over the same period as the women.

Along with local marriage goes marriage in the kin group. The local marriage records show that 14.5 per cent of the marriages were between third or closer cousins. The church considers relationships of second cousins and closer as blocks to marriage, but there are designated amounts of money for which dispensations can be secured in some cases. The more distant the relationship, the lower the amount. The *curé*, however, has the right to reduce these amounts as he sees fit. The church has adjusted itself to the local marriage configuration, so that dispensations are easy to obtain. The one-hundred-dollar payment theoretically required for the marriage of first cousins is rarely demanded in full. Other factors, such as the age and health of individuals concerned and the likelihood of their finding other mates, are considered. Even in cases where the marriage may be forbidden both by church and family because of too close kinship, such as double first cousins (the same four grandparents in common), the situations leading to choice of spouses may throw such kin together and they may feel no abhorrence of such a match. Certain matches are avoided, however, such as those between lineal descendants, with siblings of one's parents, with deceased spouse's siblings. Marriage with a sibling of the deceased spouse would seem to be desirable because of the family and economic setup and the church leniency in the case of first-cousin marriage. On the other hand, spouses use blood-kinship terms in addressing parents-in-law. The mourning customs also identify these people classified together in kin-term usage. Siblings-in-law are not completely identified with siblings in kin-terms or mourning, but the relations built up with the in-law family are so intimate that they are regarded as pseudo-blood relationships. A deceased husband's siblings may even have been in the same household with the wife. The household usually in-

cludes persons of too close kin to marry, so that this extension of the feeling of incest, in addition to the church ban,
overcomes the natural advantages of such a match.

There is no reticence about taking a wife older than one's
self, although such a situation is a basis for joking, as it is
not the most common practice. The ages of couples on the
church census of the parish show 23 per cent of the women
to be older than their husbands.[8] Analysis of cases drawn
from other St. Denis records gives the average ages of marriage as twenty-six for men and twenty-five for women.[9]
Study of age at death in the parish reveals a high infant
mortality consistent with that for the whole province. A
third of the children born die before they are five years
old.[10]

Inheritance of the paternal farm does not follow primo-
geniture. Generally the inheritor is chosen from about the
middle of the sequence of children.[11] Many female or sickly
children or mortalities in the middle of the sequence may
cause a child nearer either end to be chosen, depending
upon the age of the father. Inheriting sons marry at about
the same age as other young men. Any tendency for the
security of position to cause earlier marriage is offset by the
necessity of waiting until some of the siblings have left
home to make room for the new *ménage*. The difference in

[8] Complete data for 73 couples. Of the 23 per cent, the average superior age
of the wife is 5 years; the maximum 15 years. For couples in which the husband
is the older, the average superior age is 5.5 years; the maximum 21 years. For
the whole group, the men average 3 years older than their wives. This average is
high in consideration of other material.

[9] Material: 130 marriages since 1919. For men the maximum age at marriage
is 34, the minimum 19. For women the maximum is 33, the minimum 17.

[10] From 480 deaths, stillbirths included, over the past 39 years. One-quarter
die before they are a year old. This rate is being regularly reduced throughout
the province of Quebec.

[11] Generalization from a score of genealogies in which the inheritor was the
fifth child, on the average.

age between the father and the inheritor is about thirty-four years, and the father is usually around sixty years old when his inheriting son marries.[12]

The foregoing material is now ready to be put in cultural context as the ordinary sequence of events in the family cycle. A young man of twenty-six marries a girl of twenty-five, and in his marriage contract he receives the title to the paternal land. His father is sixty years old now and, as he is not able to work as he used to, has been planning for several years to turn over the farm to his son. The bride comes to live with her parents-in-law; and her husband moves down from a room on the second floor, which he has shared with his brothers, to take one with his bride on the ground floor, where his father and mother and grandparents sleep. The young husband now manages the farm, aided by his father and the younger brothers who are still at home. It is his obligation to use part of the first earnings of the farm for the establishment of his brothers not yet economically independent. The amount to be paid is stipulated by the father in the grant. This money may be used either to send them to college, to buy them land, or to support them in the city or lumber towns while they look for work. The father does less and less of the manual labor; and the mother shifts her responsibilities to her daughter-in-law, who is aided by the unmarried sisters of her husband who are still in the household.

All the siblings of the inheriting son are expected to leave the paternal home. A young man would not consider it honorable to live with his brother. The father is responsible for the establishing of his children. If there are any of his sons or daughters still in the house at the father's

---

[12] These average ages are drawn from samples too small to claim statistical exactitude. The manner in which they integrate with the more precise material, however, shows that they give a true conception of the actualities.

death, he will leave them small amounts of money to enable them to establish separate households with the help of what they can earn individually.

By the time the young couple have been married eight years, they have had five children, one of whom has died. The eldest child is seven years old, the youngest a babe in arms. The family cycle is so regular that native expression gives voice to such a remark as "He is just a young man. He has only four or five children." At this point the man still has the vigor of his thirty-four years to carry him over the hardest period of the cycle. Until recently he has had the partial aid of his father and the help of his brothers who were still at home. But by this time his father is dead[13] and the last brother has left the house to establish himself elsewhere. The oldest son is but seven and will not be an able farm worker for as many more years. During this time there will be only one adult male on the farm. This is where the solidarity of the scattered family is important. If one of the brothers is farming in the same or in one of the neighboring parishes he will be confronted with an identical situation. The two brothers give each other mutual aid on their two small farms until their children are old enough to do a full share. If there is no brother farming in the vicinity, some related unestablished young man may be persuaded to help for a wage. In the final event, an unrelated man may be hired; but this is undesirable. The only two tractors in the parish were bought to tide over a protracted period of this sort, when there were insufficient *mains d'œuvre*.

In eight more years the father is forty-two and the couple has had ten children, three of whom have died. The

---

[13] The further life-expectancy of persons who have lived to be 24 years old is 41.3 years. In other words, they will achieve an age of 65.3 years on the average.

eldest sons are helping in the field, and there is no labor problem. By this time the father has begun to think seriously of plans for the future of his children, for whom he is responsible. He will ultimately have to arrange for six children.[14] Obviously, one of these, a boy, will inherit the parental land and one of the girls will marry some other inheriting son from the vicinity. The selection of the inheriting son is a serious matter. He must, above all, be physically fit and intelligent enough to be capable of the eventual management of the farm. Also, the father wants to choose a boy who will be ready to marry about the time the father wants to withdraw from full-time activity on the farm. The farm should never be turned over to an unmarried son. His choice of a wife is too important. A spendthrift daughter-in-law is the perpetual bugaboo of every prospective father-in-law. If a father has acquired other land and has two farms, he will usually wait until both the sons chosen to inherit are married before he designates which farms they will receive. The parents will select the more congenial daughter-in-law to remain in the old home with them. The parents thus exert great influence on their son's choice of a wife by their mere likes or dislikes.

In selecting which son will remain at home, it must be remembered that the choice of one of the eldest boys would be unwise, as his own children would soon overcrowd the house when he married. This would also put an additional strain on the economy at a time when money is needed to help establish the siblings of the inheriting son. For these reasons a son near the middle of the sequence of children is chosen to inherit the farm. This selection is a gradual procedure, a feeling-out of the children's possibilities and of the necessities and limitations of labor, age and health, capital, and housing space. The son chosen is usually in-

[14] Forty-three per cent die before 25 years of age, according to parish records.

formally told of the fact by the time he is eighteen or twenty. Long before this, however, his activities have been directed definitely to the farm, its work, and its management. Sometimes this orientation fails, so that the inclinations of the boys must be considered in the choice. When the young man inherits, the cycle recommences.

There remain five children unestablished, two boys and three girls; one of the latter will normally marry a local farmer. The girls, as far as is financially possible, are sent to near-by convents for two or even three years to secure their *diplômes* after they complete the local schools. There is occasional opportunity for girls with such education to get teaching positions in local schools. Such work pays very little but assures an independent livelihood. Girls with convent educations are also more marriageable. A girl may go on and become a nun if she so desires. If the family has sufficient money, one or more of the boys will be given some schooling beyond the local schools. This, however, is a more expensive matter. To complete the course at the religious college twelve miles away takes eight years at two hundred dollars a year. Of those who do finish 56 per cent go on to seminaries to become priests and 31 per cent train for law or medicine.[15] The others become *agronomes*, businessmen, engineers, etc.

On the average, in each family half of the girls are sent to convent schools. Only one-fifth of the surviving boys are sent to college for any period whatsoever. One child out of every family becomes a nun, priest, doctor, lawyer, or notary every other generation.[16] The boys the father

[15] College records of the Collège de Ste Anne de la Pocatière.

[16] Computed from verbal information on parish children for the past 25 years and parish records for past 80 years, the two coinciding. This average figure masks the fact that richer families have more, poorer ones have none.

selects to go to college must show some interest in their studies in the parish schools, as the father is not going to risk heavy investment in a possible failure. A child who does show enough interest and who is not destined by circumstances to work the farm will be directed toward educational and religious interests by the whole family. Children are never told they must become priests, for such a life comes only by divine call. They are, however, oriented in that direction; and once at college, where they decide their future with priest advisers, over half enter the priesthood. The obvious function of the religious life in the social structure is to make certain individuals nonprocreative. In return for this they are given a role of great social prestige.

Thus far, the ten children have the following outlook: four die before reaching twenty-five years; one inherits the paternal land; one marries a farmer; and one (if a boy) enters priesthood, or profession, or (if a girl) enters convent, becomes a schoolteacher, or marries a professional man. There are still three children unaccounted for. The father, during his management of the farm, although passing on the responsibility to his successor in the latter's first years, tries to buy another farm or save the money for a son to get a farm somewhere. A local informant estimated that one-quarter of the farmers establish two sons on lands.[17] This failing, the father gives the boy some technical training or sends him to cities or industrial centers where he can get work.[18]

The family cycle is shown in the accompanying diagram,

[17] This is only possible because of movement from marginal farms to cities, as new lands and childless farms cannot absorb this many new farmers.

[18] See Everett C. Hughes, "Industry and the Rural System in Quebec," *Canadian Journal of Economics and Political Science*, IV (August, 1938), 341–49.

using average ages of the individuals at various stages and crises of life.[19]

This cyclical procession of events finds expression in the philosophizing of a man whose son has taken over the

THE FAMILY CYCLE

Stage Number	Years Elapsed between Stages	Family Composition	Comments
I.......	0	A♂26 = ♀25	Marriage of couple
II......	16	A♂42 = ♀41 ⌐ 10 children ¬ 0 B♂8 15	Last of 10 children born. Child who will inherit (B) is 8 years old
III.....	18	A♂60 = ♀59 ⌐ 4 children ¬ 18 B♂26 = ♀25	Son (B) marries and inherits farm. Three of his siblings have died; elder ones have left home
IV......	16	A♂76† = ♀75† B♂42 = ♀41 ⌐ 10 children ¬ 0 C♂8 15	Original parents have been dead 10 years†, and all siblings of inheritor have been out of household for similar period. Inheritor's last child born
V......	18	B♂60 = ♀59 ⌐ 4 children ¬ 18 C♂26 = ♀25	Third inheritor marries and receives farm

management of the farm and is momentarily expecting his first child. "Life is like a turning wheel. The old turn over the work to the young and die, and these in turn get old and turn over the work to their children. Yes, life is like a wheel turning."

[19] Such a diagram is only possible against the background of a uniform system, as revealed by structural study.

The foregoing scheme carries the family through two generations of thirty-four years each. Checking this against three families which have been in St. Denis for eight generations, the cycles of these families averaged thirty, thirty-two, and thirty-four years, with no tendency for shorter cycles in the earlier generations.

The following family demonstrates the principal features of the cycle as described and diagrammed. It would be placed between stages III and IV in the scheme. A more typical family could have been selected, but the following one was chosen to show how actual cases vary away from the ideal built up on averages. This family is felt to be a wide variant by the parishioners and members of the family itself. The differences from normal which they consider worthy of comment are those which we would remark upon: the presence of so many generations together, the youth of the grandparents, the large size of the family, and the lack of infant mortality. The family is composed as shown in the accompanying table. Jean *père* gave all his daughters two years of convent education. He started giving Georges a college course, but the boy had to stop because of a tubercular leg. Hospital expenses used up the money intended for his education. Now he is thrown on his own to find a means of support.

The whole social system and the family system upon which it is dependent are based upon large families and the eventual establishment of all the children, save one, outside the paternal home. To function properly there must be a continual outlet for this surplus. In France, whence came the system, the disappearance of the outlets resulted in decreased birth-rate. During the first two centuries after the French came to Canada, there was always unopened land on which noninheriting sons could establish themselves. When these lands in Quebec were taken up, there were industrial opportunities in Quebec and New England to absorb the surplus.[20] Most of these openings

Name	Age	Relationship and Residence
Marie..........	88	Great-grandmother,* mother of Jean, living with him
Jean *père*.....	60	Grandfather, still living on and working the farm he has passed on to his son
Anne.........	58	His wife
Their children and grand children:		
Céline......	37	Local school teacher until her death at 37
Claire......	36	Gray nun, Quebec
Jeanne......	35	Single and living at home
François....	34	Day-laborer at Quebec, married
Berte.......	32	Gray nun, Quebec
Lucie.......	31	Married and living in St. Denis
Georges.....	29	Living with widowed aunt; looking for employment in Quebec
Paul........	27	Living with father; farms and gets irregular employment
Jean *fils*.....	26	Inheriting son; in charge of farm
Madeleine..	28	His wife, mother of five children, all living
Julienne ..	6	
Joseph....	4	
Laure.....	3	
Thomas...	2	
Angelique.	1	
Marie Louise	24	Teacher at Levis
Jean Baptiste	18	Living at home and helping on farm
Henriette ...	17	At home

* Kin terms as used by the youngest member of the household.

are closed now, so that the surplus has little means of establishing itself. The decreasing death-rate, because of provincial public health activity, is complicating the problem by increasing the number of children who have to be

[20] There is inertia on the part of both French and English toward settlement of western Canada by the French. The problems presented by such Catholic minorities are distasteful to both groups.

established. The result has been the creation of a new economic group, as yet small. These are day-laborers and consist of the families of men who inherited no land and could find no positions. They live by odd jobs, peddling, and provincial road work. Their families are as large as farming families; but, having little economic security, the children know they must live by their own endeavors. The members of such families are more individualistic, less under paternal dominance, and tend to be less faithful Catholics. As soon as the "right" ways of life cease to be successful ways, the social system is due to shift, in an attempt to secure adjustment. In the cities the birth-rate has been falling markedly, but this tendency is much less noticeable in rural regions.[21]

Another effect has been to make marriage more difficult, owing to the economic uncertainty. There are numerous unmarried men and women to attest this fact.[22] However, the old system still holds to such an extent that these persons are obliged to leave the home of their inheriting brother.

An analysis of the one hundred and twenty households in the parish reveals both this situation and the normally functioning family cycle. By reference to the diagram of the family cycle it can be seen that, on the average, there are three generations in the household for six years and two generations for twenty-eight years. Out of all the households in the parish, ninety-one fit into the family cycle as described. Variations in longevity extend the picture somewhat from the average. These ninety-one households are composed as follows:

[21] Quebec Department of Municipal Affairs, Trade and Commerce, *1936 Statistical Year Book* (Quebec: Printer to the King's Most Excellent Majesty, 1937), p. 85.

[22] In the parish 23.4 per cent of the men and 34.1 per cent of the women over 40 years are unmarried.

68   Elementary family: husband and wife, or parent(s) and children
      (and sibling of father in 2 cases)
21   Three generations: grandparent(s), parent(s), their children (and
      unmarried sibling[s] of the male parent in 12 cases)
 2   Four generations: great-grandparent, grandparent(s), parents and
      unmarried siblings of male parent, and his children.

In these households the "grandparents" may be the parents of either spouse. It may be clearly seen how the household moves from one stage to another, following the cycle. The death of the older generations moves the household type up in the list. On the other hand, the marriage of inheriting sons soon increases the number of generations. The proportion of three-generation households is slightly more than would be expected from the cycle diagram.

The remaining twenty-nine households are divided between seven variations on the typical cycle households and twenty-two which are utterly different and demonstrate the effect on the social structure of the altered conditions due to lack of opportunity for establishment. The variations on the typical households consist of additional persons added to them. These, again, are persons who in most cases should be living elsewhere but who have been forced back on the family. Six households are of the elementary-family type but have added to them: a niece, brother-in-law, sister of the wife, hired man, aunt of husband, related hired boy, blind boarder. The seventh case is a chance anomaly, including several interrelated families.

The other cases are made up, for the most part, of households of unmarried people: sisters living together, brothers together, brother(s) and sister(s) together, men alone, or women alone. Other single cases are: brothers living together, one married; a man, his sister, and three nieces; an old woman and nephew; a man, his niece, and a hired girl; a man, his married nephew, and the latter's wife. These are all obviously makeshift households formed in an effort to live on smaller incomes.

For centuries the family cycle in rural French Canada has functioned so that all children were given the opportunity to earn a livelihood, marry, and propagate. The cycle has not changed; but the social structure of which it is an integral part has become altered, so that children no longer are assured a full social life. There are structural conflicts which can be resolved only by a return to old conditions made possible by a new outlet for surplus children or a change in the family organization itself.

CHAPTER V

THE ROLE OF RELIGION

ALL the inhabitants of St. Denis are Roman Catholics. The philosophy of this religion is ingrained in the people from childhood. Emulation of the socially powerful individuals in the community means the acceptance of Catholic ideology and behavior patterns. All the methods of orienting the child in the society are employed to develop in him emotional attachment to this particular set of beliefs. Lack of contact with persons of other convictions and the relative lack of functional problems in the mode of living mean that the particular native belief is rarely questioned.

Life in St. Denis is a flow of traditional behavior. Upon rising, there are family prayers; then the animals must be fed and the cows milked; the workers return to cross themselves and sit down to breakfast, after which the men go to the field while the women wash the dishes, spin or knit, and then prepare the next meal. Incidents in this stream of events can be singled out and designated as sacred or secular, but such distinction is not part of the native's own conceptualization of life. Nevertheless, the distinction is significant as a basis for structural consideration of the social life of the parish. The sacred ideas and acts are those which are so surrounded with strong sentiments of attachment that they may not be subjected to rational scrutiny. The secular side, then, is open to discussion and criticism. We shall be particularly concerned with that part of the sacred ideology which draws its meaning from the religion, that complex of sacred ideas and acts centering around supernatural powers and expressing ultimate social values.

One may conceive everyone in the community as living a life of participation in both the sacred and secular spheres. By renouncing secular dress, social contact, and physical pleasures, priests, friars, and nuns simulate a living death and live more in the purely sacred sphere. The newspaper announcements of girls taking vows are invariably headed "Goodbye to the world." The parishioner's life is both sacred and secular; as life goes on, he follows a road from the secular world into the sacred. Only by living this dual life can the enjoyable sacred existence be reached. *Rites de passage* mark the various stages of progress along this road. The newborn babe is like an animal, a completely secular creature. The baby, however, is an offspring of man and, as such, has a soul which an animal does not possess. A soul is a sacred element of every human being. It is a reference to that sphere which is purely sacred.

By baptism an infant is admitted into the social world—the secular-sacred world—in contrast to the purely secular one into which it was born. This is quite obvious in the ceremony and ideology of the community. The *curé* in a sermon tells his parishioners: "We are Catholics and baptized. It is our duty to struggle against sin." The fact of baptism makes them all members of a common group with common rules of life. The intimate relation of the church to the modes of life precludes the possibility of this being merely a group with only common religious ideas. An unbaptized child is not buried in the cemetery, that lot of sacred ground which expresses the continuity of the community. A baptized baby is buried by the church but without a Mass. The first rite of entrance into the social life is passed, but this is not sufficient for full membership.

The ceremony of *petite communion*, which is an unostentatious first Communion, corresponding with entrance into the schools, gives the individual more, but still not complete, recognition in the social world. The child is expected to go to church, but no Mass would be sung for his decease nor would mourning be worn. After the festive *grande communion* the status is that of a participating member of the society demanding a Mass for burial, mourning, and requiring of the individual full participation in the religious activity of the community.

From baptism through all these stages to death the individual has led both a sacred and secular life. He or she has lived by physical toil, met practical everyday problems, and has felt very much a being of flesh and natural appetites. At the same time there has been continual participation in the sacred life through prayers, Masses, confession, and penance. All these activities have as their purpose the securing of reward after the final *rite de passage*, the Requiem Mass, and burial. At this time the individual enters the purely sacred existence. This wholly sacred sphere also has a dual nature. It is divided between a happy enjoyable part and one of misery and torture—heaven and hell. As all men possess souls, everyone is referred toward the eventual sacred life, be it pleasant or miserable. The beings who people it are conceived of as being spirits, invisible to man, floating about in space and defying the physical laws of the secular world. Because of the mortal, secular nature of men on earth they describe and picture things of the purely sacred existence in terms of physical experiences. In the prayer books, the Holy Ghost is pictured as a dove, the angels with wings, God with a long beard. The actual adult conceptualization of these powers is not pictographic. These fanciful representations resulting from the limitations of drawing do, however, represent the youthful concepts. There is no conflict for youth between a catechism statement concerning God the Father and the picture of an old man. The mystical concept is learned later in life from priests and represents a definite stage in the age-grade system. The conceptualization of the dove as the Holy Ghost is like that of the gipsy bringing babies and the Christ child filling stockings on Christmas. Visualization, however, still plays an important role with the adults. The sacred beings with whom contact is the most frequent and the need of conceptualization the greatest are Jesus, Mary, and the saints, of whom there are numerous pictures and statues. According to church doctrine, which is known by the people, the saints are spirits, like God; but they are visualized in their earthly states. Jesus and Mary have their physical forms in heaven.

The sacred aspect of the social everyday life of the community is concerned with limiting the numerous possibilities of action allowed by secular human existence. The permissible modes of behavior are worked out to a nicety so as to maintain a particular form of social organization. Large families are the basis of the organization, and they are strongly sanctioned by the religion.[1] Families which do not find a solution to their life-problems in the ways of the church will vary away from accepted behavior in order to live and, in so doing, lose or weaken their religious belief. A whole society will do exactly the same thing if the sacred ways of living no longer succeed. The religion is the focal point of a body of sentiments concerning correct social behavior. Sacred beliefs support the time-tested, successful, and "right" behavior. In St. Denis the church is much alive to the fact that the local modes of life will be successful as long as all the factors in the time-tested system re-

[1] See "Kinship and the Family Cycle," chap. iv.

main the same. It looks with alarm at the growing number of unmarried men and women, at the growing city ways, at all the things which may alter the existing social setup. The sacred institutions must either stop vital changes in the society or adapt themselves to the new life. As an example of how the organized sacred beliefs are altered to fit the social pattern, the Catholic church as a world-institution has a series of dispensations which must be paid to marry close relatives. In St. Denis, however, the marriage pattern favors marriage to close kin and dispensations are easily obtained.[2]

To live a perfect social life is to adhere to all the rules of conduct which make for a smoothly running society. These rules are supported by sacred sanction and are part of the sacred ideology. Thus, for those who conform, a reward of heaven is assured; for nonconformists the threat of hell is imposed. It is obvious that even the nonconformists must have faith in the sacred doctrine for this threat to have value as a social control. All the parishioners have this faith in varying degrees. What lack of faith exists is the result of the recent changes in the functioning of the society itself.

Heaven and hell and the whole philosophy and secular-sacred behavior built up around them have another function aside from their power as a social control. The average life of a man, woman, or child in St. Denis is a hard one. It is one of long hours of toil with little reward except the continuance of life. The vagaries of nature and chance add such catastrophes as frozen crops and burned barns. Faith in the doctrine of heaven offers eventual reward for a mundane life of relative unhappiness and hard work. The reward is set in terms of terrestrial values unattainable on earth—beauty, riches, peace, and happiness. An old wom-

[2] See *ibid.*

an says: "Catholicism is a consoling religion. If a young wife has a large family and is pregnant and discouraged, she may go to the *curé* and talk to him. She will leave consoled and pass her remaining months content with her lot." The type of consolation is typified in an extract from a sermon:

Today is the celebration of St. Joseph. He is the patron of the church, of Canada and of all of us, as it is rare that a child is not baptized with the name of St. Joseph.[3] When God chose St. Joseph, he chose an humble man. The Bible says it is difficult for the rich to reach heaven. It is very understandable. They lead a life without effort or sacrifice, a life which is soft and lazy. They are interested in bodily pleasures. After death what will become of their riches, their honors? They will be in hell to suffer eternally for the sins they committed during their lives. God chose a carpenter from among all the people from whom he could choose. You are farmers, not of the rich of the earth, starting work early and stopping late. God loves you all the more. Look at St. Joseph. He was a carpenter. Don't envy those who run the streets until eleven o'clock at night going to theaters and cafés. They live low lives. In the cities there is no happiness. Love your land, the land of your fathers and your ancestors. Cultivate it; love it; love your humble calling. Your calling has been given you by God. Continue to follow it. God will bless you when you die if you till the soil and serve him. Nothing is received from heaven without sacrifice.

Here is an explicit statement to the farmers from the most respected and socially powerful person in the community that their misery on earth counts in their favor in gaining the ultimate reward. An attack on the new city values which are in a position to filter in and change life is presented here, as we might expect. The sacred sanctions must maintain the *status quo* or else change with any basic innovation.

Heaven and hell are put into a spatial context. Heaven is conceived as being *up* in space and hell *down* inside the earth. This is part of a general conceptualization placing definite value on relative height. Churches, cemeteries,

---

[3] Males only are considered in this statement.

and important buildings are placed on eminences of land. Holy statues are placed high on the walls. The altar is raised, and its steps each have significance with respect to their superior position. Contact with the earth is felt as degrading for sacred objects. Adoration is indicated by looking upward; submission, by downcast eyes. Kneeling shows a humble spirit; and prostration even more, by the intimate contact with the earth. This placing of social value on superposition is one of the most profound things in the ideology. It permeates purely secular activities. Socially important persons are conceived as higher than others. Social positions which control others are conceived as higher. The ideology of social and religious power is in terms of this basic concept.

As has already been indicated, the duality of sacred and secular is a logical one used for its value in presenting a philosophy of existence. To the *habitant* of St. Denis there is no such division in life. He could understand such a separation, but it has no part in his daily life. Nature is both sacred and secular. A crop which could grow without sacred influence is merely an idea, not a fact. To the farmer, the plowing of land, the singing of Masses for its productivity, the harrowing of the soil, the planting of blessed seed of each sort, the spreading of fertilizer, and the processions to secure the fruits of the soil are the ways to get a good crop. Some or any of them might be omitted, but with definite detrimental effect to the crop.

Another distinction which the *habitant* does not make is that between dogmatic and nondogmatic religious belief. One is equally as real and important as the other. The church, as in all societies where it is formally organized, maintains just the dogma; but other related religious beliefs are apt to grow up and cluster about it. Frequently, if these are stable enough, they become part of the dogma itself. The doctrine of the Immaculate Conception was not part of Roman Catholic dogma until 1854, after seven centuries during which it was gaining popularity as a religious belief.

A phase of the religious philosophy which is relevant to the discussion of dogma concerns the saints and miracles. The saints are the spirits of persons who are in closer accord with God than the spirits of other humans. This divine accord comes from God himself. In other words, a person cannot set out to become a saint, although he may emulate one. A saint has divine power, which is shown during life by some miracle. A miracle is some phenomenon on earth which follows the heavenly disregard for natural laws. To be a true saint, the individual must be recognized by dogma through canonization. This process usually takes a great many years after the death of the saint.[4] They are not, therefore, known as saints during their lives, although their divine powers may be recognized. After death the cult of those who believe in their power continues and grows. They have faith in the power of a person not recognized by church dogma. To use our distinction between the various types of sacred beliefs, such faith in the power of an uncanonized person is a religious belief but nondogmatic. The normal history of the creation of a saint is a movement from popular to dogmatic belief. One incipient case is worthy of study. There recently died in Montreal an old thaumaturge, Frère André, whose powers are known throughout Quebec. While alive, he healed the sick and infirm through a special relationship which he apparently possessed with St. Joseph. At present he has a large following in Quebec, who now pray to his spirit for relief because of this powerful relationship. He is part of the religious belief, not of the dogma. He may some day

[4] Ste Thérèse being a recent exception.

be canonized. If, however, during his lifetime, he had healed through his own power, rather than through that of St. Joseph—a faculty which he studiously avoided—his powers would not have been religious and he could never become a saint. Being a lay brother in a religious order and in an extremely Catholic region, he would probably never have gained his following. His cures were, therefore, due in large part to the religious context in which he operated.

As the miraculous is actually construed to mean the unusual, the intervention of divine powers in everyday life is not infrequent. All life is conceived as under divine regulation, but only such incidents which are out of the ordinary can be singled out to show divine intervention. Such intervention may be sought by certain religious acts, or it may be gratuitous. When an overheated stovepipe set a house afire and the smoke roused its male inhabitant in time to put out the fire, the fact that he was saved was attributed by his fiancée to the divine intervention of the Blessed Virgin.

As saints are obviously so potent, supplications constantly ascend to them. These prayers are usually directed to the saints and to the Virgin, although God may be prayed to directly, as in the *pater*. The relationship between mortals and saints is much more intimate than between men and God. Saints are besought to intercede with God in the supplicant's behalf. This roundabout method is explained thus: "Say that I know you and want to ask a favor of you. I can ask you directly, and you may or may not grant it. But if I know someone very well who knows you intimately, I can ask that person to ask you for me and I am more likely to be granted the request." This works particularly well in the case of prayers to the Virgin, since, following family ideology, "She is the

Mother of God, and he cannot refuse her." Besides being more approachable, the saints have special relationships with mortals. Everyone has several patron saints who look after him. The patron saint of a parish is a guardian of that parish. Rarely, however, do these two types of saints become important in the religious life of an individual. The particular saint or saints in whom a person puts his faith are "according to his devotion." This means that it is according to the particular religious experience to which he has been subject. Such devotion to a saint may arise from family or regional tradition, particularly the latter. The saint which a person selects for confidences is dependent upon the stories he has heard and experiences he has had. In a population as immobile as that in Quebec the growth of local preferences is not surprising. Ste Anne and St. Joseph dominate the whole province through the broad renown of the cures at Ste Anne de Beaupré and at the oratory of Frère André in Montreal.

Although religious behavior and thought dominate all life, and ceremonial and practical aspects of religion are frequent topics of discussion, the religious philosophy is rarely talked about except during a child's early years, when he is learning the catechism and going to school. During this time both teachers and parents discuss such matters with the child. Adults are reticent about talking of such things except with children. As the ideas are dogma and sacred, they are common knowledge and not open to question, and therefore a very poor topic of conversation. In addition, life in St. Denis puts no value on intellectual and philosophic conversation. Such things are all right for priests and teachers, but for the *habitant*—his interests do not lie in this direction. With little theological interest, related problems are not very apt to arise. When they do present themselves, they are taken to the *curé* rather than discussed openly.

To attain the final reward in the sacred hereafter and to succeed in the social life on earth, one must follow certain rules and perform certain acts. By far the most important sacred acts of the community are centered around the celebration of the Mass. The ideology here concerned is part of the general religious philosophy and is also largely dogma. All the parishioners, although members of different family groups and, therefore, sharply separated in most of their activity, have a common need. That need is the result of the religious philosophy they hold in common. They must have a priest, not only to administer the sacraments which constitute a large part of the sacred life, but also to perform the miracle of the Mass, in which Christ descends to the altar in flesh and blood. Participation in this ceremony is required of all able-bodied participating members of the society. One Mass each Sunday must be heard, as well as others on *fêtes d'obligation* or on days which have some particular religious reference. The extent to which the need for a priest is felt is easily seen in early colonial days and in the new settlements today. The financial burden of maintenance of the priest and church is clearly recognized. Frequently comments are made that the hard times in clearing and opening a new region do not begin until the parish is founded and financial obligations are incurred. Still, until such a time, life without the sacraments and death without absolution mean that the sacrifices of mortal life will not bring the ultimate reward. The lack of that close unity with the divine powers, which is expressed as "not being in grace," means less control over nature. These needs are felt so greatly that every effort is made to secure a priest, the only individual who can make possible adequate participation in the sacred life.

In St. Denis at least one Mass is sung every day, except when the priest is absent through some unusual circumstance. Even at these times his absence is apt to be resented, for the mere singing of the Mass by the priest has value in the religious life of those who attend it and of those who pay for it. The Masses at which attendance is required by dogma are given by the priest to the parish; that is, they are unpaid. The Masses of the week are paid for by individuals and are dedicated to specific purposes. High Masses cost three dollars and a half; Low Masses, which are not sung, are bought at one dollar, or fifty cents if they are to be said at the priest's convenience.

The Masses of the week, which are not compulsory, are attended by a group of about fifty persons—old maids, bachelors, widows, widowers, and other persons who are nearing the end of the secular-sacred life on earth. They explicitly feel their proximity to the purely sacred life. Like priests and nuns, many of the secular activities are closed to them, and they participate more fully in the purely sacred life which they are approaching. Most of them live in the village, close to the church, where their interests are centered. Many have moved into houses in the village for this reason alone. An extreme psychological case in a neighboring parish exhibits the extent to which this social position of sacred life on earth can be patterned by the philosophy. The case is an aged unmarried woman, a retired schoolteacher, who confesses twice a day and spends most of her days in the church from sunrise to sunset. All conversation on other than religious matters she considers sin. She is even shocked by the secular talk of the priests. She insists that visitors to her house say prayers for her father, deceased five years, for whom she

The Church of St. Denis

To Mass by *Carriole*

is still in full mourning. In a downpour of rain she refused a proffered umbrella because it had red in it. When she disrobes at night, she covers the holy pictures in her room with paper. Admittedly this is an extreme case but one which represents the pole toward which persons in her position tend to move.

The dogma which places value on participating in unrequired Masses is not the only religious belief about the matter. Most of the Masses of the week are sung to aid the soul of a particular deceased to leave purgatory and attain the happy life of heaven. If a person has led a perfect religious life on earth, when he dies his spirit will go directly to heaven. For sins on earth he must pay by punishment in purgatory, a middle ground between heaven and hell, whence he will go to heaven. A great deal of interest is naturally centered on getting the soul of a deceased person out of purgatory and in deciding when it is out. It is not unusual for priests to be asked if a certain soul is out of purgatory yet. The religious philosophy presents no way of knowing when the soul has passed on into heaven, only the assurance that any Masses or prayers said for it after this time will be divinely applied to other souls in need of help. The whole power of family solidarity makes the soul of the dead person extremely important to the relatives. Death severs no family ties; it only changes the state of some of the relatives. In addition, hearing and having Masses sung for the dead and saying rosaries for them are religious acts which help the doer himself to shorten his own days in purgatory and assure him the heavenly reward. In other words, these sacred acts are generous and selfish at once. The way this operates in the philosophy varies. Some believe that these generous actions of the mortal being will be credited in his favor by God, who will judge him less severely at death. Others believe that personal souls thus helped out of purgatory will reciprocate from their heavenly position when their benefactor is in purgatory.

Parishioners attend Sunday Mass primarily because the spiritual degradation resulting from nonattendance is as undesirable to anyone convinced of the ultimate importance of hearing the Mass as the fruits of the ceremony are desirable. We are but saying that the parishioner's behavior is in this respect motivated by the drives set up by the religious philosophy itself. The philosophy was acquired by the individual in the first place for social reasons, not because of any innate acceptability of this particular doctrine. The religious ideology expresses the ultimate values of the society and supports the forms of life of that society. As the religion is the very essence of the society, the society is deeply concerned in its maintenance.

All social forces are brought to bear on any new member of the society to make him conform to the mores and to develop in that individual a set of philosophic values which will act as an additional control on his behavior. Practically all new members of the society are the children which it produces. The social forces of criticism and ostracism, the inherent power of social leaders, and even physical force are used to make the child accept the traditional mores and beliefs.[5] The small child starts going to Mass, not because he is afraid that he will go to hell if he does not, but for other reasons: everyone else is attending, he is proud to be old enough to do what others are doing, he will be scolded and spanked if he does not, the teacher will hold him up to public ridicule for failure to attend, and the *curé*, who is obeyed by everyone, says to go. At an early age the religious philosophy is accepted for much the same reasons. Then the child goes to Mass

[5] See "Childhood," chap. ix.

partly because he is worried about his soul in the context of the ideology he has come to accept. The social forces are always ready to be brought to bear if the controls of the philosophy are not sufficient.

The Mass is a social phenomenon aside from its religious context. Nothing brings this out more clearly than a consideration of the Sunday assembly itself. Some of the religious ceremonies are private, such as confession and prayer. Others are familial rites, such as baptism, family prayers, and extreme unction. Masses are public religious celebrations whether they are Sunday Masses or Masses for marriages, anniversaries of death, burial, or special supplication. They are practically the only activity in which the whole parish participates as a group. As such, they are expressive of the social unity. The smaller social units, such as families, lose their identity only in these acts in which the whole society participates. Sex distinctions become more important than family distinctions.[6] Much of the function of the assembly for the Mass is purely secular. The Sunday Mass in its religious context asserts and strengthens the common sacred beliefs of the society, explicitly directs behavior which has its meaning in the religious ideology, and aids in the social integration of the youth. On the sacrosecular plane, the mores of the society are protected from infringement. On the purely secular level, the Sunday assembly is an opportunity for the exchange of ideas, for the dissemination of information of general importance, and for commercial transactions of interest to all. With this general conception of the function of the Mass we are ready to consider it in its full social context.

[6] The following chapter gives instances of these distinctions.

CHAPTER VI

THE MASS

SUNDAY morning the Angelus rings as usual, but at eight o'clock the bells ring out again and every quarter-hour thereafter until time for the Mass at nine.[1] The tolling from the church spire hastens the tardy and keeps all informed as to the passing of the final hour of a busy early morning. The animals must be fed, the cows milked, breakfast eaten, and the dishes washed. Then all must change from work to Sunday clothes and walk or ride to church. Most of the men of the parish, including all the males out of school, go up to the church at least a quarter of an hour early. A few of them must remain at home to drive the buggy for the women and children; but any small boy is glad to drive, so most of the men are free to go on ahead.

Many of the parishioners, both men and women, go to the sacristy even before eight o'clock to confess to the *curé*. After confession they say the prayers they have been given as penance and take Communion. In particular, parishioners who live at a distance from the church come to confess and take Communion before the Sunday Mass, as they can seldom come during the week.

In front of the church the men stand in groups smoking and discussing items of current public interest—politics, crops, or some unusual incident in the life of the parish. As a particular discussion grows in fervor, voices rise and attract other men, who join the crowd around the principal figures in the argument. On the periphery of this group

[1] The Angelus rings at five o'clock in summer, six o'clock in winter.

106

men start talking among themselves, possibly starting another knot of listeners. While the men talk quietly or argue heatedly, buggies drive up to the side of the wide church steps. Women and small children get out and walk silently along the edge of the crowd of men and on into the church. Salutations between acquaintances of the two sexes on these occasions are rare but permissible, and are seldom more than a nod. After the buggies stop at the door, the drivers go off to near-by barns and hitching rails to tie up the horses. Then they are free to join the men outside the church.

As the hour of the Mass approaches, the old doorman fulfils his duty. Distinguished by a broad red band and the five-foot black baton he holds, and supported by strong public sentiment and the frequent remarks of the *curé*, he admonishes the men to enter, since the Mass is about to start. Theoretically a guardian of the peace, empowered to eject a person from the church or separate brawlers without, he actually plays the role of a final bell. No one enters the church at his warning because he tells them to; his activity simply brings the realization that the. Mass is about to start and discussions must end. The doorman's seeming authority rests in the general social acceptance of the fact that it is bad to be late to Mass.

Only a small group of men remains outside until this final call. The rest drift into the church singly or in groups. As they pass the portals, all social intercourse ceases. Everyone takes holy water from the font by the door and crosses himself to keep away the devil during the Mass. When, on occasion, the font is empty, the gesture of putting the hand into the font is continued. The act has social significance even when the holy water, which gives it meaning, is absent. Even when the men join the women of the family in their pews or pass good friends, there is no word or look of recognition. Upon reaching the pew, each worshiper does a genuflection before entering. In the pew he kneels on his prayer bench and settles himself. Overcoats are never removed; but pocketbooks and gloves are set on the little front shelf by the women, and hats and pipes are similarly disposed of by the men. The sign of the cross is made. Until the priest and choir boys enter, one is free to look around to see who is at church and, after kneeling awhile, to sit back. A few read papers secured at the post office on the way to church. Almost everyone is at church except those who are too sick or old to come. In every household some women has had to remain at home to look after the small children. If there was an early Mass, some have attended it instead of the High Mass.

The more reverent remain kneeling for a longer time, occupying themselves with religious thoughts. A few go forward and light candles before the holy statues. Some young men, whose fathers are long dead and who are, therefore, less completely dominated by the social controls, may giggle with others for whom the hereafter is still too distant a threat to suppress such enjoyment. The *bedeau* enters in his red and black cape and lights the altar candles. The men's choir in the loft starts to sing, and the harmonium tries to follow the singers. A score or more choirboys in their black-and-white vestments enter in two single files from the doors at either side of the main altar. They walk to the front of the sanctuary platform, turn toward the center, and join, so that they return to the altar two abreast. Arriving at the foot of the altar, they execute a genuflection by pairs and proceed to the benches along either side of the sanctuary, where they remain during the Mass. The choirboys are followed by the priest, carrying the sacred vessels and accompanied by his four acolytes, selected from the *enfants de chœur*.

The Mass of the catechumens begins. Most of the parishioners follow the prayers of the Mass in their prayer-books, which give both the Latin and French versions in parallel columns. The French prayers are read silently as the priest recites the Latin. Once the Mass has begun, there is no looking about. All eyes are on the prayer-books or the altar. Every adult knows the significance of the particular color of the priest's vestments. The saint, or *fête*, to which the Mass on this day is dedicated, was announced the preceding Sunday and is marked on the large religious calendars which hang conspicuously in the kitchen of every home. The parishioners follow the movements of the Mass, which they have known since childhood—kneeling, rising, sitting as common participants in the ceremony. The choirboys execute the movements also but do not sing. Only the men's choir in the loft sings. The *bedeau* is responsible for the good behavior of the choirboys, with whom he sits.

The Mass is followed by the parishioners largely according to Catholic ritual procedure. The worshipers have always knelt during the Credo and after the Elevation, and the choirboys have stood during these parts of the Mass, following proper ritual procedure.[2] A boy in the choir sounds a wooden clapper for each movement of the Mass. Beside traditional differences of the sort just mentioned, the parishioners vary in the precision with which

[2] Local variations of this sort show the extent of parish isolation and the traditional continuance of early errors in ritual. These particular variations were just corrected by the *curé* at the bishop's request. The people felt that their religion was changing along with all the other changes in customary modes of behavior. After the *curé* announced the change, the *marguilliers* and school-teachers were the first to make the proper movement, the other parishioners following their example. It was only recently that the church, through traveling instructors, brought consensus into the manner of singing the ritual songs. Each locality had its own peculiarities, continued through its *maître chant*. "Now we can go to another parish and sing in its choir just as in ours," remarks one *chant*.

they follow the Mass. These variations follow socially determined lines. In the balcony an old-maid schoolteacher and a religious old bachelor always rise or kneel at exactly the proper instant, leading the other people. This difference is more striking in the balcony, where the less desirable pews are located, for here there is more laxity in following the Mass. Downstairs there is more precision, so that no persons are such obvious leaders, although those in the front tend to rise first. Differences between the balcony and main floor are noticeable. The balcony usually follows the people below them, the downstairs executing the movements first. It is not that the people in the balcony do not know the ritual; it is simply traditionally different behavior distinguishing these separate groups in the same church, the balcony composing about a fifth of the entire congregation. These groups do not feel any unity outside the church. Families may even be divided between pews in the two places.

The distinction between the groups is regularly shown at various points during the Mass. When the priest comes forward to asperse the choirboys and parishioners with holy water, he comes out to the front of the sanctuary three times. The first two times he turns to sprinkle the choirboys on either side; the last time he sprinkles the worshipers. When he comes out the first time, the choir, the downstairs, and a few in the balcony rise. There is a scattered rising thereafter until all have risen by the time he comes forward a second time. Those in the balcony who rise with those downstairs make themselves conspicuous by doing so. They separate themselves from the group, and such is their intention. They feel themselves "right" and occasionally win unsolicited converts. The social position of the schoolteacher both requires her to be a leader and causes others to follow her. No child would think of preceding his parents. It is true that there is a slightly less religious element in the balcony—younger men without their parents and day-laborers—but the unity derived from the isolation of the balcony includes many who are equally as faithful as those below. During the *prône* the balcony seats itself as soon as the priest leaves the altar, with the exception of the few who wait for the clapper, as do the choir and downstairs.

As the *curé* passes out of the choir to go to the pulpit, the people in the pews which he passes rise, out of deference to his position. In the pulpit the *curé* begins by a discussion of practical matters. The amount of the collection the previous Sunday is given, and the parishioners are thanked for their donations. Then follow general announcements: the place and time of the meeting of the Cercle des Fermières, the date for the auction of pews or for the election of a new *marguillier*, a request for bedding for priests in the new land settlements, reassurance as to the character of an itinerant insurance salesman, the hours the public health doctor will be at the *salle*, a request that wood for the church be hauled from another parish, religious calendars for sale after Mass in the sacristy. These are typical of the two or three statements each week. Religious announcements follow. The Mass the following Sunday is in honor of a particular saint or *fête*. The passage in the Roman ritual appropriate for that occasion is read. If any days of fast or abstinence occur during the coming week, except Friday, when abstinence is always observed, the days are announced and the regulations specified. Times and dates for confession are given. A short moral lesson may be preached on some incident in the parish during the past week: a man having cruelly beaten his dog on the public road, or strange girls in bathing suits having ridden bicycles through the parish. The priest gives verbal attention to these incidents. It is his duty to adjust all irregularities in the life of the parish. "The school children are not doing their work properly. Look at the bulletin on the wall at the school; and if your child is mediocre or below, he is not doing his best. It is up to the parents to watch their children. Children are children, and they think October is just another month of vacation." Thus are the parents taken to task before the very children they are supposed to correct.

The *curé* reads from slips of paper the dates of funerals and anniversary services to be held in neighboring parishes. "I recommend to your prayers Marie Langlais, wife of Henri Pelletier, who died yesterday at Kamouraska at the age of seventy-nine years and four months. The funeral will be Monday at nine o'clock. Relatives and friends are invited." Such announcements are followed by the Masses for the ensuing week with their donors: "The Masses of the week: Monday, for Claire Dionne, given from the money of the funeral;[3] Tuesday, for Amanda Garon, by the succession; Wednesday, anniversary service for Marie Langlais at nine o'clock instead of the usual time; Thursday, for Georges Garon, by his wife; Friday, an act of thanks by a parishioner; Saturday, a Mass of thanks and prayer by M. and Mme Joseph Gagnon on their fiftieth anniversary."

The whole kneeling congregation says a *pater* for Spain, led by the *curé*. There is a short Gospel-reading, and the priest begins the sermon. If the Mass is one of particular church significance, such as those during Lent or near Christmas, the sermon is apt to deal with the Catholic doctrine pertinent to the particular *fête*. Some of these religious topics have general appeal, particularly stories of

[3] Money from the collection taken at her funeral, to be used for subsequent Masses.

miracles and martyrs. The Sunday devoted to the propagation of the faith and dealing with missions never fails to draw feminine tears. Philosophic sermons have little interest value, but those dealing with human behavior and current events find ready listeners. The most frequent sermons of this latter type are attacks on communism, illustrated with atrocity stories from Spain. There is continual preaching against the threat of communism in Canada. The communist is associated in the public mind with the blackest of deeds and motives. Ethnic pride and unity are fostered. Quebec for the French, not for the communists, Jews, and English, is the vein of discussion. This does not mean separatism but rather the securing of ethnic rights due the French majority in the province. Such discussions often have very direct political bearing. The priest does not commit himself as to party preference, but he does feel free to support the men or the platform. The merits of the newspaper *L'Action catholique* are expounded and its policies given support. Religious and social weaknesses of the parishioners are attacked. They are told how to treat their spouses, how to rear their children, how to correct their manners. City ways are attacked, and disasters and catastrophes are pointed to as God's punishment for sin. Dancing, drinking, and superstition are attacked. The published number of foundlings in the Quebec orphanage is the basis for a morality talk. Parents are advised to watch their children more closely. Girls are advised to withhold their kisses. Mixed marriages are warned against for those who travel away from the parish. The current news in *L'Action catholique* is frequently the text of the sermon. Editorials in that paper may be cited from the pulpit. As both the paper and *curé* have the same outlook, and they are the two most potent factors in the formation of new ideas among the adults, they present a unified front against the entrance of ideas and modes of behavior which will weaken the patterns of life. The *curé* says that there are too many unmarried adults and tells the young men to get married. If they have no means of earning a living locally, they are advised to leave the parish and look for work.

The sermons are about twenty minutes long and are presented in a matter-of-fact tone of voice, rising to an angry scolding when the *curé* is put out about something. The social control exerted from the pulpit is great. Although names are not mentioned, the community is so small that any individual referred to by deed in the sermon is soon generally known. No greater social reproof can be made. "If the hat fits, pull it down on your head," is the tone in which the sermons are presented and heard. When the *curé* attacked the unmarried, bachelors of sixty flushed crimson. When the sermons deal with unapplied theology, they fall on duller ears. There are not infrequently men sleeping during the sermon but not during the Mass. Periods of great farming activity, especially during the spring, keep the farmers tired; but an ethereal sermon has the same effect on the parishioners as heavy plowing. Wives never awaken their sleeping spouses.

The *curé* leaves the pulpit after his sermon and returns to the altar for the Sacrifice of the Mass. The faithful take out their rosaries, even the youngest children carrying them, and begin telling the beads as the Mass progresses. Some glance at little cards requesting prayers for some deceased member of the family. The collection is taken by the three *marguilliers* at the proper time, but the worship continues through it. Beads slip through fingers and eyes stay on the altar. The average donation is a penny per person, change occasionally being made from the collection plate. Some of the most respected men give nothing, possibly bowing their heads over the collection as it is passed.

The Mass finished, the men in the balcony begin to file out before the priest leaves the altar. The men and boys throughout the church rise and go out silently, leaving the women in the pews. They cross themselves with holy water as they pass the fonts by the door. The *bedeau* extinguishes the tall altar candles as a few people light votive candles before statues. The women and girls follow the men out of the church. Without, on the front steps, the men are already crowding around the parish secretary and the *crieur*.

The secretary usually has something of interest to say. It may be that a house, covered by a mutual insurance company, has burned and he is distributing assessments to the company members in St. Denis. Again, there may be some official communication from the provincial government, the announcement of the date parish school taxes are due, the time of the parish council meeting, or the days on which cattle may be inspected for tuberculosis. The *crieur* then begins to cry out his information of general interest. He announces the time and place to see a visiting veterinarian, a benefit card party in a neighboring parish, the meeting of the *beurrerie* committee, or the date by which the farmers must have the roads clear of snow. More important than these announcements is the *crieur*'s function as auctioneer. He acts in a public capacity, receiving bids for the heating of the schools, selling the hay on the school grounds, auctioning the church pews and the garden produce given on All Souls' Day to be sold for Masses for the dead. He will also auction things for private individuals after church for no charge. The actual goods are not usually in evidence at this time. A man tells the *crieur* that he wants to sell a three-week-old pig, and the *crieur* calls out the offer and receives bids. He even bids himself when he finds something going for a low price. "One dollar—one dollar, one—one dollar, two—one dollar —one dollar—one dollar—three, to Monsieur Raymond. Monsieur Raymond now deals directly with the owner of the shote, discussing when he can get it. The *crieur* also handles other commercial matters which have grown out of his role. He handles the buying of a shipment of chemical fertilizer for all the farmers who want it, taking their orders at the church steps or wherever they encounter him during the week. Every Sunday he quotes the amounts a butcher in the next parish is paying for various kinds of meat, and the prices the storekeeper in that parish is asking for flour, cement, or some other special offer. These larger stores in the larger parishes even have handbills distributed after church for their special sales.

The *crieur* having finished, the men drift away from the church, talking of parish or personal affairs or some current incident which the newspaper or the sermon has made common knowledge.

CHAPTER VII

THE CONTROL OF NATURE

NATURE furnishes a livelihood, but her forces are often unkind. Sickness and death, fire and storm, drought and earthquake, constantly strike terror into the heart of man. But he is not entirely at the mercy of these rampant forces, for there are traditional controls at his disposal. Some of these are religious procedures, some are magical, while some are simply traditional acts rationally or nonrationally used.

All the techniques of living involve making use of natural forces to man's advantage. The fire in the stove and the grain growing in the field are, in a sense, controlled forces of nature. They follow natural laws, rationally used, in conjunction with other natural forces, to guide them to useful ends. A discussion of the control of nature in that sense would involve the whole technology. What we shall consider here is the knowledge and control of nature gained by supernatural and nonrational means and the relation of these procedures to rational ones.

Sickness is a natural phenomenon which is horrifying and must be continually controlled. In St. Denis there are a number of healing acts to perform for the sick or hurt which are known as "secret" cures. These have one character in common—they may be told only to someone of the opposite sex. If they are told to a person of the same sex, they lose their potency. In the whole parish there are about a dozen people who know secret cures for some malady or other. One individual usually knows only one or two. He has no personal power other than that derived from the knowledge of the secret cure. Persons with such knowledge are not reticent about imparting it to others so long as they observe the alternate-sex rule. No loss of power is felt by telling the cure to someone else; in fact, one of the secret cures is dependent upon telling it to the invalid.

The people who know cures are not known to everyone in the parish. They are only occasionally asked to use the power which their knowledge gives them. This is always done gratuitously, not from fear of losing power, but simply because one would not think of charging a friend for a simple service. Although the practitioner claims no power for himself and feels that the healings he performs are due simply to his knowledge of the secret procedure, popular opinion seems to give him partial credit. This is never explicitly stated, but people rarely try to learn the cures which they go to him to have performed. The members of his family may not even know them, although they are apt to be passed on eventually. In the popular mind the knowledge of the cure is not as important as the successful reputation an individual develops in its use.

The secret cure for goiter is full of religious symbolism. The goiter-sufferer finds someone who knows the cure, and the latter imparts his remedy to the sufferer. A middle person may be necessary if both are of the same sex. If a man wants to tell another man the procedure, he may tell it to his wife or some other woman, who passes the information on to the person with the affliction. The cure is as follows: Holy Friday, around three o'clock in the afternoon, the sufferer should go down cellar alone and rub his throat with a little earth. The goiter stops growing immediately and gradually diminishes.

There are various secret methods of stopping bleeding. No one person practices more than one method. One old bachelor has quite a reputation for stopping nosebleeds, bleeding cuts, and other hemorrhages. He lives opposite the largest school in the parish; and when the children are badly hurt in play, they are sent over to him. He says that sometimes he has failed, but the only instance he can recall is once when he tried to help someone in another parish without going there. He recalls how one young woman knew the cure but had no confidence in it. Her husband had operated on a horse and cut a vein as big around as his thumb. They had tried every other way to stop the bleeding without success and finally prevailed on her to use her "secret." She did, and the bleeding stopped. Everyone who uses secret cures can tell similar stories of their efficiency, and most of the parishioners know instances also. The cure in this case consists of leaving the room, so that you are alone, and then picking up the first convenient object and saying: "Stop."[1]

Another form of bleeding cure consists of a different sort of suggestive magic and includes the use of religious power. The practitioner recites a *pater* and an *avé* in honor of the five wounds of Jesus Christ. This he does under his breath, at the same time squeezing his thumbs and forefingers together on each hand. As greater pressure is brought to bear, the bleeding will stop. It is important not to squeeze too hard at first, as this will stop the bleeding too quickly and the person will faint. This cure may be done in public.

Another secret procedure is for ridding a horse of ticks. This must be done in private. The affliction is recognized by sores inside the horse's lips. The manner of ridding the beast of the parasite starts with a prayer: "St. Pierre, get out on your piece of ground with your golden plow. You will plow three furrows of earth. You will bury the black ticks. You will bury the white ticks. You will bury

---

[1] Other methods reported are turning a rug with the left hand or overturning a convenient object, in private, with the left hand.

the gray ticks. You will bury the yellow ticks."[2] Then the horse should be taken by the nose and stroked downward three times on each side of the belly. Three *paters* should be said in honor of St. Pierre, and a cross made on the back of the animal three times.[3]

There is another cure conceived of as similar to the secret ones but lacking the cross-sex requirement. It is a cure for horse colic and is done as follows: Take five strips of cedar bark about three inches long from the side of the tree toward the rising sun. Put these on top of one another in the shape of a cross (Greek cross) in a frying-pan on the stove. Hold them down and pour water into the pan until the cross is covered. Boil all the water away. The colic will leave the horse as the water disappears.[4]

Prayers are the most common method of propitiating the divine powers. Health, rain, good crops, children—almost any desire which does not run contrary to the religious ideals—may be sought by this means. Certain saints have developed reputations for being particularly helpful in special ways. St. Joseph and Ste Anne work frequent miracles of healing for those who pray to them. The cure of sickness is never left entirely to the saint. Remedies are given as well. Both are felt to be responsible for any resulting cure. The parish priest was critically ill and was sent to a hospital. He put himself in the hands of St. Jo-

[2] The familiar verb forms are used throughout in addressing St. Pierre, contrary to regular usage in prayers. Familiar forms are used for equals or subordinates. There is no supplication. In other words, control is exerted over St. Pierre.

[3] Another version of the precedure given by another practitioner differs in detail. Start by making the sign of the cross and then say this prayer: "Good St. Pierre, take your plow. Go and plow three furrows. Under the first bury the gray ticks; the second, the red ticks; the third, the black ticks." Open the mouth of the animal and make a cross under the tongue and a cross on the palate. After having finished this, say a *pater*.

[4] This cure is also made by simply boiling away a frying-pan full of water.

seph, to whom he prayed to be made well. He solicited
the aid of Frère André, who prayed to the saint also.
All his parishioners said three *paters* for him in honor of
St. Joseph at every Sunday Mass. After a month at
Mayo's he showed some improvement, which was attributed to the work of St. Joseph. All the parish prayed for
him on his return trip, "to give him strength to get back."

A special form of control over the laws of chance is
gained through St. Antoine. This saint has a wide reputation for helping people find lost objects. Everyone knows
of instances in which St. Antoine gave this sort of assistance. One young man lost seven dollars, for which he
searched without success. Then he went to the church and
kneeled before the statue of the saint and promised him
twenty-five cents if he would help him find his lost money.
The saint soon received the votive money in the little box
before his statue. That same day the young man went to
the store where he had been earlier in the day, and the
proprietor's children returned the money, which they had
found on his departure.

Whenever anyone is seriously ill in the parish, the *curé*
goes to pray at his bedside. Sometimes the patient is well
the next day; at other times all remedies and prayers fail.
One boy, who recovered from a serious case of typhoid
fever, during which he suffered great fear of death, believes
implicitly that the *curé* saved him with regular prayers and
the assurance that he would not die. The *curé* frequently
works in conjunction with the *remmancheur*, a bone-setter
and traditional prescriber of remedies. A woman requested
the presence of the priest to pray and give her confidence
while a broken wrist was set. A farmer, forced to stay in
bed for a month during his busiest season because of
strained abdominal muscles, was treated with an impro-
vised plaster by the *remmancheur*. Each week the *curé*

visited him and "took away some of his sickness" on leaving, finally telling him that he would be all right the next week and to come to Mass. The next Sunday the weak and wan man appeared at the church.

Beside prayer, there are still other acts employing religious procedures or paraphernalia which can be performed in an effort to cure sickness. Critical illnesses have turned for the better after the patient drank holy water, took Communion, or received extreme unction. When the priest leaves the church with the Sacred Host to visit some very sick parishioner, the big bell in the tower rings out. As its tones drift over the parish, everyone knows that "they are carrying the Good God" to the invalid.

The blessing of the priest is protective against the forces of nature and can also make nature more bounteous. During a storm the burning of beeswax candles blessed during Candlemass protects the home in which they burn from wind and lightning. They also make thunder withdraw into the distance and protect the house against earthquakes. Spruce branches blessed on Palm Sunday may be burned in the stove, and crosses made around the house with holy water to serve the same end. Religious powers are supplicated in numerous ways in an effort to control nature. Every new house is blessed by the priest to protect it from harm. Over the door in every house is a small plaque bearing the figure of the Sacred Heart of Christ with a blessing for those homes which believe in him. Sometimes houses are endangered in spite of their blessing. In such cases something additional must be done, as burning of candles or of blessed spruce. In case of danger from fire, however, the *curé* is called to pray that the building be spared. Blessed holy medals may also bring about such salvation.

Several years ago there was such a miracle in the parish.

The St. Marc's Procession for the "Fruits of the Earth"

BUILDING A FISH WEIR

Mme Gagnon had returned from early Mass on the Fête of Ste Anne so that she could watch the house and small children while her husband sang in the High Mass. No sooner had he gone, than she saw smoke coming out of the barn where the children had been playing. With the help of neighbors she got out the animals and then stood exhausted and watched the wind-whipped flames lick out at another barn only the width of a road away. Her husband, who had seen the fire from in front of the church, drove up with the *curé* at this moment. The priest hung a medal of the good Ste Anne on the endangered barn and prayed to the saint to spare the building. Soon the wind died down and the barn was safe. Even in neighboring parishes which have fire-fighting apparatus, the *curé* goes to every fire to pray for divine help, and his prayers are often answered.

Each year the fish weirs built in the tidal flats of the river are blessed so that the catch may be large. At the end of a Mass before the spring planting, the *curé* blesses a large bowl full of mixed seeds. The farmers each take a handful and sort out the different seeds at home. These are sown the first of each crop. The practice of mixing the blessed seed with the unblessed to be sown mechanically is decried, because there is no assurance that the few blessed seeds may not remain in the hopper. *Paters* are frequently said during the sowing in order to obtain the "daily bread."

On St. Marc's Day there is a church procession down onto the village road. The procession and Mass of this day are supplication for the "fruits of the earth." After the Mass there is rainfall, according to tradition. The Corpus Christi procession and ceremony in June bring divine blessing on the planted crops. The farmers of the various quarters of the parish contribute the money to have Masses sung in the spring for *les biens de la terre*. These special Masses are another way of controlling natural phenomena. The Masses are sung for an explicit purpose. No one knows how explicit this is better than a group of fishermen in the next parish. They had spent over a month erecting great fish weirs in the river to catch eels. The season came, and they were catching practically nothing; so they got together the money for a Mass. They had the Mass sung to obtain a wind from the northeast, for the eels come with this wind. That night a terrific storm came out of the northeast and destroyed the weirs for miles along the river. Now the fishermen are careful to ask for eels, not wind.

There is a body of nonrational traditional knowledge which aids in the prediction and control of natural events. Some of this knowledge is dependent upon supernatural powers, some is considered natural. The nonrational nature of many of these beliefs is recognized now because of the activity of the church in combating "superstitition." Some of the parishioners, particularly those who have intimate contact with members of their families who are priests or who have spent time in the cities, actually disbelieve this type of knowledge. They, of course, do not govern their action by it; but there are many who still do.

The principal beliefs of the disputed variety center around the importance of the phases of the moon. Planting during the waxing of the moon causes tall prolific growth, and during the waning of the moon short growth. Planting follows the type of plant growth desired. Flax and hay should be long, and grain, peas, and potatoes prolific; so they are planted during the waxing of the moon. Tobacco and garden plants, which should not go to stalk, are planted during the decrease of the moon. An even number of days after the new moon is particularly propitious for sowing, especially six or ten days. Even the believers in the importance of the moon do not follow its phases rigidly. The growing season is short; and, if waiting for the proper phase entails too great a delay in planting, the farmer would rather plant at the wrong time and be assured of some crop.

There is also a relation between the phase of the moon during which an animal is conceived and its sex. If a farmer wishes to have fillies and finds that by breeding a mare during one phase of the moon he gets male colts, shifting the breeding time a half-moon will produce fillies. Actually, it is doubtful if this knowledge is ever put to use. Children, as well as animals, born under a full moon are stronger. The phase of the moon at birth is never remembered, however. The strength of animals waxes and wanes with the moon. A horse, for example, should never have its hooves trimmed during the full of the moon, as the beast is strong then and it would be bad for its blood. The relation of animals to natural phenomena is also seen in the belief that, when the pupils of a cat's eyes are large, it is high tide; when they are small, the tide is low.

There are various ways of predicting the coming weather, seasons, and crops. Those based on quasi-natural signs blend into those for which there is some rational basis. When the Milky Way, or St. Jacque's Way, is parallel to the Coteau, it is a sign of good weather; when perpendicular, bad weather is indicated. The three days before and after the full moon are marked by bad weather, as is the last quarter of the moon. During the waxing of the moon the weather is warmer, but it is cooler during the full moon and the waning. The rainbow indicates weather for the day, following a little verse.

> L'arc en ciel du matin
> Met la pluie en chemin.
> L'arc en ciel du soir
> Met la pluie à couvert.

A "crown" around the moon means coming rain. The *Almanach beauchemin* is in many of the homes, although its weather predictions have proved themselves nonrational to most parishioners. The weather during the six days before and the beginning of the new year predicts the weather for the next twelve months. Each day represents a month, so that a heavy snow on December 26 means a snowy January, and so on. Snowfall on days representing months which have no snow indicates rain for those months. A full moon for the Christmas midnight Mass means that the barns will be empty the next fall. A poor run of maple sap in the spring also indicates poor crops. The lands will be ready to plow forty days after the first crow is seen "eating in the road."

The supernatural affords methods of predicting in advance the course of natural events. Such prediction is accomplished through the interpretation of omens and through reading the cards. The significance of omens may not always be recognized before the event occurs. Thus, two brothers, riding home one night on a motorcycle to see their sick sister, were delayed by the headlight going out. They arrived home to find the *curé* administering the last rites. Omens in dreams are recognizable in advance. Dreams of newly cut wood and new houses signify death, as do dreams of smoke. Flames and blood signify victory. Breaking a mirror or burning two lamps on the same table are signs of death in the family within the year. Because of ridicule from the pulpit, the belief in omens is very weak. Belief is shown at crises, when the omens are recalled, rather than by any show of fear at the omens themselves.

Belief in the prediction of the future through reading the cards is generally held. Anyone may know how to read the cards. The supernatural power of prediction lies entirely in the cards, but individuals vary in their ability to read what is written there. This ability is not formally passed on. Other forms of divination are also possible with the cards. Following the instructions of a reader of cards, two young men of the parish went out to the Cap in only their shirts to search for buried treasure. At midnight and by candlelight they fruitlessly dug near an old Indian grave. People are inclined to laugh now as they see the unfilled holes; but they still believe in "good" card readings. One reader finds that he has the best results on Friday. The supernatural power of this day, on which no flesh food can be eaten, is also evident in the aversion to undertaking important things, like plowing or sowing, on Friday.

As we have seen, the only individual in the parish with supernatural power in his own right is the priest. His is a derived power, but it does lie with him. He can say a blessing which is potent, while the same words from the mouth of any other parishioner would have no effect. The priest is the most important person in the parish, not only because of the powers he possesses, but because he derives these powers from the divine beings which symbolize the ultimate values of the society. All other individuals with control of supernatural powers owe their ability to their knowledge of powerful procedures, not to anything within themselves or any special relationship which they have with supernatural powers.

The care, by natural means, of the sick and hurt includes both rational and nonrational procedures. There are two local practitioners making use of their special knowledge of cures. One is the *remmancheur*, who up until this century handled almost everything except childbirth; the other is the doctor in the adjacent parish. The *remmancheur* is a farmer, but in addition he sets broken bones and dislocations and advises treatment for all ills. He is not able to charge for his services because of provincial medical regulations; so he takes whatever the patient wants to give him. This is often fifty cents for setting a broken arm. English summer visitors in a neighboring parish pay as much as five dollars. More widely known than other bonesetters, he has been sought from eighty miles away. He averages over a hundred cases a year, being called at least daily during harvesting and when the ground is covered with ice in winter.

The *remmancheur* gets all the cases of bone breaks and dislocations. The only patients of this type that the doctor sees are workmen covered by insurance which requires a doctor's certificate. By the medical standards of the doctor, the bonesetters do some good work, some bad, some purely charlatanic. On the one hand is a case in which the *remmancheur* broke and reset a leg previously badly set by a physician; on the other, are cases of falsely diagnosed fractures and dislocations. From the popular point of view the *remmancheur* is infinitely superior to the doctor in the treatment of such cases. The patient with the reset leg is reputed to be the doctor himself. Everyone knows that a little boy and a man of the parish both broke their legs about the same time. The boy went to the *remmancheur;* the man, to the doctor and hospital, where he spent months. The lad is completely well in spite of having broken the same leg again shortly afterward; the man limps. This is considered indisputable proof of the *remmancheur's* superiority. Most families have had personal experience with the bonesetter. The doctor broke the arm of a baby during delivery, and it was perfectly mended by the *remmancheur*. One woman tells how, as a girl, she lost the use of her right arm after lifting a heavy milk can. The father of the present folk practitioner replaced a dislocated nerve and then told her to make the sign of the cross, which she did with her hitherto useless arm.

The present *remmancheur* got his knowledge and technique from his father but has not passed them on, as he has no sons. One of his daughters does some nursing. The ability to heal is in the family. The father of the present bonesetter started out by helping the widow of the deceased *remmancheur* in an emergency. He learned from her and from experience. When convicted for practicing medicine without a license and fined twenty dollars, he was so poor that the parish took up a collection to cover the fine. Three of his sons learned from him, one staying in the parish. One of the sons living elsewhere is known to have been legally stopped from practicing.

The *remmancheur* requires two untrained helpers in setting fractures. Members of the patient's family or neighbors serve in this capacity. They pull on either end of the broken limb while he adjusts the broken ends of the bone with his fingers. Light padded splints are then laid along the limb and tied in place. A cloth plaster is made by beating egg whites, adding castile soap, and soaking the cloth in this mixture. The cloth is then wrapped around the splints, where it contracts and hardens. The plaster is supposed to peal off of its own accord when the limb is healed, or after forty days. For broken legs an additional box is built around the limb to keep it immobile.

Since the advent of the doctor, another folk practitioner has lost her original function entirely. She is the midwife, known as *pelle à feu* or *sage femme*. Fifteen years ago she made most of the deliveries; now she makes practically none. The doctor is called to deliver all babies. The old *sage femme* has become his helper and the postnatal nurse for the mother and child, whom the doctor does not see again after the delivery until another child is born.[5] The doctor used to get ten dollars for a delivery; now he rarely receives that much. One poor family paid him only two dollars. Reduced price and religious and provincial activity have led to the replacement of folk practitioners by the doctor. He is called now for all critical ailments of adults. The status of a doctor has always been high. In addition to the clergy and law, it has always been a highly desirable prestige profession. The prestige resulted from the long education required outside the parish and from outside recognition. Sanctioned by the church, the school and the monthly visits of the public health doctor and nurse now educate the people toward a desire for rational and trained medical care. Expectant mothers and those with babies all visit the free clinic at the *salle*.[6] Iodine and boric acid are kept in many of the homes now.

Instruction in the care of teeth is being disseminated through the same channels. Some of the school children brush their teeth, but adults do so rarely. Caries is extremely common. The general belief is that the condition of one's teeth is hereditary, and so brushing is useless. When cavities become large and painful, the tooth is extracted. There are half a dozen farmers who have forceps and extract without charge or anesthetic. A near-by dentist also pulls teeth. There is an aversion to having teeth filled. It is expensive, and then the tooth usually has to come out finally anyway. Too much gold in the mouth is

[5] For procedure before, during, and after birth see chap. ix.

[6] Simple instruction has greatly reduced the infant mortality from enteritis, the most prevalent cause of such death. Smallpox vaccination is required for school children, and free inoculation for diphtheria has reached 76 per cent of the children between six months and ten years old (Provincial Bureau of Health doctor for the region). Serums for scarlet fever and hydrophobia are also provided, and there are yearly tuberculosis clinics.

believed actually to breed decay. It is better to have the teeth pulled and then get a plate which will last.

The acceptance of suggested diet and boiled water for babies and inoculation for children and the lack of acceptance of dental instruction present an interesting problem. Why the difference? In the first place the former suggestions are stressed more by the provincial health authorities —mandatory smallpox inoculation, for instance. Likewise, the church stresses rational medicine more where life is actually concerned. Two more factors are equally important: treatment is free in one case, costs money in the other. For a people necessarily bent on every economy this is a considerable factor. The fact that the doctor is sent for in case of the critical illness of an adult but not of a small child has the same explanation. Also, around the treatment of babies and the seriously ill there has always been a great deal of traditional ritual behavior. It is a great deal easier to add items to these procedures than to start a custom like brushing teeth, where there was no previous procedure.

There is another relatively new health practitioner, the veterinarian. There is none in the parish, but one can be secured near by. He is never called except when the life of a horse is in danger. A horse represents such a large investment that paid help may be solicited. This calling of the veterinarian is just an extension of the traditional pattern of calling in a neighbor or friend who has a reputation for treating animals. Such a man usually has a large herd or flock and has learned from experience.

There are a great number of home remedies which are administered after simple home diagnosis.[7] Many of these are herbal remedies. "A woman without camomile in her garden is not competent," expresses the importance as-

7 See Appen. II for these remedies.

cribed to the knowledge of such cures. A collection of these includes a few that are new and represent the filtering-in of medical advice. The nonrational remedies are largely based on the general supposition that cold causes most common illness. Thus, heat and things associated with heat, such as soot, snuff, and hot iron, are used in the treatment of illness. Milk and iron have beneficial properties in themselves. Some of these remedies are being discarded, others adopted. The number of different cures for the same ailments shows a traditional lack of consensus. The general tendency is for the nonrational cures to be dropped. The direction of this shift has already been indicated as originating outside of the local society but entering through channels held in high local regard—the church, school, government, and doctor. As a check to this shift stand the economy and tradition—the preference for that which is well known and customary.

The regional provincial *agronome* is in much the same position as the doctor. He is a new disseminator of rational procedures. His advice is in competition with the traditional ways of farming, both supernatural and quasinatural. His instruction is given some support in the higher grades of school but is not stressed to any degree. The church is not concerned with him, as it is with the doctor. The service of the *agronome* is gratuitous; but it usually costs money to follow his advice, a retarding factor in the acceptance of his information. He again represents an outside factor pushing itself into the society, rather than any spontaneous product of the society itself. The *agronome* reaches the farmers through the Société d'Agriculture, to which they belong because of the special benefits they secure. There is also the Cercle des Fermières in the parish which is provincially organized. Fairs and contests are other ways in which the farmer is contacted. When the local *agronome* wanted to get over an idea concerning spring preparation of pastures, he adopted the commercial technique of the stores and had handbills distributed after Mass.

All the methods for the control of nature which are at the disposal of the St. Denisian are, from his point of view, either natural or supernatural. The most important supernatural procedures center around the religion, but they are not all religious in the sense of being acts in which the supplicator feels himself drawn closer to the ultimate powers through the execution of the rite. The religious experience of feeling personally better and holier because of some act which has been performed is not common to all the acts which contain religious symbolism. Attendance at Masses and the participation in processions for specific purposes is usually accompanied by such an experience. Prayers are usually religious acts in this sense, but not always. The commercial bargain with St. Antoine to solicit his help in finding something which has been lost is obviously not a religious act in this sense. It supplicates in a bargaining way a power recognized in the religion. The supplicator, however, feels no religious fervor in his prayer. On the other hand, if a sick person takes Communion or has extreme unction administered, he does so for the benefit of his soul and in hope that these acts will also bring divine aid to his sick body. When the Host, representing the actual body of Christ, is eaten with the recognition of its qualities, it is a religious experience in the full sense of the term.

The use of religious acts, ceremonies, and paraphernalia in an attempt to control nature but unaccompanied by any feeling of piety is common. The acts and objects are felt to be powerful because of their association with the religion, but in their use the person does not commune with the divine forces; he merely uses powerful procedures. Burning candles and spruce branches, putting a holy medal on an endangered barn, drinking holy water, having the priest bless a house or fish weir, and planting blessed seed are such acts. They are all associated with the power of a priest's blessing. Such blessing is a religious act for a sincere priest. For the person who uses the blessed object, it is usually only a powerful control.

Such acts as these lead directly into a consideration of magic—the direct use of supernatural procedures to control natural events. To the extent that the marginal religious acts above are religious appeals to divine forces, they are nonmagical. When they are accompanied by a feeling that the act must necessarily produce the result, they are magical. The blessing of houses and weirs is usually nonmagical, whereas sowing blessed seed, drinking holy water, and burning blessed candles are magical. The latter are not so much attempts to gain divine favor as acts which produce results. These are all obviously marginal between religion and magic. The same act may be religious for one individual and magical for another, depending upon his attitude toward it. The secret cures lack the character of religious acts. They are magical but make use of powerful religious symbols. The simple colic cure, card-reading, and the interpretation of omens are magical procedures dependent upon the supernatural but having no religious aspect.

The many techniques based on the knowledge of natural causal connections may be divided into those which are rational and those which are not. The former group includes those acts which are executed as a result of the understanding of certain causal sequences in nature. The nonrational acts assume the existence of some such causal sequence, but the assumption is held without reasonable knowledge of the causal connections. The traditional remedies, both herbal and others, fall into both groups. The beliefs about the prediction of weather and the importance of the moon are held only by those persons who do not believe that they are nonrational. The midwife and *remmancheur* practice both rational and nonrational techniques, but largely the latter. The doctor, nurse, veterinarian, and *agronome* employ only rational knowledge.[8]

Analysis of the various forms of practices and special knowledge used in controlling nature has shown them to be logically related, according to this scheme:

Supernatural:
  Religious (Mass, devout prayer, Communion)
  Magical (special uses of candles and medals, secret cures, card-reading)

Natural:
  Nonrational, quasi-natural (planting by moon, iron and soot in remedies, weather prediction by moon)
  Rational (medicine and scientific agriculture)

The features of the situation in St. Denis which are noteworthy are the dominance of religious acts and symbols and the changing trends in belief. The people of this society are intensely religious. Religious ideology permeates every institution. It is not strange, therefore, that religious symbols and forms have a certain power, or mana, because of the context from which they come. The amount of this symbolism in the magic is striking, as is the way it shades into true religious acts.

Some acts of supplication, which include true religious experience, may traditionally achieve so close a relationship between the supplicator and the supplicated powers as to amount to a practical direct control. The idea that

[8] This is true with limitations. For instance, a doctor states that meningitis and other nervous diseases appear about every fourth generation in family lines. The effects of drink and gonorrhea also appear several generations later.

rain follows the St. Marc's procession and Mass is such a case. This same phenomenon reaches its acme in Hopi rain ceremonies. Such cases as these bring into relief the fact that all that distinguishes religious from magical acts in this border line is the presence or absence of a devout feeling in the executor of the rite. True, religious acts are usually supplicatory and the result is due to the decision of the religious powers, whereas magical acts produce their results; but the foregoing cases demonstrate how these two can blend into one another.

Religion and magic being so closely allied, it is natural that symbols, which are potent in the supernatural field of religion, should also be employed in magic. The West African negroes with a background of potent magical practice were quick to seize upon the power of Catholic objects in Haiti. Bits of priests' robes or fragments of a saint's statue became powerful "fetishes" used for purposes foreign and even antagonistic to the church.[9] In Quebec, where magic does not represent a cultural background antagonistic to the church, the use of Catholic symbols is not attacked by the church. Even the dogma of the church includes many acts, such as blessing, which are frequently magically employed.

Where there is a strongly organized self-conscious church, such as the Catholic church in St. Denis, it may assert its dominance by attacking all forms of supernatural belief based on powers other than, or antagonistic to, its own. The effects of such attacks on other forms of the supernatural are observable in Quebec. In the early days of the settlement, powers of evil were in continual struggle with the divine powers of the church. The devil, in various forms, and *loups-garous* were abroad in the land and were a

[9] M. J. Herskovits, *Life in a Haitian Valley* (New York: A. A. Knopf, 1937), pp. 265–66.

considerable problem. All sort of mystical things happened. There were *feus follets*, a ghostly white mare, and a sorceress of Indian origin, right around St. Denis. Cap au Diable received its name during this time. The folk lore kept the public mind full of these evil powers, and mysterious occurrences were as frequent as miracles are now. The priests had less regular contact with the people, and even the clergy at times exhorted these evil spirits. With the growth of church control and the sophistication of the priests, these antireligious and nonreligious powers were attacked as "superstitions." Now they are almost completely gone.

We have commented that supernatural powers function as social controls as well as serve as controls of nature. In St. Denis the aspect of social control is dominated by the religious powers. The particular way in which the supernatural is used to support local custom varies in different societies, and a comparison throws light on some of the essential features. On the Melanesian island of Dobu the supernatural serves the same purposes, but most of these forces are conceived on the magical level.[10] There is magic to make nature more productive. In addition, black magic and sorcery are the most powerful social controls. Although the purpose of such magic is injurious, it is not antisocial, as the fear of magic is used to social ends just as the fear of hell is so used in St. Denis. The difference between the two systems lies in the state of personal existence to which the fear is referred and the manner in which social justice is maintained.

Considering just the supernatural aspect of social control, a Catholic sinner, or antisocial person, primarily fears misery in the life after death; secondarily, punishment on earth by an act of God. Because of his sin God punishes

[10] R. F. Fortune, *Sorcerers of Dobu* (New York: G. Routledge & Sons, 1932).

him in both ways. In Dobu, antisocial behavior causes the culprit to fear only for his terrestrial happiness. He is not concerned with life after death except that the spirits of the dead may be used to hurt him by magic. He fears that the individual he has wronged by his antisocial act will work magic on him in return, making him sick or taking his crop. In this case it is the wronged person who retaliates by using supernatural power; the punishment is not determined by a supernatural being. In Dobu the punishment of antisocial acts is kept on a social level. They are punished by the offended individual because he has received a social wrong. In St. Denis the antisocial nature of an act is overshadowed by its aspect of being a sin punishable by God.

Sickness and death in Dobu are conceived as always being the result of black magic, and diviners are called. The system goes one step farther than that of St. Denis, in that diviners attribute the source of the black magic to some person whom the victim has wronged. The punishment of sins is, thus, a terrestrial matter. This has no strong counterpart in St. Denis. If it had, the parish drunkard might actually be seen agonizing in hell. True, misfortunes which befall known sinners are popularly attributed to divine punishment, but such mortal judgments are not encouraged and are blurred by the dogma that punishment for the sins of a few is visited upon the whole group.

In many societies the supernatural powers of good coexist in conflict with powers of evil as part of the whole supernatural scheme. The conscious activity of the strong official church in St. Denis practically eliminated the evil forms. Even the social significance of the devil, recognized in dogma, has been greatly reduced. Whereas black magic dominates societies like those described in Dobu and Africa, it has no place in St. Denis. In Dobu the powers of evil are so strong that supernatural forces of good are in continual struggle to maintain themselves. On the other hand, in Quebec the religious powers are so superior that when the church decided to eliminate the powers of evil and nonreligious supernatural belief, it was thoroughly accomplished. The dominance of this one form of supernatural belief in St. Denis is attributable to the amount of time, energy, and thought which is put into acts of religious reference. These acts are ritualized, and the society is vigorous in its maintenance of these traditional rituals which continually assert the importance of the powers concerned. The beliefs in other and antagonistic supernatural forces never became so organized, never developed a body of important traditional rites, and never had a dominant role in the social life. They were loosely knit, undeveloped beliefs easily overpowered when the church so desired. That this lack of organization, ritual, and important social function was the basic weakness of the non-Catholic belief is seen by further reference to Haiti. There black magic is strongly ritualized, with a traditional place in the African philosophy. It occupies more time and more thought than the later-adopted Catholicism. No end of church effort has failed to suppress it. The Catholic supernatural powers were not dominant enough in that society.

Returning to the magic in St. Denis which employs religious symbols, its persistence in the face of loss of belief in other forms of magic is comprehensible. It derives much of its power from the very supernatural source which is attacking "superstitions." To resolve this conflict, "superstition" has come to be construed to mean anti-Catholic or non-Catholic nonrational belief, "Catholic" used not in the sense of dogma but to include also marginal religious belief. Thus, devils, werewolves, sorceresses, and fairies have disappeared; omens and card-reading are not universally accepted; and the importance of the moon is doubted by many. The doctor, veterinarian, and *agronome* are becoming accepted because of their rational nature approved by the church. The *remmancheur* and midwife persist in their rational aspects, but the group of magical beliefs which draw power from religious sources continue unquestioned. They have almost the same aroma of sanctity as the dogmatic religious beliefs. To question the power of a blessed candle to make thunder withdraw would be like questioning the ability of a saint to work miracles. Both are dependent upon the same supernatural forces.

Attention should be called to the fact that acculturation —the adoption of rational beliefs from the urban centers particularly—differs in St. Denis from the situation in Haiti or Mexico. The difference lies in the fact that in St. Denis innovations enter sanctioned by a church, which is the most powerful force in the native community. In the acculturation between people of entirely different backgrounds, the entrance of a new church is a factor. As it is new itself, it has not the same power as the native church in assisting the entrance of other new ideas. St. Denis is being acculturated from a similar society, but a society two centuries more advanced along the lines of Western industrial civilization. The fact that the parish finds support for the new ideas from within itself, in the person of the priest, explains the ready acceptance of rational procedures in matters of birth and sickness. This is the opposite situation from that found in the urbanization of most folk societies, where contacts are with an entirely different type of culture. It suggests that the sophistication of rural French Canada will take place more rapidly and completely than in these other regions.

CHAPTER VIII

THE YEARLY ROUND

THE morning Angelus at five o'clock in summer finds the adult members of the parish households already dressed and about their tasks. The men wear homespun shirts and trousers. Women are clothed in homespuns or cooler homemade cotton dresses. Family prayers are said immediately after dressing. Those who are up kneel before the black cross on the kitchen wall and say the rosary in unison. The dim light of dawn illuminates the pictures of Mary and Jesus of the Sacred Heart which invariably flank the somber cross. The prayers finished, the men feed the pigs and turn the stock out to graze, while the women start the fires, prepare the breakfast, and milk the cows. During this time the younger children rise, dress, say their prayers, and help with the small chores. A young girl may set the table, and a boy bring in the stove wood. The family eats breakfast around the big table in the kitchen. The seating arrangement around the table is expressive of the internal family organization. The seating of the head of the house at the end of the table, seating in age sequence, and division of the sexes are common features. The mother and older daughters of the house always serve the rest of the family. The women get up from the table to serve, or are seated and eat what remains after the others have finished. The morning fare consists of a fat-pork spread; bread or toast; tea, or coffee made from roasted barley or a native leguminous bean brewed with milk; pancakes made with a few eggs and eaten with maple sugar or butter; or fried eggs in their stead.

The meal finished, the men separate the milk and set out the cans to be sent to the *beurrerie*. Then they go to the fields to work, while the women wash the dishes, drying them on homemade linen towels. The bright kitchen rugs are taken up, and the room is swept. Brooms made of cedar branches are still in common use, although a store broom is usually also in evidence. The enameled stove must receive its daily cleaning. If there are no special tasks for the day, cleaning and bed-making are followed by the preparation of the noon meal. Soup is the constant basis of this meal, and its preparation must be started well in advance. The meals must be prepared for large households, an additional time-requiring factor. The usual number at the table is about ten, although there may be as many as twenty in a single home. The washing and drying of dinner dishes alone requires well over an hour's work for three people. Any free morning time is employed doing necessary sewing and mending or working in the vegetable garden, that being the women's responsibility. The female tasks in connection with housekeeping have little seasonal variation, but the rest of their work does vary with the time of year. The men's work is entirely different during the various seasons. In summer the entire day is spent in the fields. The children help the men with the harvest of hay and flax, but more of their labor goes into helping the women with the vegetable garden, which is always in a section of land adjacent to the house. Although cut flowers are never used in the houses or for funerals, flowers are grown in profusion around the houses and are used on the church altars during the summer. These gardens and the care of potted plants in winter are additional female tasks.

The women and children always wait for the men to return from the fields for the noon and evening meals. Soup is eaten every day, and usually enough is made to serve for both meals. The French-Canadian housewife is a good soup-maker, preparing it from various ingredients: vegetables, potatoes, barley, etc. Pea soup is the most common kind; and, made without stock, it is almost always used on Fridays. In addition to the soup there are boiled or riced potatoes, fat pork, and a great deal of bread. During the summer there is a variety of vegetables. Preserved in jars or dried, some of these are used sparingly during the winter also. There is more meat during the winter, when it will keep. Pork, veal, and beef are provided by the fall slaughter. Various pumpkin preparations are also made in the fall and early winter. Chicken and occasionally domesticated rabbits are used for company fare, but the usual diet includes only pork. Fish is usually eaten on Fridays during the summer. Butter and milk are constant elements of diet, as are coffee and tea. Plums, cherries, and berries are eaten in season; and apples are available most of the year.

Afternoons are spent in the same sort of activity as forenoons, and work is not abandoned until dusk. After supper the evening paper is read, and politics and the day's work are discussed. Close male kin and neighbors drop in on one another to smoke and chat, but women are too occupied in their homes to visit during the week. The small children are put to bed early, and around ten o'clock the rest of the family kneels and says its prayers before retiring.

The daily routine varies somewhat during the days of the week and also from month to month. Sunday marks a considerable change from week days. Only the necessary labor is performed; but the family must rise earlier, in order to do the house and farm work in time to change to good clothes and get to church. Saturday night the girls put their hair in curlers, and one of the family cuts the hair of those children and men whose heads are too shaggy. Sunday morning the men shave. All these activities are directed by the general social aspect of Sunday. In addition to the parish Mass, Sunday afternoon and evening are the time for general visiting among friends and relatives. Kin from other parishes may visit, and special meals are prepared in their honor.

Monday is often the time for doing the family washing, although the day varies with necessity. Bread-making is another full day's work, which must be done twice a month. The dough is made and kneaded in large troughs. When the dough is in the final stages, a fire is lit in the dome-shaped earthen oven which stands outdoors near the house. The oven is closed, so that only the smoke escapes through a special vent. When the fire has burned out, the ashes are scraped out of the inside and the loaves are put in and baked. It is not unusual for a baking to consist of two dozen five-pound loaves. The tradition of cutting a cross on the crust of the finished loaves has practically died out.

In addition to the weekly and monthly variation in tasks, there is a marked seasonal change. The variety of farm activity throughout the year is so intimately related not only to household tasks but also to the religious and social life as to be inseparable. The natural starting-point of the rural yearly round is not the calendrical one but the beginning of spring. During the month of April the deep snow over the fields begins to melt and run off, converting the deep drainage ditches along the fence rows into turbulent streams. The stream Des Bras and the rivulets along the Coteau swell to such proportions as to flood the roads which cross them. This symbol of the release from the confinement of winter is greeted with general joy, even though it ushers in a period of hard work. The beginning of the thaw is the sign for much specialized activity. When the ice breaks up along the river bank, the poorer farmers and villagers go down to dig out mussels, which are only obtained at this time of year. In the woods on the mountains to the south the maple sap begins to run. Although maple sugar is no longer made in the parish, many of the parishioners go on outings to *cabanes à sucre* in the next parish. There they can eat bread and syrup, or eggs boiled in syrup, and make *tire* by pouring syrup out on the snow. The maple sugar itself is bought locally, particularly for making candy to serve at *veillées*.

As the ice and snow covering the roads melt down until patches of road begin to show through, the farmers have their horses' winter cleated shoes removed. All the horses which have been used during the winter must be reshod, and the blacksmith's anvil rings from early until late. *Carrioles*, sleighs, and other winter vehicles remain in use until the *crieur* announces that the roads are to be opened. Then each farmer scrapes the remaining snow from the stretch of *chemin* which crosses his farm. The open weather before the land is cultivatable is an opportunity for outdoor repair work. At each house there are piles of fence posts cut during the winter. They are being sharpened and stripped of their bark. Carpentry work around the house and barns is also done at this time. A few parishioners may be completing their splitting and cording of firewood. Manure is transferred from the accumulation piles outside the barns to the fields as they appear through the snow.

Winter being the meat-eating season, there are accumulations of bones and grease to be made into soap. Lye for this process is no longer made locally but is bought at the store, along with the rosin. The whole is boiled with water in great caldrons until all the rosin and bones are consumed. The thick mixture must be carefully watched to keep it from boiling over. A little snow is kept on hand and thrown into the caldron to make the rising liquid go down. When the soap has reached the right consistency, salt is added; and then the mixture is allowed to cool in the caldron overnight. The next day the year's supply is cut out in irregular blocks.

Early spring is also the time for the *grand ménage*. All the women of the family clean the house a room at a time. Everything is removed; and the wooden walls, ceiling, and floor are all scrubbed. All the furniture is wiped over, and rugs and blankets are cleaned and hung out on the porches to air. It requires several weeks for the women to complete the *ménage*. Their progress is the main topic of conversation, just as the talk of the men centers on the weather, new horses, and other subjects relevant to the approaching plowing season. In addition to house-cleaning, the women wash and dye the wool thread which has been spun during the winter, and hang the skeins on porches or over fence posts to dry. Like the men, the women must finish before planting, for they, too, have gardens to tend. The wool itself is shorn in early spring and sent to the carding mills, hand carding having been abandoned except by a few villagers who buy only small amounts of wool. After the *grand ménage* the family moves from the winter kitchen into the summer kitchen.

The Mass of St. Marc's Day, at the end of April, has special significance for the farmers. This Mass and the outdoor procession which precedes it call for divine blessing on the approaching planting. When the Mass does not fall on Sunday, it is attended largely by farm families. Everyone goes first to his pew, and the procession leaves from the church. The choirboys, in their vestments, file after one of their number carrying the cross. They are followed by the priest and his acolytes. Behind them walks the men's choir, singing litanies. This group immediately precedes the men and boys, who, in turn, are followed by the women and girls, who wait for the men to leave the church before they join the procession. The long files move slowly through the village in silence except for the singing and the mumbling of prayers as the parishioners tell their beads. The procession returns to the church, and following the Mass the priest blesses a large china bowl full of assorted seeds. The ceremonies finished, a man from each family goes forward and secures a handful of the seeds to take home. These blessed seeds are separated into their various kinds at home and are the first to be planted as the lands are prepared for the various crops. It used to be customary for children to sow these blessed seeds and for *paters* to be said during the general sowing, but these traditions are passing with the introduction of mechanical sowers. It is usual now for the *crieur* to request orders for chemical fertilizer after this Mass, as he does during all the pre-sowing weeks.

The month of May is known as the *temps de semence*, although planting continues into June. A grain-sifter owned by the *fabrique* is used by the farmers for a small fee. The farmers employ the machine because the use of the poor seeds as animal feed pays for the sifting. The old method of obtaining seed for sowing was for the family to pick over seeds spread on the table. These selected seeds were sown in a small plot, the seed yield of which was used for the main crop the subsequent year. It is still common to start new seed lines from time to time by sowing purchased seeds in this fashion. Machine sifting has eliminated the family co-operative task of hand selection. In its place has developed a form of parish co-operation. This is the only case in which the family function has been extended to the parish through farm machinery. All machinery has, however, weakened the co-operation of the family unity by eliminating some of its activities, particularly those around harvest time.

Two generations ago there was a simple sort of crop rotation. Grain was planted on the same land for three years, and then the area was left idle for four or five years. This procedure is no longer possible, owing to decreased fertility. It is now customary to sow land in grain one year and then put it in hay for three years. Through the use of chemical fertilizers some lands are kept continually in grain.[1] It is usual to keep sandy land in potatoes. The land is usually plowed with horses, which are traditionally driven by a small boy while a man directs the plow. There are two tractors in the parish, and some farmers use their oxen. As a farmer rarely has more than one ox, it is harnessed with an old subdued horse. Bulls are hitched to carts and wagons but not to plows. During the sowing the men are up at three in the morning and frequently do not finish work until nine or ten at night. The short growing season makes it imperative to get the crops in as quickly as possible, once the ground has thawed.

As soon as a piece of land has been plowed and harrowed, it is put in seed. Most of the land is divided between oats and hay, largely timothy with some clover.[2] Wheat is

[1] According to the *crieur*, who handles the chemical-fertilizer order for the parish, the use of such fertilizer began about fifteen years ago. During recent years 25 of the 80 farmers in the parish have been purchasing it in varying quantities. In 1936 these farmers used 35 tons of chemical fertilizer, largely the least expensive kinds: 25 tons of superphosphate (16 per cent phosphoric acid); 5 tons of basic slag (as preceding); and 5 tons distributed among potash (50 per cent potash), mixed fertilizer (nitrogen, phosphoric acid, and potash), and ammonium sulphate (20 per cent nitrogen). The amount of fertilizer bought depends upon the market price of the produce the preceding year. Ten years ago the same group of farmers bought 100 tons. Fertilizer is used almost exclusively on potatoes and oats, the two heavy market crops.

[2] Provincial *agronomes* are striving particularly to get the farmers to establish permanent pasturage, raise turnips and sunflowers for cattle feed, and increase the amount of clover hay.

planted, but all of the farmers buy flour to augment their
own milled grain. Small amounts of barley, rye, and flax
are also sown. The only other large crop is potatoes.[3]
Some farmers plant small potatoes because there is less
waste in letting small ones sprout and in eating the large
potatoes. Other farmers comment: "Plant small potatoes
and get small potatoes." This skimping, to the detriment
of production, is typical of the old economy and remains
today, particularly in animal husbandry. Only small
amounts of turnips and "cow corn" are raised for the
animals.

At the end of May or early in June there is another important holy day for the parish farmers. The ceremonies of
fête-dieu bring divine blessing on the newly sown crops in
the fields. A *reposoire* is constructed in one quarter of the
parish for the ceremony. This roadside altar is placed in
various parts of the parish on successive years. It is a
bower of flowers and greenery, where the Host is temporarily exposed. After the Mass in the church all the parishioners move to the *reposoire* in solemn procession. The
order of the procession makes sharp divisions on the basis
of sex, age, and marital status. The banner of the Enfants
de Jésus leads the procession, and behind it file the choirboys and all the children of both sexes under sixteen
years of age. The banner of the Congrégation des Enfantes
de Marie heads the unmarried women of the parish.
They are followed by the married women, bearing the
banner of Ste Anne. Next, in the center of the procession, walks the priest; and the Holy Sacrament is carried
on a litter by the *marguilliers*. Older boys, under the ban-

[3] The 1930 Dominion crop report gives the following acreages under cultivation on the 80 St. Denis farms:

Timothy and clover	1,918	Barley and rye	60
Oats	1,871	Peas and beans	20
Wheat	128	Turnips and swedes	10
Potatoes	107	Tobacco	2

ner of the Enfants de St. Joseph, follow. The men bring up the end of the procession, under the banner of the Société de Tempérance and the Forestiers catholiques. The men's choir walks with the other men, but en route all the parishioners who know the canticles sing them. When the *reposoire* is reached, the Host is exposed to the kneeling group. After the ceremony at the *reposoire*, the procession returns to the church.[4]

Before and during the plowing period the farmer is also occupied with the birth of livestock. Calves, colts, shotes, and lambs are born during this period. There is a marked variation in the distribution of livestock, most farmers having good herds and flocks, while some have little more than a few horses and cows. Although the range in amount of stock is considerable, there are relatively few of the poorer farmers. Averages, therefore, do not greatly distort the typical picture. The average farm has fourteen head of cattle,[5] ten head of sheep, seven swine, and two or three horses. Almost every farm has several score of chickens, and some keep geese as well. In addition to the usual livestock, two farmers keep silver foxes. Fox-breeding is more common on the marginal lands.

Another spring activity, of specific importance to a few farming families but of interest to the whole parish, is the erection of weirs in the river to catch fish. Three or four families co-operate in the construction of the long, high,

---

[4] This account is as given by a parishioner.

[5] "Canadian" cattle are a small breed of good milk-producers brought from France by the early settlers. As they were well adapted to the new region, the provincial Bureau of Agriculture traced the purest blood lines to establish it as a pureblood stock. The purest lines were found to be in St. Denis, further evidence of the isolation of this parish. At present there are five herds of pureblood Canadian cattle and numerous individual animals in the parish. Interest in pureblood livestock of all sorts has been stimulated by provincial prizes. The cattle on all farms but two are tuberculine-tested, numerous diseased herds having been destroyed.

fencelike structures in the river bed. As they must be set up during the low tide, it takes at least a month to complete them. The family possessing the fishing rights and furnishing the materials owns the weir and takes the catch. The assisting families are paid in fish or cash. Most of the catch of sardines and eels is sold locally. As these fishermen are farmers as well, they may go for weeks with only a few consecutive hours of sleep.

Between planting and the first hay-cutting there are several slack weeks, often referred to as "vacation." Actually this time is employed sharpening mowers and repairing fences, farm buildings, and equipment. Summer is naturally the time for building new houses and barns. When the structural framework is completed, it is traditional to fasten a small spruce-tree top to the gable and to shoot it down with guns, as "a sign of joy at the erection of a new building." When the whole structure is finished, it is blessed by the *curé*.

There are two forms of summer work not related to agriculture and therefore of importance to nonlanded families. One is road work, and the other is salvaging wood from the river. Farmers play an important role in both types of work, for they are the only ones who have hauling facilities. There is need, however, for hand work which the day-laborers can do. Wood is salvaged from the beach when log booms break on tributaries to the St. Lawrence, letting the billets of pulp wood rush out into the river. Such mischance occurs not infrequently, and there is work for the unemployed all summer.[6]

Road work, organized under a politically appointed *cantonnier*, is typical of the change which has been effected in the manner of doing work of common interest to all

---

[6] In 1936, 30,000 cords broke loose over 50 miles upstream from the parish, and 1,000 cords were salvaged between Rivière Ouelle and St. Denis.

parishioners. Such work used to be accomplished by the voluntary, unremunerated group labor of a *corvée*. This institution was related to the few days of labor which the *seigneur* could require of his *habitants*. The *corvée* form extended to work for the church, and even to neighborly and family co-operation in tasks requiring many hands. With the exception of the partial response to the *curé*'s occasional request for manual help in cleaning the graveyard or hauling wood, all parish work has been changed to the pattern of taxation and hired labor. It is still customary to hire all the local labor possible, so that a road crew resembles a *corvée* formally, if not in spirit. The elimination of the *corvée* has tended to weaken internal parish unity through the loss of the *esprit de corps* of group labor for a common cause.

The remaining summer activity is in terms of the various harvests. Through July and August the children contribute to the family economy by gathering raspberries and blueberries. A few farmers have introduced strawberries. Cherries, apples, and plums ripen in that order and are gathered by the children. Youth of both sexes also help throughout the summer with the hay harvest. Girls are usually seen on top of two-wheeled *charrettes*, handling the hay tossed up by their brothers. Hay is stored, unbaled, in the barns. From late July through early September there are garden vegetables to be gathered and preserved.

The first snows come in October, and for over a month before that time the grain harvest is in progress. Autumn is a critical time, because the grain must be cut before the first frost. All the grain is harvested with small binders. The whole family co-operates in pulling up the flax stalks. This method is employed in order to leave the flax fibers as long as possible. These two harvesting methods, the binder and family hand labor, illustrate the change which has been wrought by the introduction of farm machinery. The family worked more as a co-operative unit on the same tasks in *l'ancien temps*. When the hay and grain had to be cut by hand, men, women, and children combined their efforts to accomplish the task. The families of brothers worked together on both their lands. When the grain was flailed by hand and winnowed with the wind, all able-bodied members of the family co-operated in the task for weeks on end. Today every family has its own small mower, binder, and threshing machine. Only one man is required to use the mower and binder, but the family very often still threshes as a unit. To the extent which members of the family have been freed from necessary combined labor in the same task, the great family unity, functionally consistent with such work, has been weakened.

Before the last harvesting is done, there is a series of local, county, and provincial fairs. The local *exposition* is usually that of the Cercle des Fermières. Home products of all sorts are sent to the *salle* by the farmers' wives. Preserved foods and exhibits of sewing, knitting, spinning, weaving, and rug-making are included. There are local prizes, the prize-winners progressing to the county and thence to the provincial fair at the city of Quebec. All sorts of farm produce and livestock are entered in the county fair, which is also an occasion for ever interesting political speeches. The women's interest centers in the home products, while that of the men is particularly in livestock-judging. Many men feel that the awarding of prizes for stock is influenced by politics. "The animals are judged just so it can be said they were judged," comments one breeder of purebloods.

The fair has two definite influences: it stimulates the men's interest in blooded stock and new agricultural techniques and the women's ideas in homecrafts. Modernistic designs were outstanding in the 1936 display of the county Home Economics School, although there is not a suggestion of them in the parish. They will eventually receive recognition through display and more directly through the training of girls sent to this school. Knitted dresses were prominent and have already penetrated into the parish. There are few commercial booths or special entertainment features at the fair. There is a large display of tombstones and another of enameled stoves. There is a ball-throwing game and a wheel of chance. Outside the grounds individuals are selling apples to the crowds, and one man has ice-cream cones for sale. Ice cream is not eaten in St. Denis, but this parish represents the smallest and most old-fashioned community in the county.

Before the snows, pumpkins are piled temporarily on porches, to be taken in later and stored in an unheated room, where they keep all winter if not frozen. Carrots, beets, turnips, potatoes, and onions are laid on the earthen cellar floor, where they are kept cool but above freezing. During this time the family moves out of the summer kitchen. The men, whose potato harvest is finished, use the remaining good days before winter improving their land or doing fall plowing. The *agronomes* have convinced the farmers that their lands should be slightly domed, sloping off to the drainage ditches. Many are trying to cut down the earth along the edge of the ditches. There is usually little time for fall plowing, so closely is the growing season figured. Horses and cows, which are going into the barns for the winter, are clipped to avoid overheating.

The first of November is All Saints' Day. The spirits of the dead are present in everyone's thoughts throughout the month, but particularly on the first two days. The social atmosphere is somber, a depression of gaiety equaled only on Good Friday and Holy Saturday or upon the death of some parish personage, such as the *curé*. All Saints' Day and the immediately following Day of the Dead[7] are days of obligation. Many indulgences can be gained during these days, and all unnecessary work is abandoned in favor of religious activity: Masses, confession, Communion, and prayer. The morning Mass on All Saints' Day is a first-class *fête*, and the church has out its richest decorations. Black-bordered envelopes, reading "For Our Dead," are in each pew. Contributions for Masses for the dead are made in these the following day. The traditional form of contribution was produce, which is still given to some extent. After the two vesper services the parishioners follow the cross, choirboys, and priest to the cemetery. The death knell is rung as they file into the cemetery. There the priest prays for the dead, and the men's choir sings part of the funeral chant. Before the evening Angelus the knell is tolled again, and families kneel in prayer for their dead before retiring. On the following day, the Day of the Dead, everyone goes to morning Mass. The church is decorated for a first-class funeral.[8] There is an empty coffin, covered with a pall, as there is for the anniversary death service. After the Mass the produce given for the dead is auctioned by the *crieur*. This auction is greatly commercialized now, the *crieur* having spent several years in the States. No mention of the dead is now made by the auctioneer, and the bids rarely exceed actual value, as used to be the case. Masses and prayers for the dead continue throughout the month.

Threshing may start before the harvest is complete, in order to make room for hay or more grain in the barn. It is

[7] The literal translation of *jour des morts* is here employed, as more expressive of the spirit of the time than "All Souls' Day."

[8] See the next chapter.

usually continued in short periods throughout the winter up to the beginning of March. The barns are not large enough to hold the straw, so the grain is stored and threshed as needed or as the straw is used up. Most of the threshing machines in the parish are driven by gasoline engines, although there are still a dozen run by horse-power treadmills. The head of the family often forks the sheaves of grain to an elder son, who feeds the machine. Younger boys fork the straw away, and the mother fills the sacks with the grain which issues from the thresher.

Just as flax is harvested after the old fashion, it is still flailed, to avoid cutting the fibers short in the threshing machine. The seed is winnowed after the flailing. This flailing is done in late autumn. When it is completed, the flax stalks are dried and then put through the *braie* by the men. The *braie* breaks up the pithy core of the stalk and loosens it from its fibrous sheath. The core is completely removed from the fibers by subsequently beating the stalks with a wooden swordlike object. Either sex may thus *écorcer* the flax, but only the women comb out the fibers. The combed flax is ready for spinning and weaving during the winter months. It requires about ten hours' labor to prepare a pound of linen thread from the original flax stalks.

The women in every farm household, from grandmother to the older girls, spend much of the winter either spinning, weaving, or knitting. Girls must also learn how to mount the warp threads on the warp rack and transfer it to the loom. Even small children co-operate in winding the skeins from the spinning-wheel spindles and filling spools and bobbins. Looms in the parish are largely after the old pattern; and many, which are still in use, are over a hundred years old. A few newer-type hand looms are beginning to be employed, their adoption stimulated by the convents;

The *Ecorçage* of the Flax

MUMMERS AT *Mi-Carême*

but all are made locally of wood. On most looms it is usual
to weave six feet of cloth during a ten-hour day of work.
Wool cloth for clothing is woven in simple herringbone
and diamond designs. There are family preferences for
certain designs. Worn-out clothes are unraveled and the
wool recarded, spun, and woven into rugs. Linen is woven
into tablecloths and towels.

The family routine varies considerably during the winter
months from that in summer. The Angelus rings an hour
later in the morning and an hour earlier at night. Work
being less pressing and the daylight hours fewer, parishioners rise later. The woman's day varies in the occupa-
tions she pursues in addition to the regular housework.
For the men there is a more complete change of work.
There is a new routine of chores, called *faisant le train*,
associated with the care of the livestock in the barns.
The horses and cattle and sheep, which graze in summer,
now require feeding and watering twice a day, in addition
to the care of the swine. The stalls must be cleaned also,
and the manure piled outside the barn. *Le train* requires
up to six hours' work a day. While the men are so engaged, the girls do the milking, as usual. They also cook
the caldrons full of potatoes for the pigs. The feed for the
livestock varies with what the farmer has on hand, it being
unusual to buy feed. Swine are fed a variety of mashes,
the fattening diets being largely for shotes. Cattle are
given all the clover hay available; after that, clover mixed
with timothy. Straw is fed as bulk. Chopped turnips are
also employed. In the fall there is a small amount of corn.
Horses are fed on timothy hay and oats, and the sheep
on hay alone.

Everyone slaughters in December. The kill consists almost entirely of hogs. It is usual for a whole *rang*, or
quarter, to slaughter on the same day. Five or six families

often co-operate in cleaning the animals and heating the great caldrons of water to scald them. The weights of the largest hogs are quickly known throughout the parish and are the chief topic of conversation. After the slaughter the women make blood sausage, and soon the men have new pig's-bladder tobacco pouches. Some of the meat is taken to the butcher in the next parish for sale; much is hung up for the winter.

Woodcutting and splitting is another winter activity which is started in December but which, interspersed with threshing, is continued until spring. The men must wait until there is heavy snow on the roads to facilitate hauling the wood. When the edges of the snow-covered roads are marked out with trimmed spruce saplings, and *carrioles* and dog sleds have replaced buggies and dogcarts,[9] then is the time to get the family wood. As most of the timber in the parish is cut, almost all farm families have wood lots in the mountains to the south. The able-bodied men of a family take several days' supply of food and go to the mountain wood lots. There they remain, while they fell and trim the timber they require. The logs are left in the woods to be brought down through the winter. When the wood has all been hauled home, it is sawed in stove lengths and split. Most of the wood is bucksawed, but several farmers use their gasoline engines to run circular saws. The average family burns between ten and fifteen cords of wood a year. This must all be split and corded before spring, so that it can dry during the summer. A very few farmers, farmers' sons, and day-laborers pass the winter doing commercial lumbering in the *chantiers*.

Christmas ushers in *les fêtes*, a succession of *veillées* and

---

[9] A dog is harnessed to a two-wheeled cart or low sled after the fashion of a horse. If two dogs are used, which is unusual, they are teamed side by side. Dogs are used only as means of personal conveyance, and the animals greatly enjoy their role.

religious ceremonies which last almost through January. The day before Christmas is a fastday, a fact which emphasizes the release of gaiety after the midnight Mass. During the day the *crèche* is set up before the altar of St. Joseph; but the manger remains empty until just before midnight, when the figure of the Christ child is laid in it. The figures of the Wise Men are not added until the *jour des rois*, the sixth of January. On the day before Christmas the children of the parish are brought to the church to confess. For the midnight Mass the altar and sanctuary have their richest ornaments. For a month the altar has been undecorated. Now it is covered with a gold-embroidered cloth, the paraphernalia are gold, and there are lights and bright metal flowers adorning it. The contrast is great and is reflected in the spirit of the congregation. Almost all the parish is present and beaming. During the High Mass the worshipers all take Communion, the males preceding the females. There is a special sermon by an outside priest. The High Mass is followed by a Low Mass, during which a choir of girls sings religious music.

After the church service there are *réveillons* in the homes. Wine, candy, fat pork, and bread are served to the guests and family. The stockings of the children who were too young to attend the Mass hang by the stove. They are filled with candy, so that the little ones will not think *l'enfant Jesus* forgot them. On Christmas day few parishioners go to the Masses, that at midnight sufficing. A few houses are decorated with bells and spruce, and there are one or two Christmas trees; but these things are definitely new and have been introduced through intimate contact with the cities. The local store carries no decorations, but a few Christmas cards are sold at the post office. In general, this *fête* does not receive the social recognition given New Year's.

After the last Sunday Mass of the year there is an auction of church pews. The men gather in the basement of the sacristy; and the *crieur*, in the presence of the *curé*, receives bids. There are rarely more than half a dozen pews to be auctioned, as most families avail themselves of their privilege of keeping their pews at the rentals they originally bid. The auction concluded, everyone goes down on his knees, while the *curé* prays for divine guidance of the new *marguillier* to be elected. The priest then reads the nomination made by the retiring official, seconded by the new *marguillier en charge*. Someone among the men indicates satisfaction, the *curé* asks if all agree, there is another affirmative response, and the matter is ended.

The days immediately before New Year's are full of activity. Mail-order gifts and greeting cards are being sent and received. The store and post office are decorated with colored lights, garlands, and paper Christmas trees. The store does a rushing business in candy and even some whiskey. The High Mass on the first day of the new year is crowded. The church is decorated for a first-class *fête*. During the service the new *marguillier* is inducted. Led by the sacristan, the retiring official carries a lighted candle to the pew of the new churchwarden, presents it to him, and leads him back to the *marguillier*'s pew. After the Mass, during which the priest blesses the congregation, the parishioners file out of church and greet one another on the steps. There is general handshaking and well-wishing among friends. Outside the church this is confined to each sex, although in the homes there is no sex distinction. Handshaking and kissing are formalities rarely performed except at this time of year. There is no kissing between men. It is customary to shake hands and exchange good wishes with all friends after the turn of the year. If such meetings are a week after New Year's, the custom still holds. Leaving the church, the people return home to open presents and partake of a bounteous repast with friends and relatives. In every home on this day the father traces a cross on the forehead of each member of the family and gives him his blessing.

Winter is the time for *veillées*, and they are particularly prevalent during *les fêtes*.[10] There are parties every night between New Year's and *jour des rois*. For this latter *fête*, special cakes are baked, containing a bean in one half and a pea in the other. During the progress of the *veillée* the cake is cut and served. The girl receiving the bean is the queen for the evening, and the man receiving the pea is the king. In some families, elder children put on an elaborate masquerade, as king and queen with attendants. A special feature of some *veillées* is the music. The singing of unaccompanied solos by many of the guests is an almost constant feature.[11] The most popular and amusing songs are those which come from the city. The older folk songs are rarely heard, although many are still known to the older people. A fiddler or harmonica-player may be invited to the party to entertain the guests. This kind of music is greatly enjoyed and constitutes the favorite type of radio program. The fiddler's repertoire consists largely of dance music: jigs, cotillions, reels, and quadrilles. Dancing itself meets with clerical disapproval, but it goes on *en cachette* both within and outside the parish. The quadrille, executed with English calls, is the most prevalent dance form. Like the folk songs, the folk tales are no longer heard. A generation ago story-tellers were a feature of many *veillées*. Now there is not a story-teller in the

[10] Thus, one farmer reports burning over twice as much lamp oil during *les fêtes* as during any similar length of time.

[11] There are a dozen pianos and five harmoniums in the parish, which may be used as accompaniment. Often no one can play the instruments. Radios are not used as *veillée* entertainment.

parish, and very few in the vicinity. Increased literacy
has destroyed the role of the story-teller. He was first supplanted by reading aloud, which has now been abandoned
for individual reading. Local legends have passed, along
with the *conteur de contes*. Grandparents still maintain
their belief in the supernatural happenings of the legends,
so that their mention creates arguments between the generations.

The progress and setting of a *veillée* depict an intimate
part of the winter life. The guests arrive in *carrioles;* and
the women enter the large kitchen, while the men put up
the horses. From one of the kitchen rafters hang guns,
one an old percussion-cap gun. On the wooden walls are
the black cross with a palm sprig on it, large colored pictures of Christ and Mary, and a biblical scene. There is
the usual commercial calendar. On one wall hangs an ancient pendulum clock still ticking out the seconds. Opposite the front door is the large enameled stove with a mirror
in its top. It is a very new stove, and the young son of the
house takes great pride in showing off its fine points. At
the back of the kitchen is the pump and sink. Around the
walls are long benches, rockers, and many straight-backed
chairs. White muslin curtains hang at the windows. The
salon, which opens off the kitchen, has an oil-lamp chande-
lier in the center, hanging over a small table with a lace
cover. In the corner is a harmonium. On the wall is a
composite picture of the paternal grandfather and grandmother and all their children. The picture is taken down;
and all the marriages, deaths, and relationships to present
parishioners are explained to new guests. There are several
elaborate picture frames on the wall. One contains the
picture of the last two *curés;* another, the two parents of
the husband; another, those of the wife. There is also a
composite picture of all the popes, a diploma from Laval

University, a picture of the Canadian martyrs, and a crucifix. On the harmonium are paper flowers and mounted
pictures of a priest-relative and marriage pictures of cousins, which are passed around.

As the group assembles, the women may gather around
the stove in rockers for a short while, to warm themselves
after their sleigh rides. The complete family of the host is
present, the eldest boy being home from college for the
vacation. The young sister of the wife is here on a visit
and is making herself attractive to the boys. Tonight, one
unrelated boy, a farmer's inheriting son, is here courting
her. Other guests are the first cousins of the mistress of the
house, with their wives and older children. There are some
twenty-five people in all.

The married people and the related priest, home for *les
fêtes*, go into the *salon* to see the pictures and to sit and
chat. In the kitchen the young people play and laugh.
They play a hand-slapping game, each trying to slap the
hand of the other as hard as possible. This is played between the boys and girls. They take out a watch and read
their own pulses. Then there is a discussion as to what the
pulse should be. When card-playing starts, the elders begin in the *salon* and the young people in the kitchen. There
are four tables in the kitchen and one in the *salon*. The
limited number of tables leaves quite a few nonplayers.
The players at the tables play two out of three games of
quatre septs, the losers leaving the table in favor of people
who have not yet played. The winners stay in the same
places. Oil lamps are used, one on each table except in the
salon, where there is one over the table. Upon losing, the
elders move out into the kitchen and the winning youths
into the *salon*, until they are well mixed. After there has
been almost an hour of play, the hostess passes little
glasses of wine. Maple sugar and store candy are also

passed around. The suitor and the girl visitor do not play cards but sit in the corner and talk and laugh. When not playing, the other eligible males crowd around also.

The greatest hilarity during these evenings of cards occurs when someone gets a *vilaine*.[12]   A terrible din breaks loose. Everyone yells, stamps, rattles chairs on the floor, and claps hands. Someone imitates fiddle music, and another beats on a washpan. There are comic hats, often dunce caps, to put on the pair who get the *vilaine*. Tonight the host gets a black scarf and solemnly bows to each of the players who get the *vilaine*, one of whom is the priest, and swings the scarf like a censer, three times, and bows his head again. This is a ceremony of honor in the church, given to all visiting priests when the choir and congregation are censed. The priest later returns the honor when the host gets a *vilaine*. Those getting the *vilaine* invariably try to hide it. At the end of the *veillée*, around midnight, everyone assembles in the kitchen. The host, who is in the church choir, sings a solo in a loud voice from a book of old Canadian songs. Everyone rises and sings "Au Canada," "Bon Soir," and "A la Vollette." "Alouette" is also sung, led by the priest. The men go out to hitch up the horses, the women get ready to leave, and the party is over.

As January passes, the families return to the routine and special work of winter. The gaiety of *les fêtes* is followed by the Lenten period in the next month. On *lundi gras* there is a benefit card party for all the parish in the *salle publique*. The day before the fasting and solemnity of Lent begin, there is the mummery and celebration of *mardi gras*. A score of children and young people originate costumes and make masks. The disguises represent men and

[12] If one wins tricks with insufficient scoring cards therein to count a point by the end of the hand, this constitutes a *vilaine* for both partners.

women, policemen, or important political figures. In the evening they visit through the parish, disguising their voices and identity to the best of their ability. The hosts serve wine and candy to their unknown visitors before they leave. Lent begins on Ash Wednesday, and on that day all parishioners wear the ashen cross traced on their foreheads by the priest. Early in Lent there is a *concours de confession*, during which the parishioners can confess to visiting priests from other parishes. This overcomes reticence about confessing to one's own *curé* and thus makes possible more complete spiritual preparation for Easter. During Lent everyone foregoes dancing, drinking, and parties. Abstinence from flesh food is observed on Wednesdays as well as Fridays. Fast rules are observed every day but Sunday.[13] Each person sets a certain penance for himself: giving up smoking, saying the rosary, making the Way of the Cross, or attending week-day Masses. The restraint of Lent is relaxed for a day in the middle of the period. On *mi-carême* there is mummery, with visiting and entertaining, just as on *mardi gras*. Then the strict denial of pleasurable pursuits is again resumed.

Palm Sunday begins the final week of religious activity in preparation for Easter. Everyone goes to church carrying a spruce branch, which is blessed during the Mass. Palms are blessed at the high altar and distributed to the choirboys, who carry them in a procession. The crucifix, covered in purple for mourning, precedes the procession around the church, while the parishioners stand holding their spruce branches. The congregation is admonished in the sermon of this day to increase its penance and self-mortification during the final week of Lent.

[13] Two ounces of food are allowed for breakfast, eight in the evening. The noon meal is unrestricted. Children and aged persons and those who are ill or engaged in manual labor are exempt from fasting.

The religious ceremonies on Holy Thursday and Good Friday are extremely depressing. The unusual treatment of church symbols, in which are centered intense attitudes, affects everyone. After the ceremony of the Mass on Holy Thursday, the Host is taken in a procession around the church to one of the side altars. It is preceded by the crucifix, covered with a black cloth, and the choirboys carrying lighted tapers. After the Host is deposited in the side altar, the ceiling lamp before it is lit to indicate the divine presence. The light before the high altar is extinguished, the candles are snuffed out, the altar is stripped of its decorations, and the door of the tabernacle is left open. The church bells remain silent from this time until the Mass on Holy Saturday.[14] The stripped and darkened altar and the silent bells cause many to feel that the church atmosphere is sad. At the Good Friday Mass, each person goes down on both knees, instead of the usual genuflexion, before entering his pew. The priest, wearing black vestments, prostrates himself before the altar. Later, the priest and choirboys remove their shoes and, after kneeling thrice, kiss the feet of the crucifix, which rests on a cushion on the altar steps. The congregation then goes to the Communion rail and kisses the feet of the crucifix. The main altar is then covered with a cloth and the candles lit. A procession like that of the previous day carries the Host from the side altar around the church to the main altar. The priest goes through the Mass, with the exception of the consecration of the bread and wine, the *hostie* for this Mass having been consecrated Holy Thursday. On the day of the Passion, the church does not go through the sacrifice.

[14] A children's belief in the old days was that the bells had gone to Rome. One still hears, "The bells have come back from Rome," on Holy Saturday.

At three o'clock on Good Friday, the hour of the death of Christ, the parish assembles in the church and makes the Way of the Cross with the priest.

The Holy Saturday Mass is very long, as it includes the benediction of the paschal candle, the baptismal font, the holy water, and the creation of new fire. The parishioners frankly feel that the long Masses of Holy Week are part of their penance. The benediction of the various religious symbols is conducted just inside the front doors. After the holy water has been blessed, it is left in a large tub at the back of the church. Small bottles of the water are taken home by each family. During the Mass of this day, the church bells and organ, which have been silent for two days, ring out and play once more.

After the denuded altars, the crucifixes draped in mourning, the open tabernacle, the interrupted sacrifice and the somber simplicity of the church, the Easter Mass is gay and the altars and church glitter with ornaments. The repression of Lent is over. Children's voices blend with those of the men's choir. Everyone is happy spiritually, because of the Resurrection, and gay personally, because of the end of Lenten denial and the burst of beauty in the church after weeks of drabness. On Easter the hours of the Angelus are changed to their summer routine, thus formally ushering in again the activities of spring.

This yearly round of activity in St. Denis obviously depends upon two interrelated cycles: the seasonal and the religious. Being farmers, the *habitants* are more limited by the environment to certain channels of activity during particular seasons. When the season changes to one in which economically necessary pursuits are fewer, the social patterns are less rigidly limited by the environment. The climactic points in the religious cycle, Christmas and Easter, correspond with the quiet winter period in the economic cycle; so there is no conflict with respect to focus of interest. Sacred influences are employed in the economic adjustment to the environment, such as the Masses sung for good crops; and, in turn, the religious beliefs are fortified by the economic success of the approved ways of life.

CHAPTER IX

CHILDHOOD

THE beginning of life is marked by little ceremony and only slight public interest. This social calm which prevails at birth is in striking contrast to the emotion and ritual associated with the death of an adult. In the latter case, the society abruptly loses one of its members. In the former, there is a new living being in the society, but an individual who must be made a member of the society by a long process of training. The course of life begins with this social orientation and continues through a period of active participation in the society. The difference between the reactions of any society to birth and to death is to be understood in terms of the progressive integration of the individual into the social life during his space of mortal existence.

The birth of a child causes no particular excitement because no atmosphere of novelty surrounds it. Babies are a continual part of the average household for fifteen out of every thirty-four years.[1] Children grow up in the presence of infants, and the fact of birth does not long remain a mystery. In their early years, to be sure, many children are told that a *bolomien*[2] comes to the door of the house with the baby and tries to give it to their mother. When she refuses to take the child, he breaks her leg with a club and leaves it anyway. The doctor has to be called to fix her broken leg.[3] When children approach their mother's

[1] See "Kinship and the Family Cycle," chap. iv.

[2] Local variation of *bohémien* ("gipsy").

[3] Note that actually a doctor is never called for broken limbs and that the *remmancheur* is never involved in deliveries. This part of the story seems to be new or altered to fit the new technique of delivery by a doctor.

bed, they are warned to "watch out for her broken leg." In spite of the fact that some of the families keep up this fiction with children until they reach their teens, the youngsters learn the truth years before from other children, whose parents attempt no delusion, or from older children who are no longer ignorant of the facts.

The refusal of the mother to take the baby in the story gives a subtle hint of the fact that women silently dread the long series of pregnancies which make up so much of their early married lives. To be sure, the children are loved and spoiled with parental affection; but to the wife, who must continue to run her household, another child is an additional hardship. Women cannot be outspoken in this attitude because children are "gifts of God," and his acts may not be questioned. Nevertheless, one encounters the feeling that it is the husband who wants a large family. As both parents are actively involved in the economic scheme which makes such a family an advantage, the woman's reluctance to continual child-bearing and the more active sexual desires of the man lie at the base of this attitude. Contraception is not practiced by marriage partners, and contraceptive methods are largely unknown.

There is very little prenatal care. The expectant mother continues her housework but is spared from long walks during the last months of pregnancy. Because of lack of care, miscarriages are common. This is probably the reason that the average number of births during the procreative period falls below the physiological expectation. No medical care of any sort is solicited until labor actually starts. In St. Denis, the doctor is always called to make the delivery. In addition, a *sage-femme* from the parish is on hand as an assistant. In poorer regions with less available medical aid the *sages-femmes* still make many deliveries. There are two *sages-femmes* in St. Denis, both mothers of families and past child-bearing age. They are in poor economic circumstances and assist in the deliveries and take charge of the postnatal care for whatever the families see fit to give them. They are often paid in produce. Their role includes the washing of the linens, as well as the care of the mother and child; and in addition they are often used as "bearers" for the baptism. The practice of not calling the doctor until labor is actually started means that not infrequently the *sage-femme* is forced to make the delivery before the doctor arrives.

The doctor never sees his patient again after the delivery. Besides the postnatal care by the *sage-femme*, the public health nurse makes regular visits to the parish each month. At these times she visits all the new mothers and distributes literature on the care of infants. She also tries to instruct the *sages-femmes* in the approved method of washing babies. Mothers are advised as to feeding and care. Such authoritative gratuitous advice from the unmarried nurse arouses some antagonism. "She tries to tell mothers of seven or eight children how to take care of them, as though they did not know. She says that, when a baby cries, you should let it cry and not rock it in a cradle, but leave it quiet. Rocking will make them stop crying. If she had five crying babies around her for awhile she would change her ideas." The nurse and doctor, in the baby clinics held monthly at the *salle*, advocate longer breast feeding, advising the mothers to nurse their infants for at least two months before starting feeding with diluted cow's milk. This instruction is combating the traditional practice of weaning babies as early as possible and putting them on cow's milk. The immediate use of such rich milk has been in part responsible for the frequent serious intestinal disorders of babies. The women are generally flat chested and are often unable to provide breast feeding for their offspring. But even when capability is not a question, early weaning is the rule. The fact that the mother almost immediately resumes her full load of household management after the birth of her child is doubtless related to the early weaning.

Concepts concerning prenatal influence are not highly elaborated. It is believed that the religious activity of an expectant mother will affect the child she is carrying, making it more religiously inclined. There is a check on the working of this principle. If the mother overdoes her prayers and Masses, the child will not be religious. The lack of development of these ideas is consistent with the utter disregard of the effect of prenatal physical influences.

The procedures associated with birth are admirably described in the following interview, given by one of the midwives. This woman started her practice by assisting a doctor and therefore does not represent a continuation of the old personality in the new role of doctor's assistant. Her techniques, however, show a body of traditional women's knowledge used in conjunction with that gained from doctor and nurse. Like every other aspect of life, birth is surrounded by both traditional and new rational knowledge. The midwife's account is most important as an expression of this situation.

When the husband and wife have been together and she misses her first sickness, she counts nine months from then until her baby arrives. Women rarely know the exact date, particularly the younger ones. As they get older, they are accustomed and notice the date more. When the woman first begins to feel the baby, four and a half months have passed. She frequently counts four and a half months from then and arrives at the exact date. She begins to feel the baby when just half the time has passed. At the end of the first forty days a woman may be sick and throw up, but we never pay any attention to that. Some women are never sick this way. I never was. It may last three months. At the end of the forty days the baby is alive. After seven months it can be born and live long enough to be taken to the church and baptized. I made the delivery of a baby for Mme Leblanc after seven months. It lived long enough to be baptized but died the next day. Young women who have never had children may come due as much as fifteen days sooner than the nine months. Older women may be as much as a week or two longer. In the last days before the delivery the woman cannot do laundry because it requires her to bend her stomach, but nothing is better for her than to scrub the floor. She should walk and not stay in bed too long. When she feels great pains in her stomach and back, the doctor is called. When the delivery is in the daytime, all the children are sent out of the house, particularly the girls. It's better to have young men in the house than young girls, because it may make the girls afraid to have children. If a girl in the house were about to marry, she might be afraid to. The girl's mother is rarely present for the delivery but stays with her afterward. The husband is always in the house unless he cannot be, on account of business. A wife always likes to have her husband near. At the birth of his first child the husband is usually very anxious.

When the doctor comes, he washes his hands; and when he says the entrance to the womb is open, that means that all is well. It may take a whole day before the delivery, usually three or four hours. We do not do anything to hurry it. Let nature alone. If you try to hurry it, you cause a hemorrhage. A doctor may give injections, but medicine is dangerous. I almost died after taking some when I had one child. When it's just a simple delivery, I can deliver the child. I cover my hands with a clean cloth, take the baby by the head, and "haul." When the baby has been delivered, the first thing to do is to tie up the umbilical cord in two places. It must be tied the first time tight, tight. If it is not, the baby will die of a hemorrhage. Then the cord is cut between the two ties with a pair of scissors. The baby is put in a chair beside the stove until the afterbirth arrives. After it comes, I wash the baby from one end to the other with soap and water. Instead of having to wash out the bed, we soak up the blood with newspapers covered with a clean rag. These are all rolled up and burned in the stove. The afterbirth is burned in the stove also. It should never be thrown outdoors because the children might find it. It would be covered with blood and have the cord attached to it, and it would make them ask questions.

As soon as the doctor is gone, I wrap the mother. He does not think it is necessary, but it is. I make a mixture of melted butter and camphor, black with pepper. This is put on a piece of flannel and put on the mother. If you have any, whiskey can be used instead of butter. The flannel is bound on with three layers of good yellow cotton cloth wide enough to cover the womb. The baby is bound around the stomach with a four-inch band of flannelette, doubled twice, with a layer of cotton in the center. The mother takes a tea made from juniper berries from the North. This is good for her and makes the milk come easily. She drinks it as long as she wants to. The mother must stay in bed ten days. The first three she eats only liquid food. After that she returns to her regular food. The third day she gets the "milk fever." She is given a mixture of wine and milk at this time and also when she stops nursing. You put a glass of milk on the stove in a saucepan and let it boil up. Then you take it off the stove. You let it boil up this way three times. You boil a glass of wine also, but it will not boil up. You put the two together, and they curdle. You let it cool, so that it is not too hot, and put it by the bed for the mother to drink. Castor oil should be taken after this. The mother should take the baby the day after it is born. She does not have any milk, but the baby becomes accustomed to her. Often the mother cannot give the baby milk. Then the baby is given a spoonful of boiled milk for every spoonful of boiled water. It is all measured out, half of one and half of the other. As soon as you see the baby can take richer milk, you change the proportions. The mother must be given castor oil two or three times a week, more at the beginning if she has no milk. She takes this for one month. Camphor, spread on a flannel cloth, is put on her stomach at first. I just had to do this for my daughter-in-law who had no milk. She also should take *fleurs de sirop blanc*.

The evening of the third day I give the woman a douche. Each mother has her own douche sack. I give a douche of hot water with two drops of iodine in it to disinfect. One can put in a little alum to stop bleeding if necessary. She is given a douche every evening until the tenth day. The umbilical cord of the baby dries and falls off the third, fourth, or fifth day. It is thrown in the stove. The umbilicus is powdered, and a piece of cotton is put over it. The flannelette band around the baby is left on for a year. The evening of the eighth day the mother is bathed completely and put in clean clothes, and the bed is completely changed. She is given a douche and goes to sleep. The next day she will be worse. It is just as bad for her to get up the ninth day as the first. On the tenth day she can sit up and walk around a little. The tenth day she can dress herself and go on as usual. If a woman does not take care of herself like this, it is very bad. The wife of my brother is blind and infirm because she would never let anyone take care of her when she had children.

The most important act associated with birth is baptism. It is even more important than the life of the child itself. The bodies of babies who die unbaptized cannot be interred in the cemetery, and their souls can never see heaven. Because of this dire physical and spiritual fate, baptism follows within the first twenty-four hours after birth. If the *curé* is for some reason out of the parish, the baby may be baptized at a neighboring church. When there is apparent danger that the child will not live, it is baptized by the doctor. If the child does live, it is usually baptized subsequently at the church *sous condition* that baptism was not properly performed. The church allows such baptism by laymen with ordinary water; but the priest points out that a ritual slip, such as a different person sprinkling the child from the one who says, "I baptize thee in the name of the Father, of the Son, and of the Holy Ghost," makes the baptism invalid. The only babies who are not baptized either by the priest or doctor are still-born.

The parents of the newborn child have three decisions to make: the selection of names for the child, the choice of its godparents, and the selection of a "bearer" for the ceremony of baptism. The considerations in the first two choices were discussed as aspects of the family and kinship. Naming is certainly influenced by family connections and traditional names in the lineage. In case of disagreement, the father, as head of the house, usually has his way. It is not unheard of to ask godparents for suggestions when families are large. It is extremely rare to try to aid the child by selecting godparents of influential position. The pattern of baptism here does not lend itself to such usage. As godparents are usually closely related to the child, the role of godparent is not conceived of as including duties or obligations after the actual ceremony of baptism. The "bearer" of the baby to and from the church may be the godmother or one of certain women in the parish, including several widows, who are financially aided by the dollar paid for their services as bearer. The position is not honor-ary, but a family makes a small prestige gesture by having a paid bearer for the baby.

The baptismal party, which goes to the church in a buggy or sleigh, is composed of the father and child, the godparents, and possibly a bearer. The financial obligations of the baptism rest on the godfather. He pays the bearer, gives small presents to the mother, baby, and godmother, and pays the *bedeau*. For the dollar paid him, the *bedeau* will ring the church bells for five minutes as the party leaves the church. Unpaid, only one bell will be rung a short while "for the child to hear" as it departs. Having all the bells rung has real social value. A family which can pay the doctor only two dollars for delivery will find another dollar for the *bedeau*. Comments are apt to be made if the bells do not ring loud and long. Although there are no outsiders at baptism, the baby will be dressed in special clothes with lace, if at all possible, and perfumed with rose water. The ceremony finished, the little entourage goes to the altar of the Virgin in the church and prays before leaving for home. The sound of the bells following them causes no stir in the parish. Even those who have not heard of the birth know who is expecting a baby, and the carillon only informs them that it has arrived.

During the first six years of childhood every child has his most vital interpersonal relations with his mother. It is the mother who cares for his needs, disciplines, and instructs him in these early years. An elder sister may be intrusted with his care, but the mother is always in the background as a sympathetic person to whom to appeal in case of injury or wrong. Siblings of a near age will be playmates. The characteristic feature of older siblings is that they are ever present in the family circle in its prayers, meals, work, and relaxation. They also have special relationships with the parents, with whom the youngster also has his most important relationships. Because of the control derived from the parents or because of their own superior age and strength, older siblings have disciplinary power which the small child must early recognize. The contact of the child with his older siblings is slight except in the case of shifted parental responsibility. The small child never plays, works, or eats with his older brothers or sisters. He plays with young siblings or by himself. This group eats informally around the kitchen or at a separate table from the rest of the family. They are his informal-contact group. His parents occupy the supervisory roles of authority and care. Father often relaxes and plays with the little children; and, although not directly concerned with their care, his authority over even big sister is obvious to the small child. But father is not around the house, like mother, and is therefore less important to the young child.

Outside of the family group the child under six years has few personal relations. He may play occasionally with the children of kinsmen or neighbors, but this is not usual. The family and its area of activity, the house and farm, limit the social scope of the youngster. The play activity of children is definitely patterned after adult activity. The basis of imitation is, of course, observation. Children of three and four watch the older members of the family in their work, if it is not too far afield. Threshing, woodcutting, hog-slaughter, and all the nonroutine activities are sources of great diversion. In free play time, the work of elders is imitated. A lad of three or four will mount an empty wagon and drive and work imaginary horses for hours on end. Toys reproduce in miniature objects associated with adults. A girl will tend her doll as her mother tends the baby. Already gender distinctions, marked in the manner in which the parents dress the children, begin to be accentuated by different behavior patterns.[4] These distinctive patterns are transferred by the society to the young children by first giving them a feeling of identity with their gender; then imitative behavior and ridiculed cross-gender behavior complete the distinction. This process of identification is already well defined before the age of six; but it continues until the child is grown and married, when the different parental attitudes of the father must be assumed in distinction to those of the mother. The development of the gender personality constitutes a large part of the growth of the complete social personality.

Early technical training is related to the imitative play. Small girls learn how to sew and knit. They make clothes for their dolls and even attempt some for themselves. One little girl of five knit a complete sweater for herself, the size of the task and the fact that it was for personal use being slightly unusual at this age. Very young girls are also expected to help their mothers around the kitchen, the amount of this work depending upon the number of older sisters who can assist. Small children of both sexes, accompanied by their older siblings, are usually sent to bring in the cows. Little boys will be asked to do small chores, such as getting wood for the stove from the wood closet under the stairs. For the most part, children under six have few duties. The family supports them, expecting almost nothing in return. In addition to imitative play there are traditional forms of recreation for children. They play with balls and, in winter, coast on sleds. Snow houses may be built, and dogsleds and dogcarts furnish additional

[4] The word "sex" always implies physiological distinctions. "Gender" is here used as a social grouping determined by distinctive behavior patterns—dress, language differences, special knowledges, etc. The genders are male and female, as the sexes, and normally correspond with the physiological groups. The necessity for distinguishing the concepts is seen in the fact that the child learns that it is a "boy" or "girl," defined by social criteria, years before it learns the physiological difference between the sexes.

amusement. All of the nonimitative play continues into later childhood with the addition of new amusements. Playful imitation is gradually supplanted by actual participation in family activity.

About the age of six the child begins a new phase of life. The shift is gradual in some activities but abrupt in others. The distinctive feature of this period of later childhood, which extends into early adolescence, is that the social sphere of the child expands from his immediate family to include the parish. Duties and obligations increase as the free nonproductive years are left behind. The social acts which mark the beginning of the second period are entrance into the schools and *petite communion*. Within the family the change of status is marked by the child sitting at the table with the family for meals.

The early religious education of the child starts at home, where the mother teaches him the prayers to repeat when the whole family prays together. Mother also tells the child Bible stories and introduces him to a few of the fundamental personages and principles: God, Jesus, the Virgin, St. Joseph, the Devil, heaven, and hell. Before starting school, children do not enter the church very often. They go to the children's Mass each year and occasionally accompany their parents on Sunday. At Christmas they are taken by their mothers to visit the *crèche*. There they are told the Christmas story and taught to pray and light a candle before the manger. Aside from such infrequent visits, the church plays no part in the child's life.

In the preparatory year at school, the pupils learn *le petit catéchisme* and additional prayers. This does not take the whole year, as their catechism training was started at home before they began school. After the responses of the *petit catéchisme* are learned by heart, the pupils are examined by the *curé* on the material. They take their first

Communion as a group very informally in the sacristy on the Tuesday of the last week of Lent. After this ceremony the communicants are expected to participate fully in the religious life of the community, attending Masses, confessing, and doing penance. Identity with adults is not achieved in these activities. There are special days and times designated by the *curé* for children to confess to him, school being closed for this express purpose. Half of the boys join the boys' choir after instruction in the Mass by the school teacher. Their participation in this choir during early school years serves to set their whole age group off, just as the children who attend school make up an age group commonly designated as "school children."

A sharp distinction is made between "education" and "instruction." The former designates the social and moral integration of the child into society; the latter refers to the learning of certain factual material useful in life. The primary responsibility for the education of children rests with the parents, whose home training makes the children good Catholics and good citizens. Instruction rests with the school, but it is only a factor of secondary importance in this institution, which is also concerned with the moral education of its pupils. According to the statement of the provincial Catholic education committee, the parish school system "should create moral initiative in giving the children the principles which direct the life of the Christian and citizen, developing in them the habits which orient their whole moral life."[5] The *curé* finds frequent occasion in the pulpit to warn the parents against neglecting their responsibility of education of the children at home and leaving the entire moral training to the teacher.

[5] *Réglements du Comité catholique*, quoted in Leroy Poulin, "L'Enseignement primaire rural dans la province de Québec" (unpublished Bachelor's thesis at the Ecole superieure d'Agriculture de Ste Anne, 1934).

In the explicit purpose of these schools is a definite expression of the social function of the school. Schools in any society have one basic function, that of the social orientation of the children. They often have related and minor functions as well. Where there are strong class systems, schools are elements in that system. This means simply that the society has become so complex that there must be special orienting institutions for the various social subdivisions. Another social function of the schools is to provide a concrete age-grade system through which the child moves during his progressive orientation. We are often too apt to regard the sequences of promotions through the schools as simply expressive of the increase of a child's factual knowledge and his ability to employ it. On the contrary, the sequence of school grades represents to the growing individual a series of social stages by means of which one attains adulthood. Each stage has its social unity expressed in unique patterns of behavior and defensive attitudes functioning to keep the lower group out. Once firmly established in one stage, members of each group endeavor to identify with that above by adopting its characteristic behavior and attitudes. Movement through the school system, however, is definitely controlled from the outside. Certain intellectual tasks must be mastered before the controlling adults will allow one to move on. The purely social reasons for which these materials are learned are often underestimated. If a boy were not consumed with a desire to get into the grade whose members dominate him and if his class were not going to be promoted as a group, he would have less interest in passing his course.

In St. Denis the age-grade aspect of the school is not marked, but it has become much solidified in the last generation. Less than a century ago no one went to school.

Thirty years ago it was still general to grow into recognized manhood without having passed through the school. The lad who left school to help his father in the field had an actual technical advantage over his brother who stayed in school. For this reason it is common even now for the farming sons to have less education than their brothers who contemplate living in a nonagrarian economy. The attitude has grown that some schooling is necessary for all.

To the extent that schooling is a prerequisite to accepted participation in the society, it is in a position to function as an age-grade system. As it is possible for a child to complete the six or seven years' schooling before he is old enough to take a full share of the work at home, and farm machinery makes younger hands unnecessary, it is possible under the present system to take time for schooling. In spite of the fact that all children go to school and most of them finish the series of classes, the age-grade aspect is not very strong. The fact that school attendance has only just become general is an influencing factor. In addition, and probably more important, the social intercourse among children of school age from different families is almost entirely limited to the contacts associated with going to school. Outside of school, children return to their homes and families. They do not play with one another after school is dismissed; rather, they are required to go home. Free association of youths is restricted to those of postschool age. School children play with their siblings, close relatives, or the children of neighbors who are also close family friends. The American urban phenomenon of two children playing daily with one another when their parents are barely acquainted, is unthinkable in St. Denis. Family solidarity is too great. The significance of this fact, relative to the present consideration, is that the family regulates the sequence of orientation of children within itself. Complexes of privileges and duties in the family, as well as distinctive dress, identify the successive periods of a child's social development, as we have seen for preschool children. The school, with its rigid hierarchy of classes, corresponds with the family scheme and is used to some extent by the family to introduce stages with definite limits into its sequence of orientation. Thus, when children start school, they experience an abrupt change of status, which was only gradually acquired before there were schools. Completion of school is another stage, given emphasis by the change of status of the child in the family and parish. The family does not capitalize on the minute sequence of grades to identify children with various stages of social education.

Because of the lack of social contact among school children outside their own families, the age-grade system in the school has no opportunity to function independently of the instructional scheme except in so far as the family adapts some of its periods to its own ends. School grades do not have much social unity for another reason—the one-room school. Pupils in four successive grades all sit in the same classroom. Students in the same grade do not even sit together, a device employed to keep them from cheating and to separate unruly students. The boys and girls sit in different sections; so the gender distinction is the one which is emphasized by the arrangement of the pupils. All the schools of the parish have the lower grades, but only two have the higher ones. This means that there is an actual change of school and a separate classroom for more advanced students. Boys in the higher classes do not wear black aprons to school, as the girls and younger boys do. This break comes between the ages of eight and nine. It marks a distinct mid-point between the beginning and end of schooling. The first, or preparatory, class is similarly isolated from the other classes by being sent home an hour and a half earlier in the afternoon.

As we saw earlier, the explicit purpose of the parish school is to make the children into good Catholics and good citizens, the two being synonymous in the local culture. The schools are also charged with the instruction of certain factual material. The methods of teaching fulfil both requirements. Some of the school work is purely religious study; the rest is general instruction in factual materials, presented in a strongly religious context. The pupil does not learn to speak correct French and to be a good Christian entirely separately. Moral and religious lessons, values, and concepts appear in the teaching of all subjects. Just as it is not possible to lead a purely secular life in the parish, so it is undesirable to introduce children to the techniques of life separate from some reference to moral values. In addition, the courses are planned for the rural student just as they are designed for the Catholic student. Study in the schools is organized so as to produce Catholic farmers. Concepts and values which have no place in such a life are omitted or attacked. The manner in which the children are oriented into, and fitted for, life in the local parish is best seen in the manner of instruction itself.

Each teacher instructs at least four different grades, which all sit together in the classroom. The subjects she is to teach and the time she devotes to each is predetermined by the provincial board. Classes meet five days a week, the week-ends being free. There are five and a half hours of school a day except for the *preparatoire*, which has less. In the third year after preparatory, the time per day is distributed among the various subjects as follows: French grammar, 2 hours; religion, $1\frac{1}{4}$ hours; arithmetic, $1\frac{1}{4}$ hours; history, $\frac{1}{3}$ hour; English, drawing, reading, and geography, each ½ hour once a week.[6] The relative amount of religious instruction is indicative of the emphasis of the instruction. Morning sessions begin with prayers, with all the pupils on their knees, followed by catechism study. The afternoon classes begin with a rosary and religious study. The schools give the children the material they are expected to learn and believe. Pupils would no more question the veracity of the history the teacher presents than the catechism she teaches. The rural culture can have schools which teach concrete reactions to life's problems, for the society is based on one acceptable way of life. This is in contrast to the urban community, where there is no "one way of life" for the school to pass on.

The texts employed in St. Denis schools are perfectly adapted for the orientation of the child into the local culture. The following list of titles of short readings in a French reader shows how the selections employ religious, moral, agricultural, and ethnic patriotic material in teaching the reading of French.[7] The child grows accustomed to thinking in these terms, and they are precisely those he will need in parish life. Titles in the reader include: "Une lettre à la vierge," "Générosité récompensée," "Sainte Cécile," "La Pomme de terre," "Mort de Napoléon Ier," " 'Es-tu là, Jésus?' " "Lourdes," "Héroisme de Dollard," "St. Louis de Gonzague," and "La Fuite en Egypte." Similarly, the French grammar reflects the cul-

[6] In the following years the distribution of time changes. The hours per week devoted to each subject are: French, 3 hours and 40 minutes; arithmetic, 3 hours; religion, 1 hour and 40 minutes; history, 1 hour and 40 minutes; English, 1 hour and 15 minutes; geography, 1 hour; hygiene, agriculture, manners, drawing, 30 minutes each. The school time not included in these instructional periods is spent writing exercises and studying.

[7] L'Abbé J. Roch Magnan, *Cours français de lectures graduées* (Montreal: Beauchemin, 1902).

ture in its choice of exemplary sentences: "The fear of the Lord is the beginning of wisdom"; "A well-reared child obeys his father, his mother, and his superiors"; "How good God is!"[8] These examples not only teach the child proper sentence structure and the correct use of commas and exclamation points but, by inference, teach the child to fear God, who is good, and to obey parents and superiors. To use their distinction, the child is being educated as well as instructed.

History is a discipline, the presentation of which permits even greater opportunity to give the pupils a certain religious and national philosophy. The manner in which this is achieved is seen in typical extracts from the *Histoire du Canada*, used in the last four years of school.[9] The italicized passages demark its own emphases.

The third of August, 1492, Columbus and a hundred hardy mariners came out of the Cathedral of *Palos*. They had just begged the Very High to bless their perilous enterprise. The crowd accompanied them to the port. *"In the name of Christ, unfurl the sails,"* ordered Columbus. . . . . His genius showed him there (to the west), far away, new lands peopled by idolators; his faith pressed him to subjugate these nations to the *cult of the true God*.[10]

May 18, 1642, the flotilla which carried Maisonneuve and his settlers landed at the foot of Mont Royal. They jumped to the earth, fell on their knees, and thanked God. Then they erected an altar, which Mlle Mance decorated with flowers and greenery. Father *Vimont* celebrated Mass there. All day long the Holy Sacrament remained exposed. *Jesus the Host took possession of the island of Montreal.*[11]

The piety of our ancestors was always their strength and their consolation. The thought of God dominated their life. In all the families, prayers were said in common morning and evening. . . . . The old Canadians observed Sunday religiously; they often traveled great distances to be at church on that day.[12]

[8] E. Robert, *Nouvelle grammaire française* (Montreal: Les Clercs de Saint Viateur, 1906). These and subsequent translations are my own.

[9] Les Clercs de Saint Viateur, *Histoire du Canada* (Montreal: Les Clercs de Saint Viateur, 1915).

[10] *Ibid.*, pp. 5 and 6.   [11] *Ibid.*, p. 39.   [12] *Ibid.*, pp. 137 and 138.

These quotations typify the manner in which history is presented. "History" means Canadian history to the French Canadian. That is the history he learns as a child. Through its study he learns the great pious and hardy tradition from which he sprang. He learns that the French were able to colonize Canada through constant direct divine intervention. The history of French settlement is the history of Canadian miracles. These things all strengthen the growing religious beliefs of the child. The history of the struggle with the English leaves the individual full of the proper attitudes to maintain his ethnic unity in the face of English domination. The attitude is so thoroughly imbued into these rural people, who have no actual contact with the English, that the antagonism is one that can be counted on in political campaigns. Geography, like history, gives the student the set of biases which will best carry on his culture. Contentment with the local milieu is actually taught, as is man's direct relationship to nature, upon which the local society exists.

The climate of the province, very cold in winter and very hot in summer, is agreeable and salubrious in all seasons. To live, man has need of nourishment, clothing, and shelter. That is why Divine Providence has put at his disposition the *natural riches*—animals, plants, and minerals. *Agriculture* is the art of cultivating the soil to make it produce not only the best plants for the nourishment of man and domestic animals but also those which, like flax and cotton, furnish the threads for weaving clothes. At the same time, the farmer raises or nourishes *domestic animals*, which are most useful, whether by their work, by their meat, by the milk which they give us as food, or by the wool and the leather from which we make our clothes and shoes, etc. Enjoying a propitious climate and possessing a fertile soil, the province of Quebec is particularly fit for *agriculture*, and happily working the fields is the preferred occupation of our population.[13]

This same text devotes only one-half a page to the cities of Quebec, enumerating and locating them and stating

[13] Les Frères des Ecoles chrétiennes, *Géographie illustrée* (Montreal: Les Frères des Ecoles chrétiennes, 1922), p. 21.

which are bishoprics. In a more advanced geography the
students learn the following about languages, facts which
correlate with the instruction they receive concerning
odious anglicisms:

The *French language*, because of its clarity and its precision, is the
diplomatic language of the entire world; that is to say, it is employed in
the treaties between several countries, at the courts of kings, etc. It is
also the language of *scholars*. We French Canadians speak the French
language because we are descendants of the French. We should be
proud of having the heritage of so beautiful a language, and we should
endeavor to speak it well. . . . .

The *English language* is also very widespread in the world because
of the numerous English colonies. The Irish used to speak *Gaelic*. Under the pressure of England they had almost abandoned their national
language for the English language, but today they are recommencing
with ardor to learn and speak it.[14]

Having thus warned against the danger of losing the national language by adopting an inferior one, the discussion
of human geography goes on to religions. Christian sects
are given a factual discussion which leaves the pupil with
no question as to the superiority of his own type. From
the point of view of social orientation of the child, he is
given the proper attitudes to continue the cultural tradition:

Christianity is the doctrine of Jesus Christ. During the centuries
several sects have separated from the Catholic church. These are: (1)
the *schismatics*, widespread particularly in Russia; (2) the *Protestants*,
divided today into a great number of sects. The *Catholic religion* counts
400,000,000 *faithful*, spread throughout the whole universe, and each
day the missionaries win new souls to it. *The work of the propagation of
the faith*, established throughout the world, has for purpose, by prayer
and by charity, to aid the missionaries in converting the infidels. Our
Holy Father the pope, the head of the Catholic church, resides at *Rome;*
that is why the Catholic church is called *Roman*.[15]

[14] Les Frères maristes, *Atlas géographie* (Montreal: Les Frères maristes,
1931), p. 16.

[15] *Ibid*, pp. 16 and 17.

In no subject is there any relaxation of the principle of simultaneous moral and intellectual training. English grammar accomplishes this by the lessons taught in sentence examples. The language classes capitalize on the fact that language is the expression of ideas and emotions, and teach the language structure in a context of ideas and emotions which are proper in the local society. In studying English the student uses these ideas as being of apparent equal truth:

> Champlain was a great man.
> Sin is death.
> Drunkenness is a dangerous passion.
> Virtue is lovely.
> Dancing is dangerous.
> Gold is precious.[16]

To illustrate the translation of *jamais*, the pupil studies the sentence: "I belong to God and to the Roman church forever." Likewise, the vocabularies are those with local significance.[17] Kin terms are given in their entirety. Professions and trades suggest by their order of presentation the accepted superiority of some: bishop, priest, parish priest, clergyman, lawyer, doctor, notary, schoolmaster, baker, shoemaker, etc. Foods are those eaten regularly at home: tea, coffee, soup, beef, apples, syrup. Names of holidays are those of *fêtes d'obligation* and times of fast or abstinence. A two-page list of "country" vocabulary is given, but there is no corresponding "city" section. Even arithmetic problems are given in terms of local situations. The new arithmetic text has more material of an extraneous nature than the old one and more than any other local text. Still, many of the problems in it are in terms of land divisions, crops, corded wood, steeple shadows, and other

---

[16] J. E. Chamberland, *English Grammar* (Quebec, 1915), pp. 131 and 189.

[17] Abbé A. Nantel, *Nouveau cours de la langue anglaise* (Montreal: Beauchemin, n.d.).

familiar concepts. One of these, which is by no means unusual, reflects the importance of kin patterns in the culture
in typical context:

A person leaves, on dying, his fortune to six relatives, of whom three
are fourth degree, two are fifth degree, and one is sixth degree, with the
condition that they will share in the division inversely to their degree of
relationship. The sum to be divided being $395,000, what will be
the share of each?[18]

The preceding consideration of texts is intended to show
the manner in which materials are presented in the major
school studies. The catechism was not discussed, as its
content is obviously purely religious. Its question-and-
answer form and the manner of teaching, whereby the
pupil responds to set questions with the memorized answers, pervade the other disciplines, particularly history
and geography. The materials in these two subjects, as
we have seen, are best adapted to rigid instruction, like
that in the catechism. Throughout all the studies one is
impressed with the way in which they are designed to
orient the child into his particular rural, Catholic, French-
Canadian environment. They may be accused of narrow-
ness and bias only as any culture may be similarly accused.
The fact that the local schools give no width of vision, no
world outlook, means that they prepare the children for a
life of limited scope. As long as these limits correspond
with those of the culture, the schools create no functional
problems in the society. If the children's schooling gave
them a wide, unbiased outlook full of values not achievable
locally, the children would grow into dissatisfied adults,
who would not continue in the traditional ways of life.
Any society persists only by passing on the modes of life
which have proved successful under its particular system.

[18] Les Frères des Ecoles chrétiennes, *Arithmétique* (Montreal: Les Frères des
Ecoles chrétiennes, 1926), p. 251.

Behavior not recognized in the traditional ways of life is socially undesirable because it is apt to raise functional problems in the traditional system. If such behavior is allowed or encouraged, it must be integrated into the culture and adjusted to the other mores.

Some provincial politicians feel that limited rural education, provided by $130-a-year teachers, is adequate to prepare children for the traditional rural life. However, education is such a symbol of urban progress that no man in the government dares openly to suggest that a culture which persisted for centuries without schools does not need them now in a highly developed form. Urban values are conceived of as provincial values, and more advanced education must be provided wholesale to get ahead. There is some excuse for this position. Many a rural son becomes an urban citizen. The schooling we have described ill fits him for such a role. He is not well oriented by his school training and is at a disadvantage with men of wider and more thorough schooling. This situation used to be taken care of by the system of convents and colleges, where such higher education was provided for children who were leaving the rural milieu. The expense of such training shuts out many rural sons who are now obliged to go to the city untrained, since there are no other economic outlets. Small professional schools aid to some degree. The Catholic education board for the province feels the necessity of giving the rural child a training which will better fit him for urban life; at least the trend in its policy would indicate this to be the case. Possibly educational progress is being measured in urban terms for the whole province. In any case, the elements of urban orientation which enter rural education will serve less adequately to orient the rural child destined to stay on the farm. The discontent of the rural youth with country life, which is already appearing, may well be increased by education which stresses urban culture and values.

Going to school implies more than the moral education and instruction which the child receives from the teacher. The social world of the school child includes the other children who go to the same school. New patterns of behavior must be developed with these people who are outside of the kin group. New social controls support the new behavior patterns. The ridicule of fellow-children is feared, for it temporarily isolates the child from the group. Before the child started school, he felt no unity with this group; but once a member, status must be maintained. Now voluntary isolation is unpleasant.[19]

The school children have opportunity for rather free social intercourse during the quarter-hour recreation periods in the forenoon and afternoon. These periods are largely unsupervised, the teacher intervening only in cases of physical conflict. Gender and age distinctions are those emphasized during the play periods. Boys and girls amuse themselves in separate groups, no matter what their age. Except during the winter, the recreation period is passed outdoors. Little girls have fewer actually organized games than the boys. The girls run after one another, dance around in circles, or talk and laugh in couples or groups. Little boys amuse themselves by running also, often joining hands and running down the hill in a line. They also play hide-and-seek, tag, and a game called *souris*, in which the children file between two boys who join their hands over the heads of the moving line. By dropping their arms the boys try to catch one of the "mice." Larger boys play games with balls, while the older girls usually just talk.

Indoor amusements are similarly divided but with less

[19] This is probably more the result of the early social conditioning of the child in the family than his instinctive gregarious nature.

emphasis on the gender division. Younger children make string figures and folded and cut paper objects. Making paper boats all winter to release on the swollen streams in the spring is typically a boy's amusement. Knowledge of how to make the string and paper figures is continued only in the school-age group. The young children learn from the slightly older ones, who abandon the use of their knowledge about halfway through school. By the time they leave school, the techniques are already being forgotten. These play techniques are replaced by new ones, centering around cards. The traditional game of *quatre septs* is learned by both sexes and played by both as adults. The knowledge of card tricks of a non-sleight-of-hand variety is typical of a certain social group—young men in their twenties, whose interests are centered in the city, whence the tricks have come.

In the case of both outdoor and indoor amusements it is noticeable that those typical of the older children require special equipment—balls and cards. The association of the object with the amusement of a particular age-grade is a socially important one. By acquiring the equipment the child identifies, to some extent, with the age group which employs it. Likewise by abandoning these objects, connections with lower groups are severed. The young school child wants to have cards, ice skates, and a bicycle, because these amusements are those of postschool children. The postschool boy abandons his ball and sled because they are "childish": they identify him with the younger children. In St. Denis the amusements and special equipment are little developed, skates being far from general and bicycles being used for practical, more than amusement, purposes. The relation of amusements to age divisions is allied to the concepts of physical and mental capabilities which every society formulates in terms of some age-grading scheme.[20] Thus, when the game "monopoly" was introduced in a St. Denis family, there was immediate consensus that even the advanced school children could not play it. The game was introduced by an adult and was put in the context of other adult games. The commercial aspect of the game added to the feeling that it was for adults.

It is during his school years that the individual shifts his position in the family from non-co-operative infancy to fully co-operative adulthood. Whereas almost nothing was expected of the preschool child, the school child acquires specific duties involving increasing responsibility. The girl helps her mother and older sisters more and more; the boy, his father and brothers. The patterns of division of labor are thus acquired, and gender distinctions are more firmly fixed. Young boys drive the buggy, stack wood, carry lights to the barn, bring in the cows, and assist in pulling flax. Boys nearing the completion of school tend the animals, plow, sow, cultivate, harvest, and thresh—in fact, they take over all the men's work necessary to aid father and such older brothers who are still at home. As the first sons leave to establish elsewhere, there is usually need for *mains d'œuvre*. Girls who are just starting school are expected to help at home in their free time, knit, sweep the house, set the table, dry dishes, make beds, and do other simple household tasks. As they grow older, they learn to milk, cook, wash, spin, and weave—activities which occupy them in postschool days. Force of necessity may disturb the normal division of labor. Lack of girls in a family may result in the boys having to milk or to set the table, activities which in such a case are not ridiculed in this community of close family economic units.

[20] Amusements also have significant relationship with certain social subdivisions, such as class, with which we are not concerned here. Thus, the knowledge of bridge indicates a group in St. Denis with more urban contact—priest, storekeeper, and certain young men looking for work in the city.

But if girls are in the family, no boy would think of doing these tasks.

Between the ages of ten and fifteen all children pass through two more important *rites de passage—grande communion* and graduation from the local school. These ceremonies create a definite break between childhood and young manhood and womanhood. For the religious ceremony the adolescent wears ritual clothes for the first time in a rite in which he is an important figure. Some have worn church vestments regularly as choirboys; others have worn mourning for members of their families; but this is the first time distinctive dress is associated with a change of the individual's own status.[21] The girls all wear white dresses and veils; the boys wear dark suits, white shirts, ties, and armbands. When the bishop comes to the parish for this confirmation ceremony, all the houses are decorated with bunting, religious flags, and French tricolors. Confirmation, or *grande communion*, makes possible equality with adults in the religious life. Actually, not until after school is finished does the religious behavior of the adolescent entirely correspond with that of adult parishioners, as school children always have to confess as a group and study catechism. Boys leave the choir during this period, however, and take their places in the pews of their families. This rite having been passed, death of the individual would be followed by full burial and postburial ceremony: funeral, Masses for the soul, mourning, and the anniversary funeral. Church regulations concerning fast days do not affect individuals under twenty-one, but abstinence rules are effective even before first Communion. The early religious life of all parishioners is marked by the

---

[21] Becoming an acolyte and wearing vestments imply previous *petite communion* but do not correspond with it, nor do all boys experience this ritual dressing after *petite communion*.

progressive acquisition of obligations and privileges. As the number of religious duties increases, the number of sacred and social benefits is augmented. Old age is marked by the dropping-off of obligations, while the privileges remain.

Upon leaving school the adolescent's social world experiences another change, corresponding to its expansion at the time of beginning school. This change is dependent upon the change in religious status as well as the completion of school. The social world of interpersonal contacts is extended to correspond practically with that of adults. The young man, particularly, experiences a wider range of contact. He now goes visiting, to participate in *veillées*. Such parties include the extended family-neighbor familiarity group but represent an extension of personal relations, as such visiting by school children is rare. *Veillées* at one's own house have always been a source of widened contact; but now the individual becomes a participating member of the group, playing cards rather than watching, and drawing social attention without fear of reprimand. There is still a difference in the emphasis of interpersonal relations between adolescents and adults. The adolescent's most intimate relationships outside of the family are with others of his special social group. This postschool group represents the accumulation of successive age groups which have passed out of the schools. It includes unmarried males between the ages of fifteen and thirty. The solidarity of this group is to be seen in those who gather at the post office to get the evening mail, in the knots of men who talk before and after church, and in the crowd of unmarried youths in front of the store on fair evenings during lax seasons. A fifteen-year-old schoolboy may not even receive a salutation from the postschool group, while a boy of the same age who has finished school is free to joke and playfully hit much older unmarried men. When one of these individuals marries and has children, the bonds with the old group are severed or weakened, and he associates with other married men. Whenever people gather together at a private home or public meeting, they divide into groups according to sex and marriage status, the younger children either being absent or peripheral to the groups. Thus, at *veillées* the young children are put to bed, the married adults begin the evening in the *salon*, and the unmarried young people in the big kitchen. If a man remains unmarried and stays in the community until he is past thirty, he begins to be classified as an adult bachelor, and his interpersonal relations begin to be more with married people. A married youth, however, no matter what his age, is identified with the adult group. Some feeling for the depth of this division into married and unmarried may be gained from this statement, directed against a young man of thirty and his long-promised fiancée: "They talk about things only married people should talk about." The context of this statement concerned the way this couple fraternized with young married couples. Actually, the couple, whose marriage had long been frustrated by economic difficulties, was trying to identify with the group it wished to enter. The quotation was a bit of gossip designed to force acceptance or re-assert the unobserved social usage.

Entrance to the postschool group of unmarried men means the adoption of certain new behavior patterns. Long trousers are worn without exception. Boys begin to smoke about this time.[22] The mild brand of tobacco with which they start bears the stigma of youth for other

[22] Boys begin smoking late in St. Denis, compared with other parts of Quebec. One boy in the parish started smoking a pipe before he was ten, not an unusal thing elsewhere. The pattern of postschool smoking is probably local.

smokers. Adult interests, such as politics, become very important. The group is socially designated by common membership in the religious society Les Enfants de St. Joseph. The postschool group of unmarried females has an equivalent society, La Congrégation des Enfantes de Marie. Girls experience a similar change of status upon finishing school. Although their outside contacts are markedly less numerous than those of the men, and finishing school means returning home to have really fewer outside relations than while at school, the girl's social sphere is extended by the possibility of attendance at *veillées*. She is likewise in a position to accept suitors, and her social behavior is strongly affected by this fact. Girls develop an interest in fashions and personal appearance. By the age of twenty they have started getting permanent waves, and they put their hair in curlers on Saturday nights so that it may look well at Mass the next day. Special clothes are required for this and party occasions. Both the young men and young women today follow styles in clothes which are diffused from the cities. The women are primarily concerned with finding a mate, and they follow the fashions more than the men in this competition. Men, with the exception of those interested in finding urban employment, are less interested in shifting modes.

The interests of the young person out of school become increasingly centered upon the selection of a manner of economic establishment. For the man, his establishment, independent of the economy of his family of orientation, is not only obligatory but also necessary before he can marry and assume his next social role, that of the head of a family of procreation. For the young woman, the two are simultaneous in marriage. If she does not marry, she is faced with the same problem as the man, that of setting herself up in a household independent of her in-

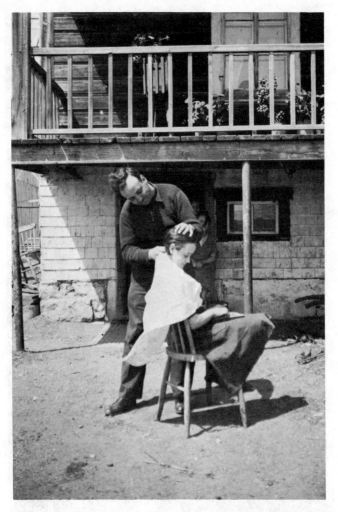

A Saturday Haircut for Sunday

An Old *Canadien*

heriting brother. Even during the last years of school, children begin to formalize their desires for the future in terms of actual possibilities. Before then children have definite ideas of what they will do as adults, but these are convictions based more upon imitation than practical possibilities. The boy playing "farmer" does so because he wants to identify with farmers. Similarly, the girl playing "mother" has little concern for the large old-maid population of the parish.

Long before the child seriously considers his own future, his parents and older siblings have done so for him. The previous study of the family cycle shows clearly that the same opportunities are not open for all the children of a family; also, that there is the definite attitude that the father is responsible to his children for their establishment. Although the responsibility rests with him, complete co-operation is expected from the child. The parent is supposed to help his offspring, not guarantee a livelihood. If the economic possibility of such parental help is slight, it devolves upon the child to look out for himself.

Because parents have in mind the eventual outlets open to a child, even when he is quite young, they can orient the child toward that particular occupation. This is true particularly in the case of male offspring, as marriage is a possibility for which girls can always be prepared. This parental conditioning of their boys is partly unconscious. The parents observe the potentialities of their children in the light of possible eventual opportunities. A child whose potentialities are directly and frequently stated to him by parents and siblings is strongly conditioned toward the employment of those abilities. As the requirements made of him are in accord with these attitudes, his interests are directed into one channel. The possible inheritor of the farm having been decided upon, or his position in the sequence of offspring being generally accepted, another child, who shows particular intelligence, may be considered worthy of a college education. The whole family will come to feel and comment upon his intelligence. He will be lauded in his grade-school achievements and excused from all possible farm work. He will be asked for help with lessons by his brothers and sisters. He will grow up to make what the parents consider a free choice as to whether he wants to go to college or not. Occasionally such orientation fails. In one case, such an "intellectual" boy, who by the distribution of male children was forced to do heavy farm work, professed a preference for farming and asked his father to pay the college money down on an available farm. The family now farms both the parental and the new farm and is grooming this and another son as inheritors. The son in question may even inherit the parental *terre*. The additional income from the second farm is making possible the college education of still another son, who is committed to the plan although still in grade school. When the possibility of this boy's becoming a farmer was raised before five members of his family, the immediate reaction of each was given these words: "He wants to go to college"; "He does not like farming"; "He has hands which are too clean"; "He has talent"; "He is too small for farming." Some of these expressed attitudes arise from the aptitudes which provoked his selection for college education. Others merely support the decision. All function to orient the child toward the goal selected. The interest of even an eight-year-old in a friendly young married woman may cause the parental comment before the child: "He should not get too interested in women, for he is going to become a priest."

Noninheriting boys know by the time they finish school that they will not receive the farm. The father may be able to assist the son, but those whose parents are financially unable to aid them must try to find some means of livelihood alone. There are a few opportunities to earn money locally. The clerk in the store is a young farm boy who eventually hopes to buy a farm. The *beurrerie* offers an opportunity to earn money and learn a trade. Road work and the *chantiers* in winter are sources of income. Government-subsidized land settlements attract a few more. Many boys develop special talents and skills on their own. Others become traveling salesmen or secure regular employment in the cities. At present, openings for untrained men are difficult to find because of unemployment in the cities.

In considering the progressive orientation of the individual from infanthood into an adult role in the society we have noted differences due to the position of the child in the sequence of children. This is not only important in inheritance, but the speed of orientation depends upon the family's need for the individual's services. First children are, therefore, apt to be called upon to assist the parents at earlier ages than later children, who are born into a family already well supplied with children helping the parents. Some of the influences these chance sequences have upon the personality of the individual offspring may be seen in the analysis of a typical household. The following list of the children with their ages attempts to characterize their most obvious personality traits on the basis of their overt social behavior:

Pierre *fils*, 27: Self-assured, frequently takes initiative, converses freely, face very expressive.
Joseph, 25: Retiring but not easily embarrassed, quiet, face placid.
Marie, 21: Quiet, domestic, gracious, dignified, efficient, assumes household responsibility and direction.
Thérèse, 20: Childish behavior, loud and ostentatious in groups, a

willing worker, some lack of initiative, more interest in clothes and jewelry than Marie has.

Georges, 18: Expressionless except for a silly smile with which he responds to kindness, very quiet and retiring, does simple manual jobs such as carrying water and wood, has great affection for animals.

Thomas, 13: Sullen, unhappy expression usually; enjoys making noise and doing things which he knows are disapproved of.

Jean, 11: Happy disposition, more sociable than Thomas but still very quiet.

Henri, 7: Happy and gay, easily embarrassed.

The temperament of each of these children is to a great degree the result of his social position in the family.

Pierre *fils* bears a large share of the farm responsibility in the family. As his father has become less active, the jobs of the farm have been thrown more and more on his shoulders. He is frequently called upon by the family to represent it officially at meetings or funerals. He has taken over his father's political interest and through it has come in contact in an active fashion with the wider circle of parish youth. His personality and temperament closely parallel those of his father, as a result of long contact and the transfer of duties and responsibilities to him. This transfer is not yet complete, but the acquisition of the social patterns of the father is tantamount to the acquisition of his social personality. Greater education and wider contacts of the son, largely made possible by the father, have given him a broader outlook. He is of a new generation and through his contacts with others of his own age he is more alive to present problems. His contact with the youths who cannot find openings in the city is more intimate than that of his father. On the other hand, he has never heard the old *conteurs de contes* or seen the big drying-ovens of flax in action. Such things have passed; and, as he has never experienced them, he feels no particular attachment to them. He will never feel their loss as his father does. Still, his father and family exert a stronger influence over him than his young village friends. Like his father, he does not smoke or drink, while many of his young friends do.

Joseph maintains the same family tradition for the same reasons. He is dependent upon his father for his start in life. This means that a complete unity of purpose and ideals must be maintained. Joseph's responsibility on the farm is markedly secondary to that of his elder brother. When feeding the animals, he may only help his father with the pigs, while Pierre *fils* is in full charge of feeding the cattle. Joseph never represents the family on any social occasion; and, when he does any responsible task independently of his father, he is usually accompanied by his brother, Pierre. Such menial work as driving people home in the sleigh after a *veillée* falls to his lot. When a *veillée de cartes* is in progress at his home, his father and brother inevitably start at the tables before him.

As Pierre *fils* acquired the duties and personality of his father, so Marie has gradually come into charge of most of the domestic work. It is she who prepares the meals, washes the dishes for her sister to dry, spins a great deal, has had a special weaving course at Ste Anne, reprimands the children when necessary, prepares the refreshments during the progress of a *veillée*, and sees that the guests are comfortable. It is Marie who already has a suitor. Her close contact with her mother in their combined domestic efforts has given her the interests and abilities of the mistress of a household.

Thérèse, only a year younger, has had a great deal less responsibility and lacks entirely the quiet reserve of her sister. She is apt to be boisterous, to call attention to herself; and her interests are still predominantly those of a child. Pictures, games, sports, and public gatherings thrill her to a greater extent. In spite of the fact that initiative has not been expected of her, she is a very frequent working companion of Anne. She is capable in her work and undoubtedly would at present respond to any opportunity for individual development of initiative.

Georges is a moron. He can go to church with the family and even was in the boys' choir for awhile until he proved himself incapable. At home he is ignored completely and cut out of all normal social contact with other members of the family. He eats with the younger children, but words are rarely addressed to him. His own statements may pass utterly unnoticed and unanswered. His mother is the only one who ever looks and smiles at him with any kindness. He is frequently sharply reprimanded; such reproaches making him cringe. This treatment has, of course, accentuated his deficiency and accounts for his love of animals, which treat him more humanely.

Thomas has no natural aptitude in school and is at present behind his younger brother, Jean, in the school system. This fact is frequently indicated by the parents in Thomas' presence, and Jean is constantly praised for his excellence in school. When Thomas is asked what he intends to become, the entire family says that they don't know what he's going to do, and express again his backwardness in respect to his brother. Thomas plays with his youngest brother, Henri, rather than with Jean.

There is a continual interest in Jean's school activity, in which he takes considerable pride. It is openly known that he is to be sent to the college at Ste Anne after he finishes school at St. Denis. He also knows that the family has hopes of his becoming a priest. His position in the family as a younger child is not altered by these facts, and so he remains a child more frequently seen than heard.

Henri, the last of the family, is still the baby and is petted and spoiled. As a result he is in perpetual good humor. Again, this spoiling does not infer that he must not submit to the age-grade superiority of his brothers. He submits, not willingly but of necessity, to their sharing of his playthings.

In addition to the influence of the role of an individual upon his personality, there is the subtle influence of unconscious imitation of others. Even this is a factor of role in the family, because those children who have the most contact with their parents will most closely resemble them in those intimate habits and mannerisms so closely identified with personality. This is particularly true between father and inheriting son. This son works in closer conjunction with his father than his brothers do. He always accompanies his father in his work and gradually assumes his duties. Even in relaxation they are usually together. Having worked together, they will come home to sit and smoke and talk. Other brothers will be helping with the farming also; and to the extent that they are thrown with their father, they, too, will tend to adopt his mannerisms and attitudes. If the father is loud-mouthed, coarse, and blustering, his inheriting son will certainly be that way too. If the father is quiet and religious, the son will follow the same pattern. Other sons, who are sent away to school or who get work outside the family as soon as they finish school, vary from the typical traits of the father. In all the families the similarity between inheriting son and father is very striking.

The close relationship between elder daughters and mother results in the same transference of attitudes and mannerisms. If these older girls marry and make room for others to be close assistants of the mother, all will experience this patterning. On the other hand, an unmarried eldest daughter may occupy this place continually, while her younger sisters marry without ever having had quite the same intimate contact with their mother. In the social life of the whole family the tempo is set by the father, the head of the house. Tradition dictates that men dominate the conversation, even in the family group, so that from generation through generation the whole atmosphere of the family gathering retains a stamp characteristic of the particular family.[23] This condition results from the transference of type from father to son and the suppression of new behavior which might result from marriage combinations introducing women of different temperament.

[23] L'Abbé H. R. Casgrain (*Une Paroisse canadienne au XVIIe siècle* [Montreal, 1912], p. 33) comments on the fact that families do preserve characteristic traits: "Le vieux type normand, avec sa tournure d'idées originales, ses allures franches, un peu brusques, avec sa jovialité et son esprit goguenard et *étrivant*, est reconnaissable aujourd'hui dans ces deux familles, aussi bien qu'il y a deux siècles."

CHAPTER X

FROM MARRIAGE TO MOURNING

AS YOUNG people begin to identify more completely with adults, they are increasingly concerned with the possibility of marriage. The young man's interest in self-establishment is greatly influenced by the fact that this is necessary before he can get married. Interest in, and knowledge of, sex has grown during school and subsequent years. The rate at which sex knowledge is acquired varies greatly among families and may even vary in the same family. Until boys of the more conservative families are in their teens, they are not even allowed to witness the serving of cows, mares, and sows or the birth of animals. In other families schoolboys are admitted to these sex-revealing situations. Women and girls are never supposed to witness them. Even in families where there is an endeavor to withhold sex knowledge from the child, farm life offers much opportunity for observing the difference of primary sex characters and witnessing the sex act among animals. Likewise, some animals have young which they nurse, while others of the same species never have young. All these things raise questions in the child's mind. When these questions are put to parents, they receive various kinds of treatment. In those families which try to continue the gipsy myth concerning the arrival of babies, the child will receive little help from his parents but will be made to feel that the questions are improper, indecent. Other parents do not try to hide from their offspring the basic truths of sex distinction, copulation, and birth. There is no detailed discussion, but the child's interest is guided to proper solutions rather than being thwarted. The idea that such matters are not proper topics of conversation is inculcated at the same time.

In all households children of the two sexes are segregated in separate bedrooms. When rather close supervision of the children's play is possible, it may be several years before a child learns the sex distinctions which parallel the gender differences he already knows. When the mother runs the house alone and has three or four children ranging up to five years of age, the normal situation in every young household, she cannot take care of the house, food, clothes, babies, and supervise the children's play in addition. Her children are, therefore, left much to their own devices. Unrestrained, their excretory functions are associated with no attitude of shame, and their performance before one another is only natural. Under such circumstances small children who have learned to distinguish between "boys" and "girls" on the basis of dress and haircut learn for themselves that there is a physical sex difference behind this gender distinction. These children learn the physiological difference between the sexes at least by the time they are four years old. Among children born later in the sequence of offspring, when their siblings are old enough to watch over them, opportunity for the discovery of physical differences is suppressed. This is particularly true in families which restrain the transmission of sex knowledge from older to younger children. Such restraint is never very effective between children of the same sex and of no great age difference. The interdiction of cross-sex discussions of sex, however, is almost completely effective. It fits into the pattern of separation of the sexes established on the basis of dress and pursuit. The gender distinction establishes dissociative attitudes with which the later acquired sex restrictions correspond. Similarly, within the same sex, attempted restriction of sex instruction is effective only across recognized division lines, such as the beginning and end of school.

As families vary in their attitude toward sex instruction, children whose parents and siblings suppress the subject can always find schoolmates who have superior sex knowledge about which they are willing or eager to talk. By the time children leave school, they are entering adolescence and know the basic sex facts. They have had no free social contact with the opposite sex since early childhood. Behavior patterns during the school years have accentuated the gender distinction by keeping them separate. With the completion of school begins a period in which the opposite sex becomes increasingly interesting. The opportunity for contact increases with the change of status. The adolescent moves with a group of young people of his own sex who frequently talk about the opposite one. Parties offer actual informal contact between the sexes, but there is supposed to be no really intimate contact before marriage. Chaperonage is strict in most families. Close vigilance of daughters is stressed by the *curé*, who also decries protracted courting periods. Ideally, the sexes should profess no interest in one another until ready for marriage, and even then the premarital period should not be long. Actually, there has always been a certain amount of premarital sexual relations. In the stricter families such a thing would be impossible, but it does occur even in respectable families. The poor families are generally conceived of as being less moral, and the actual facts support the popular opinion. The opportunities for sexual relations offered by berry-picking has given blueberry time that particular reputation. *Veillées* in distant parishes during warm weather offer further opportunity. In winter there is less possibility of privacy. Dances are under local clerical disapproval because of the drinking and intimacies which accompany them. On the whole, this particular region is probably more strict than any other part of Quebec. Local bachelors claim distant fields to be greener; and the greater informality, drinking, and dancing in the younger settlements would seem to support the idea. Still, bastard children have been born to St. Denis day-laborers' daughters. In the next parish one woman is reputed to have a family of sixteen such children. When there is a bastard birth, the *curé* tries to force the father to marry the mother "to make the child legitimate." In such cases the girl almost invariably goes to Quebec to bear her child, leaving it in the foundling hospital there.

Two new factors have increased the amount and the nature of illicit sex relations: the growing group of bachelors who never married because of economic reasons, and the increasing group of young men who must postpone marriage for the same reason. Some women in day-laborers' families are serving as prostitutes for this group of men. It is noteworthy that social degradation does correspond with economic degradation. In the young group, prolonged engagements are productive of premarital intercourse. Contraceptive knowledge is rare. The prostitutes and some of the young men who have worked in the cities know methods of contraception. A generally known abortive is a spoonful of mustard in a glass of gin or beer. It is supposed to be sure if not more than forty days have elapsed since conception. Contraceptives and abortives are not used in marital life. Extra-marital intercourse is still the exception. The average boy grows up to learn to refrain from such sinful behavior. Even transgressors usually confess, but their faith is not strong enough to correct their ways. Most boys will wait for marriage to satisfy their sexual desires in a manner which will not bring them into conflict with their society or their religion.

A young man should become financially able to marry in his twenties. From the girls he knows through parties and visits he has already chosen one who not only attracts him but whose family would probably approve and be approved of by his own kin. At this stage the girl may not even know of his interest. He then calls on her family at their home and sits and talks to the whole family group. The unusual nature of the call, that is, a single young man visiting the whole family and not just a male acquaintance, marks the visit for what it is. The girl will seat herself inconspicuously in the room and often says nothing at all. The young man talks farming and politics with her father and brothers and may leave without having addressed a single word exclusively to her. This is obviously an introductory stage when the young man is the center of family attention. Successive visits and occasions, such as dances and *veillées*, offer opportunity for the youth and girl to talk together. It is not unusual to ask the father for his daughter's hand after only a month of this visiting. The young man explains his financial situation and receives a tentative reply. The girl is not forced to marry any petitioner; but as there is no direct means for a girl to secure suitors, she usually welcomes the approach. The man is usually sure of her answer before he presents his suit to her father.[1]

After the young man has received a favorable response to his *grande demande*, the next step is to agree to terms for the marriage contract. The parents of the boy visit those of the girl at some appointed time. The meeting is strictly private between the two sets of parents. The

[1] In a recent case the suitor knew so little about the girl that when he asked the father for her hand it was only to find that she was already engaged.

couple concerned has no part in the proceedings; the parents are the only ones involved. This fact is reflected in the usual linguistic form, "I married my son (or daughter)," meaning, "I arranged his (or her) marriage." It is the fathers who marry them, by contract. The meeting of the two families is a very unstable social situation. Unless there had been some common ground of kinship, friendship, or trust, the proposed marriage would not have reached even this stage. The two families meet to seal a bond. If this feeling of unity between the groups is strengthened during the meeting, the contract binding them together through the marriage may be accomplished. If the unity is broken, the marriage is impossible, for it would link incompatible families. There is, therefore, a need for unity. The other factor is that the contract is a commercial bargain with implication as to the social value of the marrying individuals. It is a potential conflict situation. If the conflict overthrows the feeling of unity, there will be no marriage. This happens not infrequently, particularly in farming families, which have more to bargain about.

A marriage contract involves several things: the grant of the father to the son, of the father to the daughter, and the manner in which the property will be held by the new couple. The legal possibilities are understood by both families, and the contract is arranged during informal discussion between them. When the decision is reached, the contract is drawn up by a notary. If both families are poor, there may be no contract. In this case the couple lives under a *communauté legale*, each person having an equal interest in all the goods and money. Inheritance is regulated by law if there is no will or contract. Contracts are of two general types: first, community of property, like the *communauté legale* but with any desired varia-

tions, such as excluding real estate from the *communauté*
to keep it in the family name should the man die without
male issue;[2] and, second, the separation of property. If a
large money *dot*, or dowry, is given the girl, the latter form
is apt to be followed and the husband's father required to
sign over property to her. Except in unusual circumstances
the *dot* consists of household goods: linens, dishes, blankets, etc. A man may even give livestock as part of the
dot if his son-in-law has land and only a few animals. Land
never goes to the daughter. Farmers prefer *communauté*
contracts to those of separation. The wife thus "shares
in returns from her years of labor on the farm." Separation of property contracts are preferred in families which
live by commerce, so that the failure of the man in business will not ruin the wife as well. Wage-earners follow the
pattern of farmers.

As the typical farm contract is the *communauté*, the *dot*
given the girl is actually given to the couple and the grant
of the father to the son is given to both parties of the
marriage, except when otherwise stipulated. Marriage
contracts are often the documents which transfer land
from father to son. The man is the administrator of the
communauté; so the father can sign over the property he
holds with his wife as long as he provides for her support.[3]
A testamentary clause may also be inserted in the marriage
contract, and the inheritance portion so designated for the
bride can subsequently never be diminished.

The considerations of a father in a contract of marriage
are seen in the following discussion by a farmer possessing
two *terres*, both still in his own name.

[2] This clause is becoming unpopular, as it may pass on heavy indebtedness.

[3] The most widely known local notary judged that farms were deeded over
to sons when they were between 25 and 30 years old and when the fathers were
between 55 and 60.

If one of my sons were marrying, I might give him one of the pieces of land and a house, with the stipulation that he return two thousand dollars to me. Naturally, I wouldn't have to do this if there were not other sons to provide for. The farmer usually does well to place two or three of his sons and give the others an education so that they can earn a living for themselves. I might give, in addition, six cows, two horses, a vehicle, and implements. If it were a girl who was marrying, it would be quite a different matter. In that case I would attempt to secure a reasonable amount for her.[4] In giving the boy the land I would also stipulate that, if he should die within a year without children, the land would revert to me and that the wife should receive a thousand or two thousand dollars so that the land wouldn't go to a stranger.

The parish is informed of the actual wedding by the reading of banns from the pulpit on Sunday. Three banns are supposed to be read in the parish of each party on three successive Sundays. The socially proper thing is to "buy" two of them, so that only the third and last is read. The poorer day-laboring families are usually obliged to have all the banns read and to have a less expensive wedding. The marriage ceremonies range in cost from a five-dollar wedding in the sacristy to one for twenty-five dollars in the decorated church. The bells also indicate the "class" of the ceremony. The bride and groom are dressed in new clothes of a type which can later be worn for Masses and *veillées*. The couple and parents arrive and depart in automobiles, if at all possible. The cars are decorated with colored paper streamers. Custom also dictates that the groom wear kid gloves.[5] Brides do not carry flowers, and there are no attendants. The marriage ceremony takes place in the parish church of the bride. The bride and groom have special prayer benches and overstuffed leather chairs near the center of the Communion rail and in front

[4] He would only agree to a contract in which the boy brought a "reasonable amount" to the *communauté*.

[5] This whole wedding-style complex comes from the cities, partly by way of the French newspaper's social-column pictures.

of the pews. Behind and to either side are similar benches
and chairs for the father of each or his closest male relative. The couple first go to the sacristy to confess. After
they return, two representatives of the Enfantes de Marie
conduct the bride to the side altar consecrated to the Virgin. There the bride deposits her blue membership ribbon
on the altar, signifying her departure from the body of
unmarried girls and women. She returns to the groom, and
they advance to the Communion rail, where the service is
read and Communion is given. This is followed by the
celebration of the Mass.

Relatives of both the bride and groom attend this service. In addition there are many parishioners who attend
out of curiosity. After the ceremony the couple sign the
register and go to the home of the groom, where the fes-
tivities start. After weddings there is always obscene joking on the part of the unmarried men. During a delay,
while the newly married couple sign the register in the
sacristy, someone remarks: "They have probably gone to
bed for a little while." Another: "He has a big nose, but
he looks capable of doing things tonight." This joking is
expressive of the break between the groom and his old unmarried associates. During the succession of wedding
veillées, first in the groom's parish and then in the bride's,
this mild obscenity is continued before the couple by
means of songs. There are various songs sung only during
wedding celebrations. Their content is directly related to
the marriage situation. A song consoling the mother of the
groom for the loss of her son brings tears to the mother's
eyes. Other songs console the bride for leaving her home
or extol the beauty of the church sacrament of marriage.
Many more refer to the wedding night, the long sequence
of babies, or sexual indulgence itself.

A short honeymoon to Quebec or Ste Anne de Beaupré

has become customary, in addition to the *veillées*. There are wedding cakes, which are usually dark but elaborately frosted in white. Presents from friends and relatives are not very elaborate or numerous: some cut glass, table linen, and a few other practical gifts. At the *veillées* the newlyweds are embraced by members of the opposite sex. The couple sit together in their circle of friends, holding hands all evening, an act which marks their new union and which is not publicly countenanced at any other time. The new allegiance of the bride is portrayed not only in her leaving the church ceremony to go immediately to the house of her husband but also in the traditional form of attending the first Sunday Mass after the wedding in the parish of the groom. The next Sunday Mass is attended in the parish of the bride, where further parties stress the new family union which has been created.

Marriage changes the social status of both parties. Ties with the unmarried group are broken actually as well as symbolically. The couple are now adults. They must mingle with married people or confirmed bachelors and old maids. (In these latter cases, the unmarried people must be past middle age to be admitted to the group without restraint.) The change of status is marked by changes in clothing for the woman. Long sleeves and long skirts are required. The hair is usually worn long and unwaved. Clothing tends to become drab and somber. This is partly related to frequent mourning, now that there are two lineages of relatives whose deaths must be recognized. In addition, the modes of girls are considered unbecoming for married women. Functionally, the attractive garb of the girl has served its purpose and can be discarded. The function of youthful dressing is recognized to be the attraction of the other sex. Waved hair for married women is not decried as short sleeves and skirts are, but the evil influence of the city is seen therein.

For a man the most definite mark of having attained social recognition is the growing of a moustache. This does not imply that all married men have them, although the majority do. The bachelor who is economically independent—in other words, who is a recognized adult parishioner—will also be likely to wear a moustache. Those unmarried men still dependent upon their families do not have them, although a few who are partially independent do. In farm families the inheriting son often grows a moustache before he marries, and invariably it is a smaller style than that of the father. Cases are frequent of men growing them upon marriage. Almost all of the men under thirty with moustaches are either married, inheriting sons, or economically independent.[6]

Marriage in St. Denis means that a new and regularly growing family is started. This new family of procreation involves the same parent-child situations as those we have discussed for the family of orientation, but this time considered from the parent's point of view. In addition to the problems of raising a family, adult status implies new civil and religious responsibilities for the man. The management of the home and occasional social contacts with relatives and neighbors fully occupy the young wife. The husband, besides bearing the full financial burden of the family and planning for his children, must be a participating member of the community. He is expected to "buy"

[6] Two interesting cases are related to the social symbolism of moustaches. One unmarried man in his early twenties grew a moustache, which he shaved off after a few weeks. Inquiry revealed that, just before he grew it, he had signed a good contract with the storekeeper to act as clerk. The second case occurred after an election which defeated the party of the local *cantonnier*. This individual shaved off a large walrus moustache in an effort to prove himself "a different man," so that the victorious party would reappoint him.

a pew in the church and to contribute to school upkeep and road projects. He will be vitally interested in local and provincial politics as they affect him directly financially. Meetings of the *conseil* will be important, and he may eventually have public recognition by membership in it. It will be noted that these civil interests and duties arise from property ownership or dependence upon politically controlled money. Married farmers are all concerned with the management of the local *beurrerie*, as they have a like economic interest in it. These interests are typical of married life because marriage is possible only through the acquisition of property, which automatically involves participation in the civic activities. The religious status is also affected by the acquisition of property. The tithe applies to heads of farm families. The head tax and the responsibility for renting a pew fall on any family head, regardless of his economic basis. Payment for Masses for deceased members of the man's family of procreation are his responsibility, even to the Masses which will be sung for him after he dies. When that time arrives, his sons will be involved in responsibilities to their respective families of procreation.

During his lifetime a man may achieve for himself and family a certain amount of prestige by occupying the elective offices of the *conseil, fabrique,* or *municipalité scholaire*. The responsible positions in these bodies, such as the mayor and secretary-treasurer, fall to men recognized as capable and reliable. The prestige of election to any or all of these bodies is slight, as almost every farmer eventually fills several of these posts. A nonfarmer, however, must be a very outstanding man to receive such recognition. Nonlanded men are less eligible, since they have less actual interest in these bodies in terms of their own economies. Day-laborers have not, as yet, ever been elected to these official groups. Another possibility of obtaining recognition is in excellence of farming. Such recognition comes through the winning of provincial agricultural prizes and medals. The farm women submit home products to contests as well, but they derive their major satisfaction from the cash prizes. Women are not supposed to receive general social recognition apart from their identity with their husbands. Among the women of the parish, there is individual recognition. One may be known for her weaving or her ability to make paper flowers; another for her slovenly housekeeping. Such evaluations are, however, little known by the men. The excellence of a man's cattle, on the other hand, is general knowledge with both sexes.

As adults become old and shift their responsibilities to their children, their religious duties are lightened as well. Old people are not expected to go to Masses of obligation or to keep fast-rules. Abstinence from flesh food on Friday continues, just as it was one of the first rules to apply to the child. It is considered wise to keep the aged in a state of purity, ready for death, by continuing Communion and confession, although the latter is not required as frequently as formerly. In spite of the apparent laxity in the religious behavior of the aged, it is only superficial. The concessions are made because of the disabilities of age. Old people spend a great deal of time and thought in religious matters, prayer, and contemplation. They are concerned with preparing themselves to die. The greater freedom of youth in this respect is clear in the statement of a man in his sixties who refused to break a religious fast, although young people over twenty-one were doing so: "I am getting old; I must be more careful."

Death itself is succeeded by a series of ceremonies and special usages which strengthen the family and community groups. These social units have just experienced the loss of a member. The customs which follow the loss reassert the solidarity of the groups. Funeral customs are also final *rites de passage*, by means of which the individual gradually passes out of the society. Death actually becomes less abrupt thereby. Social death, in the sense of all social bonds being broken, is not completely accomplished for years after the physical death of the individual.

It is general knowledge that doctors say there are two aspects of death—apparent death, when a person is judged to be dead, and real death, when all life has passed from the body. This real death is supposed to occur about two hours after the apparent death, and it is with the passing of all life that the soul is supposed to leave the body. Final unction may, therefore, be administered shortly after persons have died sudden deaths which did not allow for administration by the priest. This sacrament is the last rite of the living, purifying them for the life beyond. It is therefore administered after death "on condition," the condition being that the soul is still in the body. Parishioners are not consistent in their belief concerning when the soul leaves the body. A person may describe the explanation of real and apparent death and follow it immediately with the statement that he thinks the soul goes to Judgment when death is but apparent. Whatever the opinion, this is a subject on which everyone has his own ideas. There is general fear of a sudden death which would send one to the beyond without final absolution. Three consecutive sudden deaths in the parish, each before remission of sins could be granted, was cause for the *curé* to tell the parishioners that God was punishing them. The post-mortem activity of relatives of persons who have so passed on is greatly increased. More Masses and prayers are necessary to get the soul out of purgatory.

The tolling of the church bells notifies the parish of the

death of one of its members. The manner in which the knell is rung indicates also the sex of the deceased. At the death of a woman each of the three bells is struck twice in slow succession. This series of six strokes, each dying away before the next is rung, is repeated three times; and then all the bells are tolled together. This whole process is repeated twice more. If it is a man who has died, there are three strokes on each bell instead of two. For the death of a child who has not yet had *grande communion*, the cycle of strokes, followed by the tolling, is only gone through once. There is no knell for babies, even if they are baptized.

The ringing of the bells is expressive of the parish-wide importance of an event. They are rung for the common prayers at Angelus, for Masses, baptisms, marriages, deaths, funerals, anniversary services, whenever the *bon Dieu* is carried to the sick, and once when the *curé* returned after a long illness. The explicit purpose in each case is different, although they all contain the common factor of public notification. It is significant that the bells are rung only to announce events of importance to the whole society. Partisan or family activities never receive this public recognition. It might be argued that baptisms and marriages are largely family affairs. From the point of view of the parish social unity, however, the beginning of a new life or of a new family of procreation is functionally as important as the loss of a member through death.

After an adult dies, his body is laid out in his home for three days. The undertaker in the next parish is called in for all but very small children.[7] The body is put in dark clothes and laid in a coffin. Tall electric or wax candles

[7] The undertaker is a bachelor. The *curé* of his parish has been trying to get him to marry, as there is considerable disapproval of his embalming girls and women. An old-maid school teacher of St. Denis stipulated in her will that she should not be embalmed for this reason.

are placed at the head and foot of the coffin, which is raised off the floor. A black crepe is hung beside the front door. A card stating the age, date of death, and time of funeral is attached to the crepe. During the three days and at least two nights before burial, the house is open to all parishioners. Visits are most frequent in the evening, when the day's work is done. Each night until burial there is such a wake. Friends and relatives of the deceased congregate at the house. One of the rooms is filled with chairs to accommodate them. Here they sit and chat, the men smoking as they talk about the deceased and his demise or any other subject of current interest. At hourly intervals the visitors go into the room containing the corpse and say three rosaries before returning to their conversation. At midnight a *petit lunch* is served. The youthful element at a wake is often playful and hilarious before the evening is over. This light vein is part of the traditional behavior pattern at wakes. Originally, heavy drinking was associated with them; but a provincial temperance movement, which originated in St. Denis, has limited the drinking at all kinds of *veillées*.

The clergy looks with disfavor on the light-hearted wakes because it considers hilarity incongruous with death. Referring to wakes, the *curé* told parishioners: "Lock your doors at nine o'clock." Nevertheless, many wakes have been continued late into the night "because they are an old custom." But even the *habitants* think that the custom will eventually lose its old character because of the clerical disapproval. Such a change will alter the social function of the institution. Family unity at the time of death will continue to be expressed, but the unity of the larger friendship group will not be strengthened by the common participation of these people in the wake. Further, the shift in the mood of the wake will be important.

At present there is ample opportunity for the expression of grief, but in addition the family and friendship group begins again its normal *veillée* behavior with its deceased member just in the next room, where they join him periodically. If the atmosphere of a normal *veillée* is removed, the shock of the loss of a member will be much greater once the regular social life is resumed.

The patterns centered around visiting the body of the deceased express varying forms of social unity between that person and other members of the society. The wake on the night before the funeral is only for the immediate family group. The other wakes traditionally include distant kinsmen, neighbors, and friends—the same group with whom the deceased was on intimate terms. Those families with whom there had never been friendship or marriage and for whom there was only dislike make no contact whatever with the family of the dead parishioner. Sympathy cards show the same divisions. These cards are bought from the local postmistress. Families who are not intimate but who are friendly toward the deceased may not attend any of the wakes. They do, however, send one or more representatives to the house to kneel on the prayer bench beside the open coffin, say some prayers for the person's soul, and leave a card of sympathy on the coffin before returning home. These cards are also left by those coming to the wake. The closest relatives and most intimate friends may leave cards stating that they have paid the priest to have so many Masses sung for the deceased. Thus the cards express variations within a wide range of social bonds.

The extended group of intimate friends and relatives is invited to come to the home of the bereaved family for prayers on the morning of the funeral. These people constitute the mourners who follow the body to the church after the prayers. The "class" of the funeral depends upon the amount of money which is paid. There are three such classes, ranging from fifty to one hundred dollars. It is usual for a man to provide for his own funeral and for that of his wife. For the first-class funeral the church is elaborately draped in purple and illuminated with purple and white lights. The High Mass at the main altar is served by three priests, while others say a Low Mass at each side altar. For the second-class funeral only one Mass is sung by three priests, and there is less church decoration. A third-class funeral Mass is sung by one priest, and the church is dark and little decorated. Second- and third-class funerals are equally effective in aiding the soul in purgatory. As three Masses are sung during a first-class *service*, it is more effective. In addition, a more elaborate funeral attracts more people to pray for the deceased. The main difference between the classes is conceived of as purely social, one of prestige. Here the explicit purpose corresponds largely with the social function of the different classes.

When a person is known to be old and critically ill, parishioners will often discuss what class funeral he will probably have. A large first-class funeral is a thing to be enjoyed. It is the most elaborate and impressive ceremony that the parish can have. Persons of moderate means or better are the only ones who can afford a first-class funeral. It is a prestige gesture supporting the family's good position in the society. The class of the funeral is announced by the *glas*. For the first class the knell rings the night before the funeral and that morning. The *glas* rung only in the morning indicates second class. Likewise, the elaboration of the undertaker's preparations is part of the same prestige pattern. Second- and third-class funerals use the horse-drawn hearse belonging to the parish *fabrique*.

Others are more likely to use the undertaker's Ford hearse. If the home of the deceased is close to the church, the mourners follow the hearse on foot. Otherwise they follow in a few automobiles and many carriages. Automobiles have social value at funerals, just as they do at weddings.

The bearer of the crepe-draped black cross precedes the hearse.[8] The bearer is the most intimate friend of the deceased. The cross is placed on the casket during the service and precedes the body to the grave. Beside the bearer of the cross walks the undertaker, dressed in a high hat and Prince Albert. Pallbearers are men selected from collateral relatives. Like the bearer of the cross, the pallbearers are marked by long black crepe ribbons on one arm. If the deceased is not an adult, the pallbearers are chosen from males nearly the same age as the dead person. Closer relatives are the chief mourners and directly follow the body. As sufficient collateral relatives of the proper age and sex are not usually available, neighbors are also asked to act as pallbearers. For large funerals distinguished individuals, such as the mayor, *marguilliers*, or councilors, may be asked to serve in this capacity. Social bonds determine the selection of these functionaries. Public indignation resulted when pallbearers for a young girl were selected from nonrelatives in the next parish.

There are modes of expressing various other social groupings. For a member of the Congrégation des Enfantes de Marie the society's banner and its members precede the body. The same is true for members of the Forestiers catholiques. The funeral Mass itself is distinctly a ceremony involving the whole parish. Unlike marriages, every family is expected to send at least one

---

[8] This symbol of the temperance society hangs on the kitchen wall of every house. The daily devotionals are directed toward it. A pressed white-metal crucifix from a coffin, palm-leaf braids, or other religious objects are often attached to it in the homes.

representative to a parishioner's funeral. Thus, upon the
death of a local school teacher, the members of a family
which had consistently tried to have her removed from her
position, because of a family feud, all attended the funeral.[9]
Her death was a parish loss, whether or not they liked her.
In contrast was the funeral of a pauper whose body was
sent to St. Denis for burial because his family had originally come from there. There was no wake; the simple coffin
was covered with a red pall; Communion was given, as the
Mass was not explicitly for the funeral; the Mass was an
hour earlier than customary; few people attended, and
they were considered curious; and the attendance of the
poor day-laborers was conspicuous. The burial of a baby
shows many parallels. A funeral for an eight-day-old baby
varies from the general form of that of an adult parishioner. There is no wake. The funeral is held in the afternoon without a Mass, signifying the infancy of the deceased. The use of white, instead of black, is to the same
end. Small children carry the white coffin and small white
cross. Others represent their families in their pews, some
with their parents. Children constitute over half of the
small group present, just as the poor attended the pauper's
funeral. Neither dead person was a real member of the
local community.

The church services finished, the coffin is carried into
the cemetery and lowered into the grave. The priest and
choir conclude the service at the grave, and those parishioners who have gone to the cemetery crowd up to look
in. It is not unusual for a member of the deceased's immediate family to request the undertaker to remove a
coffin ornament. The undertaker jumps down onto the cof-

[9] Their obvious lack of grief at the funeral increased hard feelings between
the families. The bereaved family actually blamed the death of the teacher on
the mischief of the school children from the hated family.

fin, still in his high hat, and pries off a crucifix, name plate, or handle. This souvenir of the departed one thereafter adorns the family *salon*. The family continues to express its relationship to the dead member through prayers, special Masses for his soul, and by wearing mourning. It has recently become customary to take up a collection at funerals to pay for further Masses. This system was started to aid those poor families which could otherwise have no subsequent Masses sung. Masses for the soul usually terminate with the anniversary service. This Mass is sung about a year after the funeral, but the approach of winter may cause the family to assemble for this service months before a year has actually passed. The anniversary service is an exact reenactment of the funeral service up to the point where the body is removed from the church. There is an artificial coffin, covered with a pall, which is censed and sprinkled just as the real one was. The classes of anniversary Masses parallel those of funerals, as do the preceding knells, decorations, attendance, etc. By this second burial the dead member of the society is further cut off from the society. Even this is not a complete severance, as his kinsmen may continue to wear mourning and to pray for him for a time after this ceremony.

Mourning customs have changed a great deal in the last fifty years, but the proper periods of mourning for women are about the same. In the old days it was the practice for a woman to wear full mourning for two years after the death of her husband and half-mourning at least another year. Wives past middle age very frequently wore full mourning for the remainder of their lives. Full mourning consisted of an entirely black dress with a veil from the front of the hat to the hem of the dress. This veil, thrown back over the hat, is still worn by one widow in the parish. To mourn the death of a father or mother, full mourning is worn for one year and half-mourning the next year. Half-mourning dress consists of white, gray, or heliotrope, but never red. Mourning for grandparents is for six months. In this and the following cases half-mourning is worn about the same length of time as full mourning. The local explanation of half-mourning is: "You're too accustomed to wearing black to change into bright colors at the end of the mourning period. That's why you go into half-mourning." For adult siblings the mourning period for women was six months with the veil in front and six months with the veil pinned back on the right side of the head. Men wore full mourning for six months for deceased siblings. Children wear mourning similar to adults and are mourned in full black for two months by parents. Deceased siblings and offspring must have finished school to be recognized by mourning. Men used to mourn by wearing a black suit or, if they could not afford that, a black armband. In addition, they wore black ties, black and white shirts, black-bordered handkerchiefs, and a three-inch square of crepe on the right side of their hats. These were the customs up until fifty years ago. Since that time they have changed, having become more "modern" through contact with industrial cities. Catalogues, which are closely followed for styles, may have also had an influence. Women who have been in contact with people from the States reflect the new attitude that the extreme mourning customs were "crazy" and that "it was terrible the way women used to be encumbered."

The major change in these customs has been the disappearance of the mourning veil. This gradually became shortened, so that twenty years ago it just reached the shoulders; and now a rudimentary veil is fastened to the hat but does not cover the face. Twenty years ago the mourning veil had changed from crepe de Chine to net. There has been a change for the men also, in that they

rarely wear the patches of crepe on the hat or the armbands but still wear black ties and black and white shirts.
There is a general tendency for shortening of the mourning
period. This is more true in the cities. Children wear
black; girls have black dresses and boys black ties at present. Boys rarely wear armbands now. Seemliness used to
require that the mourners observe certain taboos of action. They were not allowed to go to public meetings, to
play cards, or to go to weddings or other parties. These
restrictions were observed all during the time of *grand
deuil* but now only during the beginning of the mourning
period. Black-bordered handkerchiefs and stationery are
still used for both sexes. For *semi-deuil* the black on the
handkerchief leaves the severe border form and becomes
black embroidery around the edge. When one mourning
period is finished, mourning clothes are packed away for
the next *deuil*.

The mourning periods are here shown diagrammatically.

RELATIONSHIP OF DECEASED	MOURNING PERIOD	
	Until 50 Years Ago	Now
Spouse..........	2 years of full mourning and 1 year of half-mourning required. Most women kept full mourning all their lives	The present condition is marked by great reduc- tion in the length of mourning by some indi- viduals. There is no con- census. The more conserv-
Parent..........	1 year of full mourning and 1 year of half-mourning	ative families adhere more closely to the old periods. Men have practically
Adult sibling (out of school)......	6 months of full mourning and 6 months of half- mourning	abandoned mourning, ex- cept for their wives. The long veils for women have disappeared
Grandparent.....	Same as sibling	
Grown child (out of school)......	2 months of full mourning and 2 months of half- mourning	

Parents-in-law were recognized just as blood relatives. Thus, one would mourn for a mother-in-law as one would for a mother, no matter whether one were a man or woman. "They could not have half of the family in mourning and the other half not. Imagine how it would be if the husband sat quietly in the corner while his wife danced like the demon." Another informant states that siblings-in-law were mourned only three months in *grand deuil*.

Computed on the basis of the average ages in the individual life-cycle, a person spends an average of about twelve years in mourning, with a maximum of around twenty years, should he be a tenth child married to a tenth child. With the exception of mourning for grandparents, most of this mourning time is grouped in the latter years of a person's life. It is little wonder that women frequently kept the mourning for their husbands to their graves. The drab, usually black, dress of married women is probably related to the long mourning years under the old system. The function of the mourning dress and the restrictions are clearly to identify the relatives, according to their degree of relation, with the deceased. These relatives withdraw as much as possible from the local society, so as to continue their association with the person who has left the physical social circle of the community. It is noted that persons who are aged and are preparing to die do the same sort of thing. Their interests and activities are centered around the cemetery and the church. Therefore, it is consistent that these two times of withdrawal from society should coincide in old age. The fact that some large part of the mourning years comes before there is this voluntary retirement of old age in preparation for death creates a strain on the young mourners, particularly the women, who are under greater restrictions. Therefore the contact with the States, where mourning was not so exacting, was all that was necessary to throw over the system and result in the expressions against the way women used to be "encumbered." Young women, who were forced by precedent to go into mourning, still were living their lives with their values more in terms of social than religious rewards. This structural situation created antithetical attitudes—a desire to withdraw from social life and a desire to remain. All that was needed to bring about the change in mourning custom was the stimulus from outside contact. These mourning periods may not be thought of in terms of grief alone. Long after the grief is over, a person is in black merely as a symbol of respect to the dead person. That is to say, black singles the person out and connects her with the deceased.

Functionally, mourning is the positive means by which a society can react to the loss of one of its members. The reaction to the loss is proportional to the loss the deceased represents. One has only to look at the old lengths of mourning periods to see this. Infant children had practically no value socially; adolescent children were recognized more. Grandparents also were not a marked loss, for their usefulness was passed. The longest mourning period was for a deceased spouse. This is, in fact, the most vital relationship in the society, and therefore its rupture is responded to the most vigorously by the society. Thus, not only do the lengths of the mourning periods denote the importance of individuals of different ages in the society, but they also show the relative importance of various relationships in the society. We just stated that the marriage bond is the most important socially.[10] After it, in importance, is the parent-child bond, from the point of view of the child. From the point of view of the parent

[10] The importance of the marriage bond is also shown in the identification of parents with parents-in-law in the length of mourning periods.

it is much less important. What social importance is recognized in the child is as a member of the working unit, the family. The relationship of the grandchild to the grandparent is about equal to that between siblings. In spite of the shortened mourning periods, these relative times still hold.

For the individual who passes through his span of life in St. Denis, that life is full of hard work. The drab cycle of years is lightened by incidents which are unusual, those happenings which have not become commonplace through repetition.[11] Many of the *rites de passage* are at once unique experiences and forms of social recognition for which the individual has been striving. Ultimate satisfaction is achieved in terms of two great goals: a well-established posterity and a heavenly hereafter.

[11] See autobiography in Appen. III.

CHAPTER XI

OLD AND NEW

IN EVERY phase of life in St. Denis one finds cultural changes which have come about in the last one or two generations. Every society becomes altered through the years, but rural French-Canadian culture has changed more in the last forty years than it did in the preceding century. An intimate analysis of the parish social structure showed the direction of these changes and also indicated the reasons for these altered folkways. Here we shall devote our attention explicitly to the problems associated with this breakdown of old traditions and the diffusion of urban traits into the country.

The social organization of the rural French in Canada is losing its folk character. Folk songs have lost their place in the life, and folk tales no longer have their old appeal. Folk medicine is giving way more slowly, but the doctor and public health nurse are making inroads. Many of the old culture traits are so closely allied to the thrifty, close-family economy that they have resisted change to a remarkable degree. Thus, flax is flailed, wool is spun and woven, and clothes are made from this local *étoffe*. The family bread is baked in outdoor ovens. The soap is made in great caldrons. Some of the traits have resisted change, but for each of these there is some complementary alteration of custom. Every farm has its threshing machine. All wool is carded at a mill. Some clothing is bought from the store and by catalogue; city fashions have local social value. A baker passes through the parish twice a week. Soap is bought in some quantity from the local store, and the lye for home soap-production is no longer made. These trends are toward industrialization and urbanization, toward the acquisition of city manners. The reason for the change is not simply the proximity of the urban culture to the rural; nor is the change to be understood simply in terms of improved standards of living, for the standards of day-laboring families have declined.

Fundamentally the culture shift is toward increasing dependence of the local society upon the great industrial civilization of which it is becoming a part. The old social structure, its sanctions, and its mores were based on an independent, self-sufficient farming economy. With the exception of a very few items obtainable in trade, all an individual's needs were satisfied through locally practiced techniques and locally produced materials. As long as this local independence was maintained, there was no concern about social or economic conditions in the rest of the world. This self-sufficient economy was made possible by a family system which provided adequate *mains d'œuvre* to feed and clothe the *habitants* without the use of farm machinery. Such tools and simple equipment as were necessary were made locally. This economy and family system were structurally dependent upon a continual supply of new land upon which surplus children could be established. New France provided these conditions for over two centuries.

During the settlement and expansion period the rural parishes were not dependent upon a money economy. The money which was used consisted of the currency of half a dozen different countries.[1] If a man wanted to buy a *carriole*, he could use either crop capital or the money into which it might have been converted. Transportation diffi-

---

[1] Words used in referring to the present standardized currency reflect the variation existing well past the conquest. *Piastre* and *sou* are used for "dollar" and "cent"; and *trente sous* carries the connotation of its old equivalent, "twenty-five cents." The term *louis* has died out in the last fifty years.

culties favored money exchange in preference to barter in kind over any distance. But the large cities were easily accessible only to a few parishes. The remote parishes had less use for money, as their inhabitants never got to the city. Even commerce with the itinerant peddler was often in kind.

In the latter half of the nineteenth century young men were forced to go farther and farther afield to find land on which to settle. In those times rural sons were rarely given advanced education, as there was not the capital with which to train boys for professions. New settlements, such as that around Lac St. Jean, absorbed some of the new generations. The movement was toward more and more marginal land. The shift from a self-sufficient to a dependent economy is best understood in terms of this increasing land pressure. In other words, the basic human geographic conditions upon which the social structure was built were being altered through the operation of the social system itself. The changed land conditions in turn created problems in the society, which was based upon specific geographic requirements, and the society changed to meet the problems.

It is a commonplace that social systems change to meet their structural problems. When the traditional ways cease to solve the problems of life, social behavior varies from the old ways until a solution is found. If the new ways are successful, they in turn will become traditional. Thus, when the English suppressed female infanticide among the Toda, traditional polyandrous marriage could not take care of the increasing percentage of females. A type of adelphic "group marriage" grew up to meet this new structural situation.[2] The social changes in French Canada are to be understood in the same light. In this case, however,

[2] W. H. R. Rivers, *The Todas* (London: Macmillan & Co., Ltd., 1906).

structural problems in the society are due to the operation of the traditional system itself.

This suggests another consideration in the study of cultural integration. Not only must the degree of integration within the society be considered but also the degree to which the culture is adjusted to its habitat.[3] If this adaptation of the society to the environment is bad in terms of the immediate economy, the integration of purely social elements based on the economy will be weak. If the adjustment is poor from a long-term view, the integration of the purely social elements may be of a high degree for centuries.[4] A consideration of cultural integration should not be content with only the investigation of the interadjustment of institutions and mores but also with the integration of these with the habitat. The extent to which a society is internally well integrated expresses the probability of conflict and change. In the same way the degree to which the integration between the society and its habitat is satisfactory, even from a long-term point of view, is expressive of probable conflict and change.

Those cultures which have been long isolated from outside factors, which might change the basic conditions upon which the culture is based, are usually highly integrated both in the purely social sense and in terms of a long-term economic adjustment. Plains Indian tribes restricted their bison kill so that the faunal feature of the habitat upon which they depended was not exhausted until after white contact. A highly socially integrated tribe might have existed for centuries with economic traditions demanding wasteful kills. In terms of the complete cultural adjustment, the degree of integration would have been low.

[3] The former has been designated as "internal integration"; the latter, as "external integration."

[4] Such cases would involve some exhaustion of the local habitat.

French-Canadian culture was one which had a high degree of internal social integration based on a short-term adjustment to the environment. It took two centuries for the weakness of the territorial adjustment to appear. The problem having arisen, the society has tried to adjust itself, to integrate itself more adequately to its environment. In so doing, it has seized upon elements of American social environment, in contrast to the purely physical environment on which French-Canadian culture was once founded. The growing dependence on this new and unstable environment has made the culture subject to the vicissitudes of an industrial society whose own integration is very weak.

Land pressure alone created the structural problem in the society and accounts for the necessity for change and some of the actual cultural changes, but an even greater amount of change is only indirectly related to the basic structural problem. The growing lack of land forced parents to seek other outlets for their children. The society was experiencing trial-and-error behavior in an attempt to find a solution to its problem. The conflict between the old patterns of establishment and the lack of land was a gradually growing one. There was no sudden disruption of the traditional ways, only an increasing attempt to find other ways. All the new ways involved dependence upon the industrial civilization surrounding the old culture. The diffusion of elements of material and nonmaterial culture from the cities to the country has been a feature of this growing dependence of the latter on the former.[5] Good unsettled lands being rare, one way of placing children was to educate them or to buy farms from farmers willing to move to more marginal land. These two simple possi-

[5] A unique feature of diffusion from industrial society is the concerted effort of this type of culture to inject its material culture into the borrowing society—the attempt to "create a market."

bilities implied basic social changes. Each necessitated capital in money. The only way to secure such capital was to sell produce to the cities. Traditional modes of agriculture did not even furnish a surplus of produce. Agricultural methods were changed in order to develop a surplus. These changes were aided and abetted by representatives of the urban industrial society which was to absorb the surplus. Primary among the changes was the adoption of simple farm machinery: harrows, mowers, binders, and small threshing-machines. Crop rotation was also introduced. These innovations made possible the development of a crop surplus. The raising of animals for market was less dependent upon outside factors other than the market; but the crop surplus made the feeding of more animals possible. The crop and animal surplus did give the farmer money with which to establish his children, but he had lost his old independent economy and had become dependent upon items of material culture which he could not produce but had to buy with part of his surplus. Even more vital, the placement of children now became increasingly dependent upon the fluctuating market from which the farmer got his money. He is now doubly dependent upon the cities—not for the support of his family, for the old economy did that, but for the placing of his children.

About the same time that these changes in agricultural method were being effected, another outlet was found for unestablished children. This was in industrial and urban employment. The need for workers in these places caused the great emigration of farmers' available children from the country to cities in the United States and Canada. This new form of economic establishment completed the solution of the structural situation produced by the exhaustion of available land. It will be noted that this solution, like the others, was based on a new type of environment—a social, rather than a physical, environment. That this new environment was unstable, as the old one had not been, was discovered with the economic depression. Farmers might occasionally lose a crop from adverse weather; but never was their whole economic basis destroyed, as was the case with farmers' sons in the city. This outlet for children did not diminish gradually as the land had done, but closed almost at one blow. The markets for crop surplus also fell; and investments, another feature of the new economy, were lost. Still, the *habitant* suffered less than almost anyone else in North America, for he had clung to a great deal of his independent economy. Inbred conservatism had kept him from one-crop farming. Households could still be fed and clothed no matter what industry did, but the *habitant* was faced anew with his old problem of providing for the establishment of his children. The society's adjustment had failed. Rural French Canada is in this structural conflict position now.

Before discussing the recent social responses to the problem, let us consider what the change from an independent to a dependent community is doing to the culture. The loss of stability resulting from the shift in economy has already been noted. An alteration of social values has resulted from this change. In the old culture pattern, a young man aspired to have a farm like his father and therefore modeled his behavior after that of the farmers with whom he would eventually identify. Now a large part of the youth knows it can never farm and that it must find work in the city. The values of this group are increasingly influenced from the city. Urban ways have definite value to these young men, for the closer they can identify with the city, the better is their chance of success there. The old culture patterns are sufficiently strong to keep young women from going to the cities in search of work as the men do. The old patterns are not strong enough, however, to keep a girl from desiring such work, finding it through relatives and friends, instead of personal search, and going to the cities to fill positions. The movement of women into urban employment is less than that of men. In order to compete for the men with city-turned eyes, rural girls are adopting city fashions and customs. Thus, urban values are becoming important for the girls also. If the young people oriented toward the city came from a different group of families from those oriented toward the country, one might find the development of two groups differing in styles and customs. Members of both of these groups actually belong to the same families. There is then, because of family solidarity, a diffusion of city ways among even the rurally inclined youth. Still, those young men whose dress and behavior are most strikingly of city origin are men interested in getting to the city. There is a separation into two groups of families whose interests are different, as suggested above: the landed and nonlanded or day-laboring families. The very limited economy of this latter group tends to repress the tendency to adopt urban modes.

In addition to these factors influencing change of values it must be remembered that a number of adult farmers and *rentiers* spent several years in cities in the United States. This breaking of the isolation in which the old culture was maintained has had its effect. Even a short time spent in the industrial centers resulted in altered values, in spite of the fact that much of the old life was continued in these cities. The change in mourning customs is best understood in terms of this return movement from the cities. The diffusion of urban ways received its start through these various channels. The growth of literacy and the introduction of the newspaper, radio, and advertising have maintained and developed the consciousness of the value of the city manner of doing things. The diffusion of these patterns has but started, having been restricted by the close family economy. The loss of isolation through increased social mobility of all sorts has set up the conditions of social contact through which cultural diffusion is possible. The forced change to a dependent economy has motivated the acceptance of new culture patterns.[6]

The adoption of the urban elements makes the local society dependent upon the urban centers to maintain its new mixed culture. The new traits are altered to fit into the old culture pattern. This alteration in the process of diffusion is the usual thing between any two cultures. When the difference between the cultures is great, the two contexts into which a single trait is put vary considerably. Even when the difference is as slight as this between two Western cultures, there is alteration of borrowed traits in adoption. The fact that the English play croquet gives the game class significance when borrowed by the French. A knowledge of bridge is likewise a mark of sophistication. Borrowed food ideas get social significance from their origin and become "company" dishes in many cases. The new association of the culture trait does not always depend upon the larger English-French or urban-rural context. An electric motor may be mounted on a spinning-wheel frame, giving a novel, yet natural, combination of new and old culture elements. A harmonica-player adopts the foot-patting technique and the repertoire of the fiddler. The harmonica slips into the culture pattern of the violin. New combinations of new elements are made and become established as proper. Spats worn over rubbers are practical in keeping melting snow from running down into the shoes.

[6] See Appendix IV for a list of present culture traits divided into "old" and "new."

This combination is generally accepted by the young men as the proper way of wearing these articles.

The old culture background is capable of reacting to these new borrowed elements. Cultural needs are now usually met by borrowing. Before this was possible, the local culture was capable of producing its own answers to its needs. Naturally these answers were new traits—but local ones based on the local culture. Necessity gave the *platée* accepted meaning as a unit of measure on a par with any other. Curved roofs developed naturally from straight ones; galleries from raised porches. New weaving designs and *boutonné* bed covers grew from older, simpler manners of weaving. The new traits, however, which are entering from without, are based on a foreign background and are, therefore, dependent upon the outside culture for development. The threshing-machine was first run by windmills, then by horse treadmills, now by gasoline engines; and there is talk of electric ones. Each of these steps was originated outside the parish. The farmer adopted the changes in time, although the lag in adoption of traits often lasted long enough to bridge one of the steps. With each step he became more dependent. At first he needed only elements with which he was familiar: wind and horses. Then he had to buy gas, and soon he will be paying for electricity. He is becoming more and more dependent on the products of the outside world. To accomplish this he has to sell an equal value of local produce, thus putting himself in relation to the consumer market over which he has no control. When he was independent, he had control of all the economic factors which affected his life.

Possibly no single technique is as useful in indicating the type and origin of culture-borrowing as the analysis of borrowed words. Such study gives but little insight into the dynamics of diffusion, but it may be used to advantage in conjunction with an investigation of the manner of diffusion. Anthropologists frequently resort to the study of borrowed words to learn about culture-borrowings. The basic tenet of such a study is that words which are borrowed are adopted because of their association with borrowed traits of material or nonmaterial culture.[7] An analysis of words, therefore, will indicate the nature of the more concrete cultural diffusion which took place. The application of this technique to the body of English words in use in French Canada does point out clearly the nature of the diffusion. As the culture traits typical of the industrial city are here associated with cities dominated by English and Americans, the linguistic diffusion indicates not only anglicization but urbanization as well. Of the seven hundred basic English words in use in Quebec, only half are current in St. Denis.[8] The remaining half is known in the cities but not in the country. The list of words known in St. Denis is exclusive of any knowledge obtained in the schools. It may be said that practically no English words get into the vocabulary through this source. Farmers in the parish who have worked in the United States have a wider knowledge of English words. The native is unconscious of the fact that he is not employing a French word in the majority of cases, although he may speak of a *black aie*

[7] A simple illustration is the use of French words in English to refer to culture traits associated with food and its preparation and service. The words were adopted from France along with the actual *cuisine*.

[8] N. E. Dionne, in *Le Parler populaire des canadiens français* (Quebec, 1909), includes 945 words of English origin. This list contains duplications which have been eliminated to obtain the list of 700 words. Variations in pronunciation (*marshmallow* and *mâche-mâlo*) and derivatives of the same stem (*grocerie, groceries, groceur*) have been excluded. This basic list has been only slightly augmented in rural regions since 1909, although in that year the percentage known in the country was much less than now, as the major contact has been since then. Borrowing has always been greater in the cities where there is more contact. New words not included (*zippeur, radio, gaz*) are largely associated with innovations in technical material culture.

in fun, deriving part of the amusement from the mere use of the English words. The wide variance in the sound of this expression from French adds to the amusement.

A classification (see accompanying table) of a large unselected sample from this list of words not only shows the type of cultural-borrowing but also the difference between that in the city and country.[9] This distribution indicates

Cultural Association of Words	Percentage of All English Words Known in St. Denis	Percentage of English Words Known in Quebec but Not in St. Denis	Percentage of All English Words Known in Quebec
Technical and mechanical......	20	14	17
Transport mechanisms....	(9)	(3)	(6)
Clothes.....................	13	8	10.5
Business, correspondence, travel.	11	8	9.5
Food and drink..............	7	6	6.5
Amusements.................	5	7	6
Medicine, drugs, barber........	5	1	3
Government and politics.......	4	1	2.5
Others.....................	35	55	45
Total...................	100	100	100

immediately one thing: the English words known in St. Denis are associated with a narrower range of cultural phenomena than are the words known in urban places. The first four categories include 51 per cent of the words known in St. Denis from this sample. They make up only 43.5 per cent of the total for all the French Canadians. Exemplifying the same thing, only 35 per cent of the words known in St. Denis do not fall in the seven categories, whereas 45 per cent fall without when all Quebec is considered. There is definite indication, then, that the parishioners of St. Denis get their words from a narrower

[9] The sample consists of the 200 words listed under "B" and "S," the two most numerous initial letters. The borrowing of English words does not, of course, mean bi-lingualism.

range of cultural contexts. We see that 20 per cent of the words enter the parish associated with technical and mechanical objects and concepts. This is quite in accord with what we observe in the borrowing of culture objects themselves. New things must have names, and the vocabulary is borrowed along with the objects. In St. Denis there are very few English words used for objects or concepts which used to be referred to in French. A few such words do get in, such as *stuff* for *étoffe;* but they are little used and occur much less frequently than in the cities. There, words like *slice, short, sharp,* etc., replace the traditional French words, indicating a different sort of diffusion process.

The first two columns of the foregoing table give a relative idea of the extent to which St. Denis has acquired the English vocabulary known in all Quebec. Words associated with food and drink and with amusements are as frequently known as not. English words associated with technical things, particularly vehicles, and with clothes and business and correspondence are more familiar. This indicates greater contact with these objects and concepts. Remarkably better known is the English vocabulary related to politics and government. The apparent knowledge of pharmaceutical and medical words is probably misleading, as Dionne does not include many words, particularly trade names, known by the French of the cities.[10]

The relatively large borrowing of words related to machinery and techniques bought from, and learned from, the English is what we would expect. The fact that the country Frenchman knows almost as many borrowed words associated with his country's bilingual government as the city Frenchman is not surprising. Politics is one of the major interests of the rural people, exhibited both

[10] *Op. cit.*

in their political activity and in the papers they read. The only other interest which can compare with this is religious. This interest is entirely separate, even antagonistic to the English; so there is no borrowing there. Political events are followed in the papers, assemblies, and over the radio, just as the city French follow them. The only difference is a slightly more conservative paper, linguistically, in the country. The borrowing of business terms, clothes, and foods is related to the new economy and the growth of value on city ways.

The manner of entry of the various types of culture-borrowing and their associated words may be stated with considerable accuracy. At the base of all the culture-borrowing is direct contact of some sort between the individuals of the two language groups. The industrial and class dominance of the English in the cities makes the adoption of their traits by city French desirable. We have already indicated that the borrowed political words, usually associated with some new idea, such as *trust*, are transmitted to the rural population from the urban borrowers by means of the newspaper and speeches. Amusements require a more intimate setting for their diffusion. This again starts in the cities and moves out into the country through visiting relatives and contacts in the higher school system. Words linked with clothes are definitely introduced by English and French stores alike. Both the local parish store and the mail-order house with its catalogue are modes of entry for these words. The same are responsible for words dealing with medicines and drugs and, to some extent, for food and drink through trade-names. These food items with English designations are adopted largely through the more intimate contact of the *chantier* or of French emigrants in the States. The adoption of the word *bean* to refer to baked beans owes its origin to this latter movement, in all probability. Again, the connotation of the new word is so definitely associated with only the new feature that is the baked bean that one hears the following: "Je veux avoir des fevres pour faire des beans." Business terms and travel expressions are originally the result of direct contact with the English or greatly anglicized French. Again the importance of the English in commerce is the basic cause. Technical language borrowing comes through various channels—returned workers from the mills and plants of the States and from the bilingual lumber camps. Trade-names and the English names for parts of machines are adopted with the machines themselves.

These influences do not all affect everyone in the community the same way. There is, therefore, a range to the number and type of words known. The grandfathers who used to cut their grain by hand instead of with a binder have much less of the mechanical vocabulary. They also do not know the new English games. Of travel terms they know very few, as they may have been on a train but once in their lives. The fathers who have been to the States know more English words than the average youth. The sons of other farmers have had more contact with boys from college and have traveled more than their fathers. These things and their interest in new machines, born of their lack of other tradition, give them a wider English vocabulary than their parents. There is evidence that words have vogues. Thus, in a single family, the parents who had read their newspapers before prohibition-repeal knew the words *smoggleur* and *boudelage* ("bootleg"), while their children did not know them. There are also sex differences in the words learned. Thus, the boys of the family knew *badge* and *black aie* while their mother and sisters were unfamiliar with these words. Likewise the girls knew *banne* ("band") and *salve*, whereas their mother and brothers did not. Again, *brécer* ("to brace") and *boullé* ("bully") are known to the parents and boys but not to the girls. Words associated with female techniques, such as knitting, are not known by the boys, just as those associated with male activities are not known by the girls.

To return to the structural changes which brought about the condition favorable for the diffusion of urban traits, the developments of the last generation are important. During the decade ending in 1931, 49 per cent of the 406,800 persons who moved from rural to urban districts in Canada were residents of Quebec.[11] The net rural-urban movement for the decade in the province was 19.2 per cent of the whole 1921 rural population in the province. During the decade the farm acreage in the province increased only 1.09 per cent, and the number gainfully employed in agriculture but 3.8 per cent. These figures show conclusively what was becoming of the farmer's noninheriting children.[12]

With the practical closure of the urban outlet, which is even now very small, attempts are being made to accommodate the rural surplus through the opening of new lands in the province. The reason for not settling the lands in western Canada has been mentioned.[13] According to the superintendent of colonization for the Canadian National Railroad, there are 75,000 young men in the country who are potential settlers. This number is augmented each year by 8,000. If all possible lands were opened with govern-

---

[11] Jean C. Cameron and W. B. Hurd, "Population Movements in Canada, 1921–1931: Some Further Considerations," *Canadian Journal of Economics and Political Science*, I (May, 1935), 222–45.

[12] This is an old movement. In 1881, 77 per cent of the population of Quebec was rural. Only 37 per cent was rural in 1931, and the actual rural population had hardly changed (Quebec Department of Municipal Affairs, Trade and Commerce, *1936 Statistical Year Book* [Quebec: Printer to the King's Most Excellent Majesty, 1937]).

[13] Chap. iv, "Kinship and the Family Cycle," n. 20.

ment aid, they would amount to 150,000 new farms.[14]
This would obviously constitute but a short-term answer
to the problem.

The only other solution to the structural situation beside new outlets to land or industry is to cut the native
birth-rate. This possibility is strongly opposed by the
church, which plays such a vital role in the rural parish.
The birth-rate in the cities is falling rapidly in response to
the same problem, but in the country the old culture has
not been disrupted to the same extent, and the traditional
sanctions are stronger. Even the rural regions show a decreased birth-rate only in part due to increase in unmarried
population. The decrease in rural birth-rate lags behind
that of the province as a whole. The decreasing death rate
in the country, owing largely to lowered infant mortality,
is keeping pace with that of the province. Combining these
two rates, we find that the rate of natural increase in the
country has remained much more stable than the decreasing rate for the province.[15] The small decrease in rural
birth-rate is almost offset by the decrease in death-rate,
so that the population pressure remains the same.

The present configuration of the general social organization of St. Denis shows what changes have been wrought

[14] Speech of M. Lanctot reported in the newspaper *L'Action catholique*,
April 5, 1937.

[15] From Quebec Department of Municipal Affairs, Trade and Commerce,
1921 Statistical Year Book and *1935 Statistical Year Book* (Quebec: Printer to
the King's Most Excellent Majesty):

RATES PER 1,000 POPULATION	KAMOURASKA COUNTY		PROVINCE OF QUEBEC		CHANGE OVER 16 YEARS	
	1919	1935	1919	1935	Kamouraska County	Province of Quebec
Increase.............	21.03	19.3	19.66	13.9	−1.73	− 5.76
Birth................	36.27	30.2	35.04	24.6	−6.07	−10.44
Death................	15.24	10.9	15.38	10.7	−4.34	− 4.68

by this internal pressure. The broadest social divisions of the parish are shown schematically in the accompanying figure. The circle represents the entire local community. The various divisions designate roughly by their area the part of the population included therein. The arrow accompanying the circle represents prestige, the greater prestige position being at the top. This section, marked *A*, includes all those persons who are socially so far removed from the

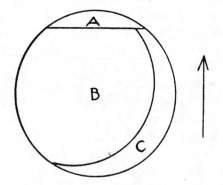

society of the parish that they cannot carry on personal social contacts with the other parishioners. If they do attempt it, there is a distinct feeling of strain or lack of ease. The section includes the *curé*, his relatives, the relatives of past *curés*, and the senator and his family and relatives. These persons do not owe their position to anything within the immediate society. Their position is due to contacts which they have had with the world outside the parish, from which sphere they have received recognition far higher than anything the parish can give. It is clear, therefore, that persons can move from the sections below to that above. It would be quite possible for the son of a family below the line to go away to college and receive the necessary recognition. Any professional man would probably enter this class. Because of the outside contact of this group, their manners of living, social graces, and behavior are foreign to the parish.

The section of the circle marked *B* includes all the owners of farms. Prestige in this group is a matter of wealth. This prestige is a very weak affair, however, as it is never a block to free social contact between the farmers' families. Family and political lines are much stronger than any benefit derived from possession of wealth. A poor relative of a fellow-partisan is far better company than a rich political opponent of an unrelated family. The prestige is thus weaker than other factors and may show itself only in marriage preferences. It is true, however, that the families at the top of the section will be more likely to be able to give their children the advantages which lead to their qualification for the upper sector. The parish is so small that the chance is slight that they would return to it once they had made good outside. Section *B* may be visualized as broken up into family and neighborhood cliques. These cliques are almost constant from one generation to another and run from top to bottom of the section of the diagram and include also individuals in *C*.

The crescent *C* includes all the nonfarmers. As has already been pointed out, this group lives exclusively in the village. It includes *rentiers*, day-laborers, banker, small tradesmen, gardeners, and the like. They also have prestige according to wealth. Those at the bottom are less religious. There are several families of peddlers and traders who are so low socially that they are not welcome in the homes of other parishioners. The position of the part of the crescent in the figure at the very bottom indicates this situation. They are poor, dirty, hard-drinking, lying, stealing people who frequently do not even grow a garden. At the top of the crescent are the banker-carpenter, merchant, blacksmith, etc. In this section the type of household varies, as it includes bachelors, old maids, and childless couples in addition to the usual form of households. There is a tendency for movement from the farming group *B* into the nonlanded group. Sons who cannot be established may join the day-laborers or craftsmen.

So far as recognition of prestige with public office is concerned, people in the top sector are not elected to these positions. Everyone knows they are actively interested in the parish; and, in truth, they have done more for it than any others. They are actually too big for positions on the church or school boards, or on the council, or for the position of mayor. These offices are bestowed on persons from both *B* and *C* who are not identified with the bottom of their sectors.

In the very early days of French-Canadian settlement there was only the division between *A* and *B*. The *curé* and *seigneur* and his family were distinguishable from the *habitants*. There was less reserve between the two groups under pioneer conditions than later, when life was less rigorous. The upper group once farmed, whereas they do not today. The longer-settled parishes soon attracted tradesmen, who made a living from their specialized work. They constituted the first persons of section *C*. They differed from the farmers only in their economy. Their other modes of life were identical. This was the situation up until population pressure began to make itself felt as a result of lack of outlet. Unestablished sons began to settle in the village and to earn a living by odd jobs and day-labor. Unmarried and married persons of both sexes accumulated enough money to become *rentiers* in the village. These people expanded the nonlanded population of the parish. In contrast to the families of tradesmen, their households were unlike those of the farmer. The poorer day-laborers sometimes adopted illegal and immoral practices to live. This at once isolated them from the rest of the parishioners. The traditional and religiously sanctioned ways of life were insufficient to provide a living for these people. Along with the breaking of traditions and disregard of religious sanctions, there developed a disrespect for those sanctions which opposed the ways of life of these day-laborers. This marginal economy group came to be looked down upon by the rest of the parish. This feeling developed from, and further emphasized, the asocial behavior of the few families. Their change of attitudes and the extent to which they ignore the social controls is illustrated by their abnormal behavior. Not only do they carry on local illegal liquor traffic, but they indulge in prostitution and produce the parish's illegitimate children. Their weakened religious faith is expressed in lack of confession and Communion and irregular church attendance.

An examination of the day-laboring group as a whole shows that its marginal economy finds expression in the beginning of an interest in methods of birth control. In terms of the economy itself, its difference from that of the farmers creates an open rift in the parish on questions of public works. A recently proposed highway through the parish is acclaimed by the nonlanded group, which sees in it an opportunity for road work. The same road finds disapproval among the farmers. Their lands will be severed, their springs filled, and their pastures isolated from watering-places. The dissension over such a project arises directly from the growth of this new population type, which in turn arose from forced location in the parish. The problem of economic placement has changed the unified nature of the parish and has weakened the effect of the social controls on the new part of the population. These effects are most obvious in the second-generation nonlanded parishioners, who have been oriented into such life since childhood.

Except for the larger cities, such as Quebec and Montreal, there have developed no distinctive urban-rural dissociative attitudes. The French population of the smaller towns and cities is drawn to so large an extent from rural regions that the family solidarity precludes the possibility of "rube" and "city-slicker" attitudes. Every urban French Canadian has close relatives in rural parishes. Should the urban outlet remain closed for several generations, one might expect the growth of such attitudes. At present the rural clergy tries to maintain the old traditions by attacking city values, but the social necessity of these values to farmers' sons weakens confidence in the church.

The analysis and history of the social structure of St. Denis has brought into relief the interdependence of the various parts of the society. The present changes in customs and attitudes are not to be perceived in terms of any single factor. They are, rather, the result of the operation of a definite form of social configuration in a particular socio-physical environment through a series of historically determined contacts. Neither structure nor environment nor chance can explain the changes involved. The study of St. Denis has demonstrated interrelations which show that true understanding is distorted by the omission of any of these factors.

CHAPTER XII
POSTSCRIPT

THE preceding description of St. Denis pictures it as it was in 1936—a community recently caught up in the expanding web of urban influence. The processes already at work were destined to accelerate change, and the advent of World War II further stimulated this trend. To study these changes, a brief survey of the parish was made in 1949. This Postscript records what St. Denis was like at that time and considers new forces working in the society.

Today, of course, St. Denis is still more altered than it was just after the war. Innovations such as television have spread readily into the community. Not only are new things coming in but the members of the older generation have been dying out and, with them, the old traditions. The children of yesterday, with their greater education and wider experience, are the adults of today. Life is now less "like a turning wheel," as an old *habitant* described it, for the repetitive cycle of life no longer returns to the same point with each succeeding generation. In addition, the forces of urbanization alter the life of the adults themselves. The degree to which this is true is evident in the changes which had occurred by 1949.

The returning visitor is immediately struck with the changes in material culture. The principal road to the parish, once graveled and rough, is now part of the macadam-surfaced route from Quebec to Gaspé. The automobiles of Canadian and American tourists stream through the community, out of which a motorcycle policeman now operates on road patrol. The two hundred and fifty autos which passed through the village during one hour on July 4 inescapably impressed the residents with the date of that American holiday. Few tourists stop in the parish, however, except to purchase gasoline at one of the two pumps.[1]

The road means easier communication, and year-round autobus service is now available. Eight trucks and sixteen automobiles, including three jeeps, are now owned by parishioners, in contrast to the five automobiles in St. Denis in 1936.[2] The number of farmers who have tractors increased from two to thirteen in the same period. The dual utility of the horse for transportation and field work is still retained to a degree with the tractor. It is not unusual to see farmers driving their tractors to town. On the other hand, the oxcart has disappeared.

The village is illuminated by street lights, and the roads are now paralleled by electric and telephone lines. There are forty telephones in the parish, whereas formerly there were two. While previously almost no farms had electricity, now they are practically all electrified and there are radios in almost every home. Even electric washing machines and refrigerators, while not general, are to be found in many a farmhouse. There are some fifteen electric milking machines in the parish—a radical innovation. Local explanation for their introduction is that they facilitate the work of women who have many small children. "They are not expensive; only cost a couple of hundred dollars," commented one farmer, who twelve years earlier had operated on a largely self-subsistent basis. He also recently finished building a forty-by-eighty-foot barn, the materials for which cost $5,000.

[1] One of these pumps sold 22,000 gallons of gasoline in 1948, including that for farm use.

[2] The number of motor vehicles registered in the Province of Quebec rose only from 197,917 to 298,688 between 1937 and 1947 (Quebec Department of Trade and Commerce, *1948 Statistical Year Book*, p. 485).

Farm technology has felt still further changes. Threshing by horsepower, which was general, has completely given way to threshers operated by electric motors or gasoline engines. The old threshing machine may still be employed with the new source of power. Milk was separated at the local butter factory in 1936. Electrified farms now have their own separators.

Houses may be supplied with running water, provided by electric pumps in the old wells, and wash basins and toilets are found even on farms. Homemade clothes of homespun, once typical, are now uncommon. Clothes are purchased from the store or, most commonly, from mail-order houses. Some farm wives even buy their bread from the wagon which passes their door semiweekly, instead of baking it themselves. Commercial soap flakes are used in households once entirely dependent upon homemade soap. Ice cream, not eaten in 1936, has become a popular food.[3]

The county fair in 1949 exemplified the changes which have occurred. Visitors now arrive predominantly by automobile instead of by carriage. Major commercial exhibits have shifted from tombstones and wood stoves to electric water heaters, refrigerators, milkers, pumps, separators, and radios. Wood stoves are still shown beside electric and oil stoves. Overstuffed suites of furniture are on display to tempt the farm wife, and farm machinery is set out to draw her husband.

The exhibits of preserved foods and garden produce show no marked alteration, nor does the livestock competition. The sewn and woven articles in the competitive displays, however, are far from the traditional patterns and forms. Linen towels are all that seem to have persisted. Lace-trimmed underclothes are boldly exhibited. Bridge-

[3] The consumption of ice cream in the province almost trebled between 1938 and 1947 (*1948 Statistical Year Book*, p. 364).

table covers and zippered, woolen baby-wrappers are popular items, along with knitted garments, which were already in evidence earlier.

The growing dependence of St. Denis upon the wider society of Canada is highlighted by the shift from manpower and horsepower to electricity and gasoline. All the other changes in material culture also represent a loss in self-sufficiency. Such increasing dependence upon the outside is but the local view of the growing interdependence of the parts of a larger social whole. This is very evident in farm production.

Agricultural data are not available for St. Denis itself, but statistics for the county of Kamouraska may be taken as representative. Basic crops changed little, in contrast to minor ones. Hay and oats are still the major crops, occupying about 90 per cent of the cropland. Between 1941 and 1948, farm acreages devoted to oats remained about constant, and those in hay increased only 4 per cent. But wheat acreage declined a third by 1947. Livestock showed marked changes. The number of hogs increased 40 per cent over the seven years and cattle increased 13 per cent. The latter are primarily milk cows, cattle for slaughter being unimportant. Consistent with technological shifts, the number of horses decreased almost 10 per cent.

Aside from the decline in horses, the other changes resulted from the activity of the Dominion government. In 1941 it undertook a war program designed to curtail wheat production and increase that of livestock and dairy products. Through publicity, marketing quotas, and agricultural subsidies, the production of pork and milk was more than doubled and the contribution of wheat to farm income was halved. Annual Canadian bacon exports to England rose from 192 million to nearly 700 million pounds between

1937 and 1944.[4] Although the role of Kamouraska County was a minor one, it is clear that the agricultural changes in the county directly reflected the Dominion program.

Wartime inflation contributed to the value of expanded farm production. Between 1938 and 1947, the value of field crops in Quebec increased 140 per cent, and the value of hogs 180 per cent. The cost-of-living index, however, rose by only one-third during the period.[5] Nor was such increment the only source of new income. Under the Canadian Family Allowances Act of 1944, lower-income families received from $5.00 to $8.00 a month per child under sixteen years of age. The amount varied upward with the age of the child, but benefits declined progressively for higher-income groups.[6] St. Denis, with its average of ten children per family, also experienced an increase in cash income from this source.

These economic changes are of importance in understanding the shift from self-sufficiency in rural Quebec. The religiously sanctioned large family was long a prerequisite for farm operation with the traditional technology of hand labor. Mechanization was blocked by the large-family system, as the greater efficiency of the machine could not make itself felt through decreasing the number of family farm workers. Then suddenly and with only minor alteration of the old agricultural system, cash income increased beyond the old requirements. It became possible both to mechanize the farm and to rear a large family. The increased cash income of St. Denis has had ramifying effects in the local economy. One young man

[4] V. C. Fowke, "Canadian Agriculture in the Postwar World," *Annals of the American Academy of Political and Social Sciences*, CCLIII (1947), 46–47.

[5] *1948 Statistical Year Book*, pp. 337, 347, 544.

[6] Harry M. Cassidy, "The Canadian Social Services," *Annals of American Academy of Political and Social Sciences*, CCLIII (1947), 194–95.

who was unemployed but desirous of marrying in 1936 has become a life-insurance salesman and is happily married. Almost half the parishioners are now insured with him. Several other young men have since become representatives of insurance companies.

A major development has been in the organization and expansion of co-operatives. This change is the direct product of intense promotion from outside the parish. The co-operative movement, which is a half-century old in Quebec, was encouraged from the start by provincial legislation, but its development has been slow and irregular. La Coopérative Féderée de Québec was reorganized in 1930 and the whole movement given new impetus, although consumer co-operatives were particularly slow in developing.[7] In 1940, however, provincial promoters succeeded in interesting a group of parishioners of St. Denis to purchase, on a co-operative basis, the only significant general retail store in the parish. The enterprise is now shared by 275 members, including people from almost all families in the parish and even some from the neighboring three parishes.

L'Active, as the co-operative is called, also operates a nonprofit flour mill for the benefit of the members. Even building materials and plumbing are purchased through the organization at substantial savings. In 1949 assets amounted to $46,300, against which a $14,560 debt was carried. Gross sales were approximately $140,000 in 1948, representing an increase of 59 per cent over the first year's operations. Shares in L'Active sell for $5.00, and no member may have more than forty shares. Membership may even be secured for $1.00, the complete share being paid for from subsequent dividends. The annual dividend paid to each member is based on the amount purchased by him

[7] Albert Fancher, "Co-operative Trends in Canada," *Annals of the American Academy of Political and Social Sciences*, CCLIII (1947), 184–89.

at the store during the year. The dividend rate has been increasing by 1 per cent a year and in 1949 amounted to 8 per cent. The manager, who is a native of St. Denis, does not bill his members, who purchase largely on credit. He takes action to collect only long-standing debts. Yet, at the end of January, 1949, only $1,900 was outstanding. Rarely do the members collect their interest or dividends, preferring to let their investment increase.

Since 1932 the provincial government has directly subsidized the promotion of the Caisse Populaire, which is a mutual savings and loan association. This co-operative provides the only bank in St. Denis today, having replaced the former, small, private banking enterprise. The Caisse operates out of the dwelling of its woman manager, who also runs a small drugstore in another room of the house. Beginning with ninety-three members and assets of $9,000 in 1940, the Caisse of St. Denis now has 423 members and assets of $200,000. Loans to parishioners amount to $21,000.[8] Between L'Active and the Caisse Populaire, the average family in St. Denis has $2,000 invested in co-operative enterprise. In addition, the local butter factory has also become a co-operative, owned by the farmers who once sold their cream to the proprietor.

Demographic changes in St. Denis are less obvious than those in the economy, but they have been profound. The population had been declining regularly from 1871 to 1931, but between 1936 and 1946 the parish experienced a 13 per cent increase.[9] The average annual birth-rate for the dec-

---

[8] The experience of the Caisse Populaire of St. Denis is fairly typical of peoples' banks throughout Quebec. The number of such banks almost doubled between 1940 and 1946; the number of depositors more than trebled. Assets rose 600 per cent. While the assets of the St. Denis Caisse are somewhat above the Quebec average, loans outstanding are only a quarter of the average amount (*1945–46 Statistical Year Book*, p. 535; *1948 Year Book*, p. 580).

[9] The population was 700 in 1936; 792 in 1946.

ade 1937–46 was 28.4 births per 1,000 population, compared to the 24 per 1,000 rate of the previous decade. The rural birth-rate throughout Quebec experienced the same trend.[10]

For the forty-year period up to 1937, 25 per cent of the deaths in St. Denis were at ages of less than one year; 33 per cent under five years; 43 per cent under twenty-five years. For the period between 1937 and 1948 these percentages changed to 17 per cent under one year, 18.7 per cent under five years, and 22.8 per cent under twenty-five years.[11] Not only has the mortality of infants and young persons been thus reduced, but the total life-expectancy of those who reach the age of twenty-four years has increased from 65.3 to 72.1 years. The county and province show the same sort of change. Infant mortality in Kamouraska County, however, has decreased more rapidly than the rural average.[12] Declining mortality rates were also found at the time of the earlier study. The apparent suddenness of the decline noted above is partly a product of the long time period for which the earlier rates were computed..

The general health improvement indicated by altered mortality is possibly also reflected in the increased birth-rate, through fewer miscarriages. Birth control is not practiced, but the mother of a poor family may welcome, rather than seek to avoid, a natural miscarriage. Still, the increasing birth-rate and the declining infant mortality have led to a 43 per cent increase in the number of children in St. Denis under the age of fifteen. Other age categories also show shifts.

[10] 30.6/1,000 in 1926–35; 36.4/1,000 in 1946 (*1948 Statistical Year Book*, p. 120).

[11] Data consisted of 123 deaths.

[12] The Kamouraska rate was 74.7/1,000 in 1936 and 47.5/1,000 in 1945. The provincial rate fell from 82.6/1,000 to 62/1,000 during the same period. Rural and urban rates became about equal (*1948 Statistical Year Book*, pp. 131–32).

During the last decade, there was a continuation of the emigration of persons between the ages of twenty-five and thirty-five, but at a much reduced rate.[13] A larger proportion of the farm children remained in the community. The fact that there were 43 per cent more women between the ages of twenty-five and thirty-nine in 1946 than there were in 1936 might account for the increased birth-rate, but this does not appear to be the case.

Because brides settle in their husbands' parishes, it is the marriage rate of local men which is significant for the birth-rate in St. Denis. The number of local male residents who marry each year could not be ascertained, as marriages are performed and recorded in the parish of the bride. So far as marriages performed in St. Denis are concerned, an increased proportion of them have been between parishioners,[14] but otherwise girls have gone farther afield to find mates.[15]

The marriage rates for the province and county have been generally, but irregularly, increasing.[16] This trend, previously operative in St. Denis, was not discernible there over the last decade,[17] and the proportion of the local popu-

[13] In 1936, the age group between twenty-five and thirty-four years equaled 60 per cent of the group between fifteen and twenty-four years. By 1947 this percentage had risen to 91. Only 24 per cent of those who were between fifteen and twenty-four years of age in 1936 had emigrated by 1947, and 4 per cent had died.

[14] They were 29 per cent of all marriages in St. Denis in 1898–1936 and 35.6 per cent for the period 1937–48.

[15] The proportion of marriages in which the groom came from within twenty miles of St. Denis was 84 per cent for the forty-year period prior to 1937. Since then, only 77 per cent of the grooms have come from within that radius.

[16] The marriage rate of Quebec increased from 6/1,000 population in 1934 to 10.1/1,000 in 1946. The rate for Kamouraska County rose from 4.7 per cent to 8.0 over the same period (*1935 Statistical Year Book*, p. 97; *1948 Year Book*, pp. 110, 116).

[17] The number of marriages per 1,000 population, by decades, has been: 1907–16, 4.5; 1917–26, 5.5; 1927–36, 6.6; 1937–46, 6.7.

lation which is of marriageable age has increased. It is obvious that even the expanded economy is still proving insufficient to provide an economic base for the marriage of children who do not remain on the farm.

Lest change be overemphasized, let us consider a few of the ways in which the old ways mingle with the new. Increased communication with the outside world is reflected in the growth of correspondence by mail. The number of letters entering and leaving the parish has almost doubled since 1936. Parcel post has also increased with augmented mail-order buying. Many parishioners living outside the village have availed themselves of the new opportunity to have rural mail delivery, yet the postmistress continues to respect the living patterns of those who collect their mail at her residence. She refuses to be bound by the official hours of Quebec post offices and insists that, if the mail train arrives so late that mail cannot be distributed before closing time, she must remain open later. In defense of her practice of also opening the office early, she says, "Can I expect people who go to early Mass to come back to the village later to get their mail?" Her relationship with parishioners remains personal despite pressure from her counterparts in more urban parishes.

There are other indications of an increasing use of literacy. Between 1936 and 1946 the number of subscriptions to daily newspapers increased one-third. The strongly religious *Action catholique* continued to hold three-quarters of the subscribers. The proportion of subscribers who take papers which directly or indirectly support the Liberal party remained about constant, despite the rise to national power of the Liberal French-Canadian, Prime Minister St. Laurent. The traditional division between Conservatives and Liberals in the parish was likewise little altered by the introduction of the unsought privilege of woman suffrage.

Women do exercise their right to vote, however, and it is even rumored that some wives do not vote as their husbands do!

A new doctor has just come to the neighboring parish of St. Philippe, making five medical practitioners in the immediate vicinity of St. Denis, in addition to two dentists. Even in 1936, the sole doctor had replaced the *sage-femme* at childbirth. With the increase in the number of practitioners, the *remmancheur*, or bonesetter, has been forced to discontinue his practice, which has long been illegal. His daughter has become a nurse and is said to use some of her father's skills. Folk remedies remain in use, particularly when the doctor fails to effect a cure. One local farmer, stricken with rheumatism, tried to find relief both through prescribed medicine and by wearing a brass chain on his right wrist, but to no avail. He then went to a Quebec hospital, a step taken only in grave emergencies in 1936.

On the beach, where a small summer colony once represented the sins of the city incarnate, a new chapel has risen. There a priest says daily Masses during the summer. The small resort hotel has burned, and the *curé* has successfully obstructed attempts to renew this focus of undesirable transients. The half-dozen beach cottages of 1936 have increased to two score summer dwellings occupied by respectable families.

The church continues to act as an agent in the control of nature. In early August, 1949, the parish was threatened by a plague of grasshoppers. Masses were said in the various quarters of the community, and religious processions were organized to pray for deliverance. The grasshoppers departed. Late in the summer a severe drought caused the bishop to request that Masses be sung throughout the province "for the fruits of the earth." The rains came before the local Mass was scheduled, but, as the *curé* pointed out, all areas had not yet been so fortunate.

The *curé*, who has long been ill, attributes what strength he has regained to the prayers of his parishioners. He is still not well enough, however, to give the sermons. The priest who replaces him in the pulpit chose for his theme, during the summer months, the distinction between proper veneration and improper supernatural beliefs and practices. The power of the saints was clearly limited to intercession. Their physical representation in statues was likened to "pictures of ancestors," with no power residing in them. The primacy of the high altar over those of the saints was stressed. Folk beliefs in methods of foretelling events and working magical cures were derided.[18] The role of the priest in suppressing superstition was noted earlier in connection with the decline of belief in *loups-garous* and *feus follets*. Now clerical influence is being exerted against the magical use of religious symbols.

It would appear valuable to conclude our re-examination of St. Denis with a general appraisal of earlier conclusions about social change in the light of what was subsequently found. The focus of the original study was the community and, in so far as the larger society impinged upon it, outside influences were dealt with as constants—a methodological fiction. Although consideration of the changing content of these influences was beyond our scope, their growing importance in the community was obvious. The local problem of population pressure loomed large in 1936. Nonlanded sons of the parish and even farm girls, the future of most of whom lay outside the parish, looked to the cities

---

[18] Basically, he assailed those supernatural practices which were defined as "magical" in chapter vii. While there was some understandable adverse clerical reaction to this section of the book when it appeared, these sermons, given twelve years later and begun before the author's return, seem to substantiate the earlier record.

and towns for ultimate establishment. At the very least, urban ways of life were of value in making a local, nonfarm adjustment. Other trends were those toward increasing literacy, decreasing infant mortality, and the decline of folk medicine. The growing dependence of the local society upon industrial civilization was clear in technology, styles, foods, and amusements.

Comparing this projected view of the future with what actually took place, the nature and direction of change were no surprise.[19] If we search for unforeseen aspects of change, several things stand out with regard to the amount of change and the form it took. In spite of the fact that the earlier analysis of borrowed English words showed the major diffusion to be of technical and mechanical items, the rapidity of technological change was greater than would have been anticipated. In addition, these borrowings affected farm families more than was expected. Finally, the development of co-operatives was not foreseen. The provincial and Dominion governments were the precipitating agents of change in each of these cases.

It is particularly noteworthy that the economic shift took place with little alteration in the old pattern of production. High prices, subsidies, and family allowances poured cash into the parish. The principal production change was the increase in the number of milk cows and hogs. These were but modest expansions of the old system.[20] It was possible to be conservative and still reap cash benefits. There has been no boom in the sense of greatly increased operation on credit.

What was the cash used for? Where additional farms

[19] The increased birth-rate is an exception, but this is probably temporary.

[20] For example, two sows, averaging two litters of fifteen shoats each, now bring one farmer $3,000 a year. Previously he raised only enough pork for his family's needs.

were available, they were purchased. Buildings were re-paired. More children were sent away to school. All this was in the old pattern of expenditure. The acquisition of cream-separators and milking-machines contributes to the expansion of the dairy economy. But the displacement of the horse by the automobile, truck, tractor, electric motor, and gasoline engine is much less of a productive change. The machines are used to cultivate much the same crops on the same farms and are largely a convenience. Only part of the time which they free is used in economically productive ways. Even more surprising introductions are such pure conveniences as telephones, plumbing, wash-ing machines, refrigerators, store-clothes, and commercial soaps.

A decade ago any awareness of conveniences was not expressed in terms of their desirability. The traditional family economy made their acquisition almost literally un-thinkable. How did it come about that things not then desired are now required? The suddenness of the change was possible only because it involved no fundamental al-teration in the local social patterns. The only slightly modified economy suddenly produced profits beyond the requirements of the old system. The increment was used to facilitate the labor of the farm family. The work skills of home and field, as well as hard work itself, were virtues only so long as their productive contribution was essential. It is also significant that the decline in the necessity for such labor took place in a situation of increased awareness of the greater ease of life in the cities.

Today one hears discussed, for the first time, the prob-lem of "keeping the children on the farms." There has been growing resistance among unmarried girls to assuming the burden of bearing and rearing a family of ten while cook-ing, housekeeping, gardening, milking, carding, spinning, weaving, making clothes, and helping with the harvests and threshing. In the present glow of economic expansion, a girl can assert her preference for an easier life, and everyone can lighten his labors.

What does the future hold for St. Denis? Certainly there will be more change in the direction originally indicated—increasing dependence upon the surrounding industrial civilization and all that this implies. The development of a surplus farm population seems destined to continue until economic pressures result in birth control, already evident in the cities. The new mechanization of the farms makes a luxury of the large family which was once a necessity. The establishment of the landless youth depends upon expansion of the nonfarm economy, either locally or elsewhere. It is apparent that St. Denis will pay for her conveniences with vicissitudes she never knew before. This is no nostalgic plaint, for the seeds of change were in the local system itself.

APPENDIX I

AGE-SEX DISTRIBUTION OF THE POPULA-TION OF ST. DENIS, 1936

Age	Total	Total Male	Total Female	Married Men and Widowers	Married Women and Widows
0–4	71	38	33	....	....
5–9	70	37	33	....	....
10–14	62	29	33	....	....
15–19	83	38	45	....	1
20–24	71	31	40	2	4
25–29	58	30	28	8	10
30–34	35	18	17	10	10
35–39	27	14	13	10	7
40–44	34	19	15	12	13
45–49	24	10	14	7	7
50–54	33	13	20	9	14
55–59	34	13	21	11	13
60–64	25	11	14	10	6
65–69	23	12	11	9	9
70–74	20	6	14	6	9
75–79	16	8	8	7	6
80–84	10	1	9	....	6
85–89	3	....	3	....	2
90–94	1	1	....	1	....
Total	700	329	371	102	117

APPENDIX II

TRADITIONAL CURES AND REMEDIES

The following is a list of common ailments and their modes of treatment:

Bad cold.—A spoonful of pine gum in three-quarters of a cup of whiskey and a cup of maple syrup. One spoonful three times a day.

Sore throat.—A pint of water, well salted, boiled with a teaspoon of vinegar. Gargle.

Gargle a mixture of alum and water. Apply a bit of mustard and roll the neck in a piece of flannel (preferably red).

Pleurisy.—Drink milk which has almost come to the boil, with molasses added. If at the end of a half-hour perspiration has not started, take another dose. Take frequently in small quantities during perspiration.

Drink stove soot mixed with milk. Heat the sore portion with oatsacks of ashes.

Pleurisy or grippe.—Put the feet in hot water, containing a spoonful of powdered mustard, for twenty minutes. Repeat this bath three times at half-hour intervals. Change clothes when perspiration is too great. Rub the stomach with mustard ungent. Finally give Bromo Quinine,[1] or ginger brew, or some other hot drink.

Cold in the head.—Take some snuff to heat the nose.

Cold in the chest.—Rub the chest with a mixture of skunk grease and fuller's earth.

Sickness from autumn humid cold.—Take an infusion of camomile. Do not take too often, as it is weakening.

Indigestion.—To accelerate digestion, make an infusion, like tea, of plantain weed seeds or flaxseeds, and drink.

For indigestion with or without vomiting and diarrhea, take a good cup of black coffee, that is, without milk. Coffee is also good for those who have smoked too much.

Acute indigestion.—Take a teaspoonful of mustard in cold water.

Constipation.—Eat the berries of the service tree.

Persistent constipation.—Prepare a liquid from everlasting flowers and take a spoonful morning and evening for five days.

[1] Trade-mark.

Stomach cramps.—Milk cut with water. Drink by long drafts. Apply hot cloths to the sore part.

Colic with diarrhea.—Drink camomile tea.

Worms.—One teaspoonful of gunpowder in a tablespoonful of molasses taken three successive mornings before breakfast.

Make an infusion of aspen bark and give in small doses.

Milk boiled with garlic skins gives good results.

Inflammation of the lips (feu sauvage).—Put coal oil on the lips.

Eczema.—Take a piece of sulphur, the size of a pea, in a spoonful of molasses nine consecutive mornings on an empty stomach. Do not drink cold water during these days.

Itch, pimples all over the body.—Make a mixture of fat, sulphur, and gunpowder. Apply this ungent, before retiring, every night for three nights.

Boils and furuncles.—Make an infusion of wild-rhubarb roots. Take this infusion with a little gin.

Tetter.—Burn a twist of paper on an ax. The oil which appears gives a complete cure.

Rub around the affected area with a rag used for oiling boots.

Bathe in water from a blacksmith's tempering trough.

Bathe with a boric-acid solution.

Warts.—Rub the wart with a piece of pork and then bury the pork. As the pork rots, the wart will disappear.

Tie a silk thread tightly around the base of the wart and allow to remain until the wart falls off.

Moisten finger with saliva and dip it in salt. Then rub the finger around the wart seven times in each direction.

Whitlow.—Caused by a drop of blood adhering to the bone. Take the membranous skin of an egg and stretch it tight around the finger and over the whitlow. Allow it to dry and tighten. Put on a new egg skin every half hour until the drop of blood comes to the surface.

Running sores.—Wash or dip sores in a very weak lye solution.

Cholera.—Drink milk boiled with starch.

Wine boiled with iron in it is preferable.

Drink a decoction made of raspberry twigs.

Diphtheria.—Apply coal oil with a flannel and leave as long as necessary. In a few very serious cases the invalid was given a teaspoonful of this oil.

Whooping cough.—Mix poplar buds, dragon's blood, pine gum, and camphor and rub with this preparation.

Appendicitis.—Take the following brew: two tablespoonsful of chimney soot, three tablespoonsful of water, and two tablespoonsful of milk. Boil, sweeten, and strain before drinking.

It used to be customary to move the patient up to the stove and heat his side.

Kidney pains.—Rub the kidneys with mustard ungent. Apply a hot flannel to the affected part.

Apply a Red Cross[2] mustard plaster and allow to remain for two weeks.

Frequent urination.—Make an infusion of cherry stems and drink until cured. Pumpkin seeds and flaxseeds also give good results.

Bed-wetting by adolescents.—Feed the child a mouse skinned and cleaned and cooked as a patty. Do not tell the child what he has eaten. This is a hearsay remedy.

Hemorrhoids.—Put hot coals in a night jar with a little rosin. Sit over this for about fifteen minutes until hot. Avoid chills.

Boil spruce buds in a liter of water and drink in big doses.

Jaundice.—Sheep dung, mixed with butter and spread on bread and given to patient without his knowledge. Hearsay remedy.

Painful joints.—Melt butter; put it on a flannel and apply to pain.

Eye inflammation.—Wash eyes in water of white roses. Milk is also a good remedy.

Earache.—Put a piece of fried onion in the ear with the aid of cotton.

One drop of chicken fat or tepid glycerin. Rinse out the ear in the morning.

Paralysis.—Rub affected parts with vinegar.

Burns.—Immediately put olive oil on parchment paper and place on the burn. The patient must not eat too much for several days if the burn is large. If pus forms under the paper, remove it and wash with cooled boiled water containing peroxide or baking soda. Allow to dry and apply another piece of parchment paper. Drink olive oil.

Cuts and tears, particularly on bony parts.—Take a marigold stalk and make an infusion like tea. Apply as a compress.

Cuts and contusions with black-and-blue spots.—Make an infusion of yarrow and apply as a compress. Take a single dose internally.

Arnica des P. P. Trappistes[3] is preferable but must not be used straight.

Freezing.—Apply a compress of wartwort prepared in liquid form or put the member in the liquid. The plant must be gathered in summer and dried in the shade.

Cold feet from poor circulation.—Place in the socks or shoes a pinch of powdered mustard. The blood will quickly be drawn to the extremities.

Nervous excitement.—Take an infusion of camomile.

---

[2] Trade-mark.   [3] Trade-mark.

Headache.—Take camomile tea.

A Red Cross mustard plaster on the back of the neck is effective.

Fever.—Take an infusion of camomile. Follow by a purgative.

Fainting.—Rub the members of the affected person and wash his face with cold water.

Swelling or cold in wounds.—Apply a poultice of flaxseed.

Dip the affected part in boiled bran.

Put on a hot-water compress.

Falling hair.—Put on a little coal oil.

Rub with birch sap.

APPENDIX III

THE AUTOBIOGRAPHY OF AN *HABITANT*

The following autobiography was given orally by the farmer of a *terre* on which six generations of his family have lived before him. He is the father of seventeen children, fourteen of whom are still living. He is a better-than-average farmer and very religious. The religious side of his life he did not give. He is always extremely close-mouthed about his religion. He writes his name and reads with some difficulty. Having never heard of a life-story, he asked for explicit suggestions as to the type of material desired. The following items in the story were suggested: work as a child, school, first Communion, family reunions, marriage, death of parents, land improvement, travel, and membership in the council. These suggestions had to be given to obtain the story. His idea of the relative interest of the various topics is indicated by the length of time devoted to each. Original ideas, such as the section on his two years in the *chantier*, his shock upon seeing his first *morte*, his health, the mayorship, etc., bear additional weight by virtue of the fact that they were unsuggested. Anyone sophisticated enough to write an autobiography would be atypical. This autobiography could be duplicated in form and general material by any of the local farmers.

Among the first things I remember was playing at my uncle's house. I was only three or four years old, and I went to play with my little girl-cousin. There were a lot of children there. We all played, and my hands were very dirty. I remember when we played with wooden blocks in a big tub. We put them on top of each other, built them up into buildings and points. One Sunday in the afternoon we went to my uncle's house to see a cousin who had died. That really struck me. Oh!

That struck me! I can see her still, perfectly. I never was afraid of the dead and have gone into the cemetery at night. There are people who are afraid of the dead. I've heard of people in the old days who, when there was danger, went and lay in the cemetery. That was sensible; there's no danger there.

We played, but we worked a little too. We all began to work early. As soon as a child could cut a little with a sickle, he would go out and cut grain. When he started, he would just cut little paths in the grain, across the *planches* that the men were cutting. We did all sorts of things at our house. Mother was all alone,[1] and we were four men. You have to help the *créatures* a little. I did all the things one can do around a house. We had a curiously arranged family. There were two girls first, and then followed four boys. The girls married young, one at nineteen and one at twenty. When mother used to go to her father's at St. Pacôme, we were left alone. I was able to do everything around the kitchen. My grandfather on mother's side was at St. Pacôme. Their paternal lands were opened by the Dubés. My mother was a Dubé. They don't come to our house often. Her mother was a Langlais. My brother Jean is related to his wife through both families. One is a relationship of three; the other of four.[2]

We all started plowing early. Jean was the first. I didn't plow before my first Communion. I was too young, as I took my first Communion at ten. The day we took our first Communion was the day they started on the new steeple. They wanted to start earlier; but Curé Brochu, who was *curé* then, asked them to wait. He was afraid there might be some accident. Just as soon as we left the church after the Mass, they started work on the steeple. The brother of the contractor was a Oulette. They carried the rocks on two poles. I remember him saying: "We just strain our faces, not our arms." They used to cry "Ou" when they were just carrying a small rock. My brother Jean was strong enough to try a test of strength, but he never did. He was strong enough, but he never wanted to strain himself. For these tests they used to try to lift something like a big sackful of sand. Once they were playing games of strength, and my uncle won. They were playing *tirer de poignet*.[3] He "broke" all the others' arms. There was one time his hand was hurt so badly that the doctor said it would have to be removed, but it started to get well. He was at our house, and his hand was still swollen and blue. He put a folded handkerchief in his hand to

[1] She had no daughters to help her.

[2] Second- and third-cousin relationships.

[3] The contestants grasp right hands and put their right elbows together on a table. Each tries to force the other's arm down on the table. This is known as "breaking" the opponent's arm.

protect it and was still a little stronger than any of the others. Those games of strength are like all games. They're not talked of for some time, and then it takes hold and everyone plays them. All of a sudden it starts, just like lifting weights. It used to be done a lot. This winter there has been no talk at all of games of force. When they load grain, there is often competition in strength. They had a big bag of wheat in the village once—and wheat is very heavy—that nobody was capable of loading. They had a man come from way down at the end of the *rang* to load it. We could have loaded it, but nobody asked us. We've loaded many just as heavy at our house. The heaviest I ever saw loaded was by my brother-in-law. He was a thin man with deep-set eyes, deeper than mine even; and he was strong, strong, strong.

For Communion we all wore black suits, collars, white ties, and bands on the arm. I was old when I took my first Communion. There was only one older than I. He was the eldest, then there was myself, then the son of Pierre Dionne, and then the brother of Joseph Garon. We all sat in the same pew together, the same pew that our family has today—The Four Apostles (*he laughs*). I was tall, as I grew like a locust. At twelve I was taller than my elder brother. Just today I saw a boy who took Communion with me, the brother of Ambroise Franck. I say "boy." He has fifteen or sixteen children. He was three months younger than I. In those days the boys who took Communion together were more united. There was always a half-hour catechism before vespers. Those preparing for their Communion always sat in the front together. Later they moved back to make room for another set, but they always sat together. Now the *curé* goes to the school to give the catechism and has a meeting the first Thursday of every month. Some people said they lived so far away and it was hard to come. There are always those who can find difficulties. We found those catechism meetings *beau, beau*. They recalled things which had happened, and we were all together. There were often a lot of people there. There were visiting priests in the summer, and we liked that. There was one nice old priest who used to come and visit. He liked the children, and we liked him. I worked at my catechism. I knew every word; but aside from that, I didn't learn anything at school. I was too bad to be kept at home; so they sent me to school when I was six. I didn't go any more after my first Communion. The teachers then had their diplomas from *our* school. Our school was renowned and had a good name. Girls came from other parishes to get their diplomas here. Now I don't know what they're about to do. They want all the girls to get their diplomas from normal schools.

In winter we used to make a slide and slide *des veillées de temps*. There was no end to it. When there was a full moon, we used to slide even at night. My little fellows slid all day yesterday, even going to the hill to the north, where there is a long slope. They could slide for five *arpents* there.

In my youth boys about the age of seven or eight began to drive the horses. The farmers always had small boys drive their horses for them when they worked. If they had no small boys of their own, they hired them. That is the reason we missed so much school. We could not go to school during the spring sowing. After the sowing there was such a short time before vacation that we didn't go back to school but stayed at home. In the fall there was mowing, then potatoes, and it was often November before we could even start school. During the winter there was threshing, for which we had to miss school. The generation of my father had so little schooling that only about half of them could write. Work was all by hand then, and it took longer. Remember the Beaulieu woman, he called her Hudon I think, that the *curé* recommended to our prayers? She was one of my teachers. She married when she was old, and married nothing but a widower, a Desjardins.

When I was about sixteen, our barn was completely repaired. It was all done in one summer, which was a lot of work. It used to be right next to the road. The new barn was completely new—new posts, walls, and everything except the wood in the roof. I worked a lot of the stone myself. That was the first piece of work which Georges Lavoie ever worked. He was eighteen then, two years older than I.

At nineteen I went to the *chantier*[4] with my brother. We had never been out before. At the first camp we were with a lot of English. We could not understand them, and they could not understand us. We were there one day, and the next day we went to the second camp. There was a big lake between the first and second camps. I had brought two horses up to work, and I had to take them to the other camp. There was no road around the lake, so we just followed the shore; and when the trees were right down to the water, we would go out into the lake. The first work we had at the second camp was cutting wood for the "cook." Then they took us out into the forest. If I ever had any experience in the *chantier*, it would not have been so hard to understand the directions they gave me in English. After a few days I had to take down[5] a horse which had gotten a bad foot, I think from keeping its feet in the water so much when we came around the lake.

It has been talked about recently, the big wind, the "puff" that came that winter. It was just at noon, and we were at dinner. We had to cut down the trees to keep them from falling on us. They would be bent over and we would give them a few chops, and they would fall. It was the worst *coup de vent* that has ever been seen. It blew over several windmills. Where we were it blew the tops out of the trees.

[4] Lumber camp.   [5] Down out of the mountains to his own parish.

The hard thing about work there was the long walks. We walked three or four miles a day to get to work. That was bad. Sundays we played with axes on the lake.[6] You swing the ax low and let it go, and it will slide far, far, far. There are other men still farther away to slide them back again. One man, Louis Dionne, who was really *capable*, big, and strong, used to play in only a shirt and pants with bare head and feet. He kept moving all the time *par exemple*.

The second year we understood a little, and it was better. It was not the wood which was difficult but the language. We had had lots of experience cutting wood for our own family. One day a big storm filled a little stream so that the men would not have been able to get back to camp without wading through it. The "foreman" came and tried to explain it to us, wanting to know if we knew how to make a bridge. We couldn't understand a thing he was saying; so I went with him to see what had happened. He showed me the stream; and at first I thought the word "bridge"[7] must mean "stream," but then I realized he wanted to make a bridge. It's aggravating not to understand anything. It was worse for them to hire a man and not have him understand anything. That "foreman" was always smiling and laughing. The "foreman" at the first camp looked "rough."

The prettiest pine I saw while I was there was eleven inches through at the end of sixty-two feet. It got smaller so gradually that the sides were almost like that stick over there. There is much better wood in other regions, but that's the best I ever saw. I saw a cedar that was four feet through. It was so large and got small so quickly that the "foreman" told us to leave it alone.

The second year I took up two horses; and when I arrived at the camp there was no one there. Later in the day a "foreman" came there. The next day he told me to take care of the horses. I told him that was easy: I had spent my life taking care of horses. My brother and he went to a place on the lake where they were opening a new camp. They went in a small steamboat. There were two Indians at the new camp to help them. The next day my brother and I took the horses down to the new camp. There was a road cut around the lake this time. On the way it began to rain. When we arrived at the camp we found that the Indians had taken a piece of birch bark about three feet square and set it up slanting on four posts. They and two other men were all standing under it. We couldn't get a piece of birch bark to cover us and the horses, though (*laughing*). Making the new camp was the nicest work I ever had while I was up there. We knew the "bosses";

---

[6] The lake was frozen.

[7] Here the informant could not remember the English words and used French. Elsewhere in this account, words in quotations were given in English.

and if there was any hard work, they would give it to someone else. That was the nicest time during my two years in the *chantier*. Sundays we would *promenade* on the lake. Louis Dionne had hollowed out a log and made a boat. A boat like that "rolls" M'sieur! We would take his "logue" when we could not get one of the "boats" of the camp. He even put a birch-bark sail on his boat. I stopped the *chantier* because I had to work for my uncle at Mont Carmel. I would have kept it up until I got married had it not been for that. A lot of families went to the States in the summer and left their lands uncultivated. Then they would return in the winter when there was nothing to do, and spend part of the money they had earned. We always thought it was better to farm in summer and then go to the *chantier* in the winter. I never went to the States because there was always plenty to do at home.

My uncle was one of the best men in Mont Carmel. I worked for him for three years and didn't like it. I started working in haytime. After I had been there about two weeks, he dislocated his shoulder when he was mowing and his scythe hit a mound of earth. I was all alone then. His shoulder was dislocated six or seven times after that, and he had to have his arm strapped to his side, so I had to do all the work. One spring, after I had plowed both *terres* at our own home by myself, my uncle in Cacouna wrote my father a letter and told him he had only half his sowing done. I went up and plowed and harrowed for him.

The biggest family reunion we ever had was in 1900. That was when my uncle Hermenegilde was there. All my father's brothers and sisters were there, and all their children were invited. They couldn't all get there though. I don't know how many there were, but the house was full, full, full, full. I remember they had a big discussion about whether it was the end of the century or not. Some said the century was ended; others said it wouldn't end until the end of the next year. Everyone yelled his opinion at *pleine tête*. That was the biggest reunion that was ever had at our house. Father's family alone counted sixteen— not all living, of course.

There was a shoemaker in St. Denis who lived in the house there in the garden of Ludger Pelletier. I knew him very well. He came from Kamouraska, and his parents still lived there. We used to go there quite often. They were neighbors of the Hudons, and that's how I came to know my wife. I went to a *veillée de danse* in Hauteville near her house. She was not there, but she has always said if she had been there I never would have married her. At that party they had the most beautiful girls I have ever seen around here. It's rare they ever have such beautiful girls. My brother Jean left home when he was twenty-nine years old. He left in October, and I was married right away that winter. The first time I went to the Hudon's house was the second Sunday of

January; and we were married *lundi gras*, the fifteenth of February. I
went to her house two or three Sundays and often during the week before I made the *grande démande*. Once having made up your mind,
you shouldn't lose time. After I had made the *démande*, father went
with me and arranged the contract. It was arranged that I should have
one or the other of the two *terres*.[8] After that was in the contract,
father had to give me one or the other. That is how the old ones would
arrange it. That way they could choose their daughter-in-law. It did
not matter which boy would remain in the house. It was the wife
that made the difference. At that time the boys always made the
démande. Now they may arrange it so the girl will ask her father.
They used to give the bride a complete *ménage;* now they give less.
People are poorer since the depression.

For the wedding a cousin came from Trois Pistoles, and all the relatives of *maman* in St. Pacôme came. All the close ones of father were
there. I don't want to brag, but the biggest wedding papa made was
mine. Oh, but we had a tempest that day! It started as we were coming back from Kamouraska. It continued all that night and the next
day. The Thursday after the *lundi gras* of our marriage I had to take
our little cousins to the convent at Rivière Ouelle. Robert[9] was taking
another load of visitors to the train; so I had to go. The snowbanks
were so deep that the horses couldn't go through them. I had to walk
in front, and they followed me. Sometimes they were almost buried in
snow, and I had to look around for the branches which marked the
road. My father was even better with a horse than I. He used to go
through snowbanks like a bird. Winters are milder now than they used
to be. Even during my time I can see the difference. In the old days
the snow was so deep they had to dig tunnels into the houses. It was
because the land was not completely cleared. You have heard of the
trouble they are having in Abitibi with frozen grain. It is always
that way with the new settlements. When Lake Temiscouata was
opened, they could grow nothing but "buckwhit." Now they grow
grain, just as we do here. I never used to get cold then. I could go
all day in the snow. I get chilly now. It's changed, and I don't like
tempests.

Robert married two years after I did. He had one child before he
moved into the house where he is now. We built his barn the summer
before I got married. We built his house with the help of a workman
the summer after I got married. The house on that piece of land needed
a lot of repair; so papa had sold it and said: "When we want one, we
can build another." When a boy marries, he moves downstairs if there
is any room. We had three children when my parents decided it was

---

[8] Two lands belonging to his father.   [9] His next younger brother.

too much work for the mother to take care of her children upstairs; so they made over the dining-room back of the salon into a bedroom. In the early days there were no rooms above. It was the grain that was put up there. Not here, but in St. Philippe, I've seen a house without any partitions in the old style. The people were poor, poor, poor.

It was a surprise for everyone when my father died. He was a big man and sixty-two years old. Four of his family died at sixty-two. That doesn't happen very often. *Maman* died two years later. With grandfather and grandmother it was the same. He was stronger than papa. Papa had no more hair and *dents à porter*. It was only four years ago, with Curé Lallemand, that they began selling lots in the cemetery. Before, if there was room to put relatives together, it was well. If not, there was nothing to be done.

Before us no one had improved the land. It had been cleared and then used. The crops were always diminishing. In father's time we had several pieces of land which could not be used. They are as good as any now. To improve the land, one must work all the time, particularly in the autumn. The land used to be divided into small sections, owing to the way the plain had been drained. We made these sections into long fields, cleared out the rocks, and made fences.

Thomas[10] has considerable talent, but he works hard for what he learns. Baptiste[11] has the real talent. Joseph[12] is bright, but he would be about like Thomas. Baptiste is the one of real ability. I wanted to send him to college, but he didn't want to go. He said that if we were two we could work more land; so I bought the *terre* in the southeast. Having missed so much school, I never let any of my children miss any. Missing six months a year, one is always behind the rest. You're put back and always stay in the same class. I was the fifth in our family, and there were five after me. We were not rich, and we had to help.

When Thomas was ordained, there were too many people at the house to have the banquet in it. We put three long tables upstairs in the carriage house. We covered the ceiling with paper and the walls with pine branches. The tables were arranged around three sides, and there was a table for the children in the center. Our family alone counted fourteen. On my side, at the right of Thomas, were all my relatives. On the left was my wife and all her relatives. That was the day after he was ordained. We all went to Ste Anne for the ordination—all, all, all. Little Pierre was only three years old, and he went along.

[10] Eldest son, a priest.

[11] Eldest of the sons at home, 27 years old.

[12] Next youngest son, 24 years old.

When the son of my brother Jean was ordained, I went to Montreal—
the only time I ever went. I visited the oratory of St. Joseph and met
Frère André.[13] I never traveled much. I went as far down as Campbell-
ton, New Brunswick. I took a bull of Robert's there. My father
went farther than that. He went with a carload of animals, not just one.
He went to the ferry which goes to Prince Edward Island. They wanted
him to make the crossing, but he didn't want to. The first Canadian
animals that the government station at Ste Anne had were furnished
by us. The brother of Thomas Chapais, Charles Chapais, commis-
sioner for Milk Industries, gave us the chance. He was a good, fine
friend. He used to bring his own sick animals down to us and have
us take care of his colts.

It was at the time of the changing of the municipal codes that I
was elected to the council. They changed all the rules governing the
elections and selected all new members. As some of us had to go out
of office after one year and others after two, we had to decide among
ourselves which ones would stay, as this was the beginning of the system. We drew straws, and I was unlucky; I had to stay two years.
Above all, we started the repair of the *routes*. We had a mayor who
did not want to repair them, but at the first meeting we started talking
about it and never had any trouble. It was there that the *routes*
started to be repaired, have sand put on them. Just beyond the *terre
grise*, beyond Ignace Dionne, there was a very bad piece of road. We
started putting sand on it. We didn't have any sand; so we hunted
around for it and sent it to the department to be analyzed. Since then
they have struggled with me, trying to put me back in. They've tried
to make me mayor several times; even this year they tried to make me
mayor. Every year I am kept busy trying to see that I am not caught.
One year I went into the woods one Monday night. They came up to
our camp *en voiture* to tell me they had proposed me for mayor. I
wanted to come down, but I had gone up for a week's work so we decided to stay. They had proposed me against Lionel Rossignol. We
came down Saturday at the end of the week, and I asked at home:
"Have you heard anything in the village this week?" They said: "No";
and I said: "Good." The next morning I went and gave Denis Martin
my resignation.[14] When you can't do otherwise and are caught, it's
all right; but I don't like public positions like that. There are those
who like them and feel they are directing the parish. They are also
responsible for the welfare of the parish. They must take only the
interest of the parish; they cannot follow their own ideas and interests
as when they are not so charged.

I was an inspector and assessor and got criticized a lot. We made

---

[13] Thaumaturge, who died recently. [14] Withdrew his name.

a lot of changes. Some had not enough evaluation; others had much too much. Our neighbor, Pelletier, who had one-half an *arpent* clear to the sea, not just a half-*arpent* long, was not entered at all. Lionel Rossignol had received the prize for agricultural merit, and they were always talking about his *belles terres*. There was no reason for his being charged more because he had a *belle terre*. We lowered his evaluation. We rearranged several that year. Just last Wednesday I was in St. Philippe, and a man said to me: "Why aren't you at home, occupying yourself with your election to mayor?" I said I had regulated that all right.

I am beginning to lose my strength some. The other day old Marius Dionne told me he was as strong as ever. I said there is something wrong, as I am only sixty and already beginning to be weaker. I have been well all my life up to about three years ago, when I got sick. I could not eat anything. It was in the fall, and I was on the hill north of the house burying some drain pipe. There was just a little more to do, but I was so weak I could not finish. I had to call my boys, who were near, to come and finish it. I went to the doctor's house two or three times, but he was never there. I decided: "Well, if he's not going to be at home, I'll cure myself"; and I did. I was sick again like that this fall, but I am good now.

There are other lives a great deal better than mine. My life isn't very interesting. I've never traveled. I've always worked. Early to rise and late to bed has been my life. When I was working in Mont Carmel, I have seen people arrive to *veillée* and I was still in the field.

APPENDIX IV

OLD AND NEW TRAITS IN ST. DENIS

The following list divides various culture traits found in St. Denis into old and new. Those listed as old were existent at the beginning of the nineteenth century, many having been present a century earlier. They are largely associated with the conditions of isolated pioneer farming life. The new elements, which have entered into the pattern of life since 1800, originate almost exclusively in the cities. They are the result of urbanization and industrialization. As these processes were largely due to English stimulus, many of the new elements are characteristic of English and American life. The asterisk (*) signifies decline or lack of general acceptance, several asterisks indicating even greater lack of acceptance of the trait. The new traits are listed and starred from the point of view of the farming household. There is a greater total number of traits and a wider acceptance of new ones to be found in the village households of *rentiers*, day-laborers, and tradesmen. Canned goods are used to some extent by the village people, and meat is bought from a passing butcher and bread from a baker.

AGRICULTURE AND HUSBANDRY

Old	New
**Flail threshing (now of flax only)	Mechanical shears, cream-separator, binder, mower, sower, raker, spring harrow, thresher
Bucksaw and buck	*Circular saw
Blessing of seeds and sown fields, Masses for success of	Seed grain mechanically sifted, *chemical fertilizers, simple crop rotation

Old	New
crops, *paters* during planting	Advice of *agronomes*, interest in pure blood animals, tuberculosis-testing
*Moon-phase determination of animal sex	*Veterinarians for sick horses
*Moon-phase determination of sowing time	
*Magico-religious cures for animal sickness	
Local men with experience in handling animal sickness and birth	

FOOD AND DRINK

Local bean and barley "coffee"	*Catsup
Pancakes	Puddings
Bread	Riced potatoes
Pea soup made without a stock, and other soups	*Home-preserved meats
Doughnuts	Tea
Fried eggs	Coffee
Potatoes—*boiled, *fried, and ***baked	Jello
Meat pies	*Jelly roll
Cold pork patty	
*Salt pork	
Butter	
Milk	
Maple-sugar candy	

HOUSE

***Straight steep roofs	Curved roofs, French roofs, flat roofs
**Embankments around foundations	Box houses with two stories
*Long low barns	Two-story barns
**Birch bark under shingles	Tar paper under shingles
**Peg locks for doors	Mechanical locks
Double doors, windows	
Winter entryway	

FURNISHINGS

***Candles	*Kerosene lamps, *electric lights
Woven carpets over entire floor	**Wall paper
	Stoves

Furnishings—*Continued*

Old	New
Braided rugs	**Washing-machines, sewing-machines
Wool blankets	
Linen towels	**Inside toilets
Flour troughs	**Running water
Benches, tables, rockers, and straight chairs	Spring beds, mattresses
China and tableware	

Male Clothing

Bottes sauvages (moccasin boots)	High- and low-cut shoes
	Rubber boots, leather boots
	Felt boot–fillers, rubbers
*Homemade shirts, trousers, overcoats, and suits of *étoffe*	Overalls, blue-denim coats, shirts, ready-made suits, cotton shirts
Home-knitted socks and underwear	Caps, felt hats, derbies
	*Leather and cloth jackets
	Ready-made overcoats
	*Gloves, scarves, neckties
	*Tie clasps
	*Stiff collars, spats

Female Clothing

Aprons	*High-heeled shoes
Knitted petticoats, underwear	Felt and straw hats
Wool stockings	Corsets, brassieres
*Dresses of *étoffe*	*Cotton cloth for dresses, ready-made silk and cotton dresses
	Silk and wool stockings woven in mills
	Purses, gloves
	Ready-made coats
	Beauty aids: powder, *rouge, **nail polish,** permanent waves, **baths (weekly), **freckle cream

Smoking
(male)

*Pipes (stubby "Irish" and clay)	Pipes (long slender stem and elbow)

Old	New
Home-grown and shredded tobacco	*Cigarettes (tailor-made and *Polak*)—younger men particularly
**Hot coals for lighting	
*Pig-bladder tobacco pouches	Tobacco pouches of rubber and leather
	Lighters, **matches
	**Store tobacco (used solely in cigarettes)

(FEMALE)

**Pipes for old women	**Cigarettes for young women

HOME-PRODUCT TECHNIQUES

**Hand carding	Wool carded at the mill
Spinning	
Weaving	
Dyeing	
Rug-making	
Brayage, *écorçage*, *épinglage* of flax	
Homemade soap	Lye bought at the store
**Hewn wooden shovels	Bought iron shovels
*Hand-sewn clothes	Sewing-machine
**Hand churning of butter	Mechanical churns and butter from *beurrerie*

VEHICLES

***Traineau*	Bobsleigh
Work sled	Sleigh
Carriole	Wagon
Charrette (two wheeled with side frames for hay and grain)	Buggy
	*Big surry
	*"Rubber tire"
Tombereau (two wheeled with deep bed)	Sulky
	Bicycle
Play sled	**Motorcycle
***Calèche* (still in city of Quebec for tourists)	**Automobile
***Cabriolet* (springs differ from the foregoing)	

CARE OF SICKNESS

Old	New
Remmancheur (bone-setter)	*Doctor
Sage femme (has become doctor's aid)	Red Cross mustard plaster
	Iodine
Traditional herbal and home remedies	Boric acid
*Magical and religious cures	

MEASURES

Minot	Pint
Pot (about 2 quarts)	Quart
Platée	Gallon
Arpent	Inch
Botte (15 pounds)	Foot
Aune (ell)	Mile

GAMES

Quatre sept	**Baseball
***Brisse*	**Croquet
	**Hockey (common near by)
	*Bridge
	*Poker (not for money)

MUSIC AND DANCE

Violin	Harmonica
	*Victrola
	*Piano
	*Harmonium
	*Radio
Allouette and a few others sung occasionally	Popular songs from the city
Cotillion, salut des dames	Quadrille, reel, sets

BIBLIOGRAPHY

BARBEAU, MARIUS. *The Kingdom of the Saguenay.* New York: Macmillan Co., 1936.

———. *Quebec, Where Ancient France Lingers.* New York: Macmillan Co., 1936.

BARBEAU, MARIUS, and SAPIR, EDWARD. *Folk Songs of French-Canada.* New Haven: Yale University Press, 1925.

BLANCHARD, RAOUL. *L'Est du Canada française.* 2 vols. Montreal: Beauchemin, 1935.

BOUCHARD, GEORGES. *Vieilles choses, vieilles gens.* 2d. ed. Montreal: Beauchemin, 1926.

BOVEY, WILFRED. *Canadien.* Toronto: J. M. Dent & Sons, 1933.

BRACQ, JEAN C. *The Evolution of French Canada.* New York: Macmillan Co., 1924.

CAMERON, JEAN C., and HURD, W. B. "Population Movements in Canada, 1921–1931: Some Further Considerations," *Canadian Journal of Economics and Political Science,* I (May, 1935), 222–45.

CANADA, BUREAU OF STATISTICS. *Seventh Canadian Census, 1931.* Ottawa: J. O. Patenaude, 1933.

CASGRAIN, L'ABBÉ H. R. *Légendes canadiennes.* Quebec: Brocusseau, 1861.

———. *Une Paroisse canadienne au XVIIe siècle.* Montreal, 1912.

CASSIDY, HARRY M. "The Canadian Social Services," *Annals of the American Academy of Political and Social Sciences,* CCLIII (1947), 194–95.

CHAMBERLAND, J. E. *English Grammar.* Quebec, 1915.

CLERCS DE SAINT VIATEUR, LES. *Histoire du Canada.* Montreal: Les Clercs de Saint Viateur, 1915.

DIONNE, N. E. *Le Parler populaire des canadiens français.* Quebec, 1909.

DOMINION BUREAU OF STATISTICS. *Chronological List of Canadian Censuses.* Ottawa, 1933. (Mimeographed.)

FENCHER, ALBERT. "Co-operative Trends in Canada," *Annals of the American Academy of Political and Social Sciences,* CCLIII (1947), 184–89.

FORTUNE, R. F. *Sorcerers of Dobu.* New York: G. Routledge & Sons, 1932.

FOWKE, V. C. "Canadian Agriculture in the Postwar World," *Annals of the American Academy of Political and Social Sciences,* CCLIII (1947), 46–47.

GÉRIN, LÉON. "L'Habitant de Saint-Justin," *Mémoires et comptes rendus de la Société royale du Canada* (2d. ser.), IV (1898), 139–216.

HERSKOVITS, M. J. *Life in a Haitian Valley.* New York: A. A. Knopf, 1937.

HUGHES, EVERETT C. "The French-English Margin in Canada," *American Journal of Sociology*, XXXIX (July, 1933), 1–11.

———. "Industry and the Rural System in Quebec," *Canadian Journal of Economics and Political Science*, IV (August, 1938), 341–49.

———. "Position and Status in a Quebec Industrial Town," *American Sociological Review*, III (October, 1938), 709–17.

JUNEK, OSCAR W, *Isolated Communities.* New York: American Book Co., 1937.

LAVOIE, JOSEPH A. *La Famille Lavoie au Canada.* Quebec, 1922.

LYND, ROBERT S., and LYND, HELEN MERRELL. *Middletown.* New York: Harcourt, Brace & Co., 1929.

———. *Middletown in Transition.* New York: Harcourt, Brace & Co., 1937.

MAGNAN, ABBÉ J. ROCH. *Cours français de lectures graduées.* Montreal: Beauchemin, 1902.

MINER, HORACE. "Changes in Rural French-Canadian Culture," *American Journal of Sociology*, XLIV (November, 1938), 365–78.

———. "The French-Canadian Family Cycle," *American Sociological Review*, III (October, 1938), 700–708.

MOORE, W. H. *The Clash.* New York: E. P. Dutton & Co., 1919.

NANTEL, ABBÉ A. *Nouveau cours de la langue anglaise.* Montreal: Beauchemin, n.d.

PARKMAN, FRANCIS. *The Old Régime in Canada.* 8th ed. Boston: Little, Brown & Co., 1880.

PEATTIE, RODERICK. "The Problem of Communication in the Lower St. Lawrence Valley," *Journal of Geography*, XX (January, 1921), 1–12.

POULIN, LEROY. "L'Enseignement primaire rural dans la province de Québec." Unpublished Bachelor's thesis, Ecole superieure d'Agriculture de Ste Anne, Québec, 1934.

FRÈRES DES ECOLES CHRÉTIENNES, LES. *Arithmétique.* Montreal: Les Frères des Ecoles chrétiennes, 1926.

———. *Géographie illustrée.* Montreal: Les Frères des Ecoles chrétiennes, 1922.

FRÈRES MARISTES, LES. *Atlas géographie.* Montreal: Les Frères maristes, 1931.

GÉRIN, LÉON. "La Famille canadienne-française, sa force, ses faiblesses," *Revue trimestrielle canadienne*, XIX (March, 1932), 35–63.

QUEBEC DEPARTMENT OF MUNICIPAL AFFAIRS, TRADE AND COMMERCE. *1931 Statistical Year Book.* Quebec: Printer to the King's Most Excellent Majesty, 1932.

———. *1935 Statistical Year Book.* Quebec: Printer to the King's Most Excellent Majesty, 1936.

———. *1936 Statistical Year Book.* Quebec: Printer to the King's Most Excellent Majesty, 1937.

QUÉBEC, MINISTÈRE DE L'AGRICULTURE. *Le Québec agricole 1932.* Quebec: Printer to the King's Most Excellent Majesty, 1933.

REDFIELD, ROBERT. *Tepoztlán.* Chicago: University of Chicago Press, 1930.

REDFIELD, ROBERT, and VILLA R, ALFONSO. *Chan Kom.* Washington: Carnegie Institution, 1934.

RIVERS, W. H. R. *The Todas.* London: Macmillan & Co., Ltd., 1906.

ROBERT, E. *Nouvelle grammaire française.* Montreal: Les Clercs de Saint Viateur, 1906.

SIEGFRIED, ANDRÉ. *Le Canada, les deux races.* Paris: A. Colin, 1906.

SOCIÉTÉ DU PARLER FRANÇAIS AU CANADA. *Glossaire du parler français au Canada.* Quebec: L'Action sociale, 1930.

WILLIAMS, MICHAEL. *The Catholic Church in Action.* New York: Macmillan Co., 1935.

INDEX

PHOENIX BOOKS
Sociology, Anthropology, and Archeology